POLITICAL PHILOSOPHY NOW

POLITICAL PHILOSOPHY NOW

Poverty, Ethics and Justice

H. P. P. [Hennie] Lötter

UNIVERSITY OF WALES PRESS • CARDIFF • 2011

www.uwp.co.uk

British Library Cataloguing-in-Publication Data
A catalogue record for this book is available from the British Library.

ISBN   978-0-7083-2400-4
e-ISBN 978-0-7083-2436-3

Typeset in Wales by Eira Fenn Gaunt, Cardiff
Printed in Great Britain by CPI Antony Rowe, Wiltshire

For Emma, colleague and friend, whose support
and critique improved this book

Contents

Acknowledgements

I am grateful for the role of my parents in so many ways. My late father and my mother are exemplars of persons who developed and used their capabilities to build flourishing lives.

My heartfelt thanks to Trix and Lisa, who had to sacrifice a lot of family time and endure the hours I spent working on this book for many years, but nevertheless gave their utmost support.

Trix shared the emotional upheavals that accompanied the stresses and strains of this lengthy, at times disturbing, project. She was always there to talk to. In this way she made a long and arduous journey easier.

I have deep appreciation for David Braybrooke (emeritus professor of Philosophy at the University of Texas at Austin) who read the manuscript thoroughly and with deep insight. He gave lots of helpful comments.

Part of the research for this book was done at Oxford University during September 2004 to March 2005 whilst I was on a generous Commonwealth Fellowship. The late Professor G. A. Cohen was my host.

This book has been brought to publication with the kind assistance of the Publication Subvention Programme of the Research Management Committee of the Faculty of Humanities at the University of Johannesburg.

Chapter 2 was published in an earlier form in September 2007 in *HTS* (*Hervormde Teologiese Studies*), 63, 3. An extract was used as a chapter in my book called *When I Needed a Neighbour Were You There? Christians and the Challenge of Poverty* (Wellington, South Africa: Lux Verbi).

Chapter 4 was published in an earlier form in 'The moral challenge of poverty's impact on individuals', *Koers*, 72, 2 (2007).

Chapter 5 was published in an earlier form in 2008 as a chapter in my book called *When I Needed a Neighbour Were You There? Christians and the Challenge of Poverty* (Wellington, South Africa: Lux Verbi).

Chapter 6 was published in an earlier form in *Public Affairs Quarterly*, 22, 2, April 2008, 175–93.

Chapter 12 was published in an earlier form in *Politikon: South African Journal of Political Science* in June 2005.

Introduction

Ever since time immemorial poverty and war provide evidence that our species willingly allows millions of our members to die preventable deaths and suffer all kinds of harms and humiliations. The fight against our inhumanity must never stop. With every breath we take we must work against our dark side that inflicts pain, suffering and death on our fellow human beings. In every awake moment we must engage our energy against our cold hearts that are unmoved by the dreadful conditions we find so many of our kind have to deal with.

Throughout my life I have seen how friends, acquaintances and strangers struggle to make life meaningful against the odds stacked by the easily recognizable condition of poverty. I could not fail to observe how others respond: some think they understand exactly how people got themselves into such a mess, blaming the poor for their unfortunate condition and its obstinate persistence. Others ignore the obvious suffering and congratulate themselves and perhaps praise their gods for their own success and prosperity. A few compassionate hearts make brave attempts, with more or less success, to change the lives of people negatively affected by a condition sometimes only vaguely understood.

There is no doubt that our understanding of the phenomenon of poverty has increased exponentially in the last century or so – at least within the ranks of human scientists and some smart policy makers. However, despite numerous attempts by individuals, organizations, governments and international institutions, suffering caused by poverty persists on a massive, alarming scale throughout the world.

In this book I aim to contribute to the struggle to eradicate poverty everywhere. I use the results from numerous studies by human scientists over many decades to present a profile of poverty and its effects on human lives. In contrast to the more abstract philosophical ways of dealing with some select, narrowly defined issue that excludes a view on the full impact of poverty on human lives, I choose a holistic approach that portrays the wide range of dimensions complexly assembled in every case of poverty. Only a profile expressing a comprehensive grip of the multidimensional nature of poverty that highlights the diverse range of harmful impacts poverty might have can provide the proper background for a deep understanding of a seriously troubling condition. Only such an understanding can be an appropriate illumination of the salient issues for moral evaluation as a prelude for aid and action.

The core argument of the book runs as follows. Poverty is a complex multidimensional phenomenon amongst humans that violates a host of ethical values and can only be eradicated through a similarly complex suite of responses based on a comprehensive evaluation by means of a generally accepted set of moral values. In Part 1 of the book I show the full complexity of poverty as a moral issue. I first set up an argument in chapter 1 to demonstrate that poverty anywhere is a concern of human beings everywhere. I then proceed to provide a definition that depicts poverty as a serious moral wrong that undermines the human dignity of its sufferers and threatens their health.

Next, I argue that poverty is a complex phenomenon playing out in different ways in different instances that has a wide ranging series of negative impacts on individuals and societies. The main point about the conditions and consequences of poverty is that poverty undermines the human dignity of its sufferers. Poverty must thus, first and foremost, be eradicated for its inhuman consequences, because these consequences make it so much more difficult to build flourishing lives and use available opportunities to realize one's potential.

I understand the main effect of poverty as being a threat to the human dignity and self-respect of its sufferers. I thus propose that poverty can best be understood from a variety of ethical perspectives through using a diverse group of metaphors and descriptions that unpack every dimension of its possible harm to human life.

In the light of the complexities of the symptoms, effects and causes our understanding of this multidimensional phenomenon generates, I argue that full eradication of poverty can only be accomplished through a diverse set of individual and collective actions based on a comprehensive series of moral evaluations that present a correct understanding of the moral requirements for aid and empowerment. These complexities also imply eradication can best be done through collective human action. I argue that we must re-imagine and revise the goal and purpose of political institutions and reformulate the purposes aid ought to be for. Aid for full eradication must include a suite of diverse human interventions that must meaningfully involve everyone: rich and poor, scientific expert and layperson, political leaders and their followers, global institutions and local street committees, highly organized groups and lone individuals, aid givers and aid receivers.

I build my argument as follows.

In the first section of the book I intend to show the negative impact of poverty on human beings. I look at the phenomenon of poverty through different ethical perspectives to expose in detail why poverty is such an unacceptable condition for humans to live in. First, I define poverty as a distinctively human condition. Next, I show the link between poverty and inequality and argue for the moral urgency of the inequality between rich and poor. I then show how the condition of poverty impacts negatively on the lives of individuals and why the condition of poverty violates several universally accepted moral values we apply to all human societies. I furthermore explain poverty from a different angle by noting its harmful impact on different kinds of environment that directly affect people in their everyday lives. Finally, I point out to what extent poverty is in conflict with the fundamental moral values accepted as foundational for democratic societies.

After having shown the ethically unacceptable consequences of poverty, I explain the phenomenon of poverty by offering a theory that intends to illuminate the complexity of poverty and clarify why it is such an intractable problem that evades simple solutions. In this book I use the word 'theory' as follows: I see a theory as a systematic framework of ideas that aims to account for a specific series of phenomena to provide insight and understanding therein and possible explanations thereof.

Through the above chapters I present an argument that goes as follows. Both the ways that poverty violates the human dignity of its sufferers and the serious nature of the harmful consequences poverty has for their lives establish a *prima facie* moral duty for non-poor people to assist poor people in their attempts to escape the ravages of poverty.

In the second section of the book I present arguments to support and guide the eradication of poverty. It is not good enough to merely depict in detail why it is so deeply objectionable for humans to live in poverty. The important question is what guidance our ethical values provide for appropriately, humanely and effectively helping people trapped and engulfed by poverty.

Against a simplistic understanding of aid to assist poor people, I define a conception of aid that embodies moral prerequisites for the eradication of poverty on a sustainable basis. Then I focus on our responsibilities to accurately identify poverty and the goals which any aid aimed at eradicating poverty must serve.

I furthermore look at poverty through the lens of contemporary theories of justice and demonstrate the degree to which poverty could be prevented and fully eradicated if a society has a comprehensive, fully functioning conception of justice. I show how a retrieval of the value of solidarity in politics must play a crucial role in getting rid of poverty permanently. To exemplify this role of solidarity, I present a proposal to re-imagine the governance functions in human society so as to define the state and related institutions, from local to global level, as the crucial instruments to rid society of enduring poverty. I rethink our collective responsibility for poverty by redefining the role of the state and related institutions or organizations, with a local or global focus.

Once we have clarity about political and related institutions and organizations, we can face the issue that poverty often has its roots in past injustices. I thus examine the tricky issue of whether we should compensate people who were impoverished by past events. I set out arguments to determine responsibilities for eradicating poverty caused by past injustices. In conclusion I present a brief overview of the broad theory of poverty I develop throughout the book. I indicate how poverty thus understood ought to be eradicated through aid and cooperation guided and motivated by core ethical values I developed through a comprehensive approach to the complexities of poverty.

It might seem as if I am ignoring the ethical issues about the moral obligation of rich countries to assist the poorer nations of the world. In a sense I am. One reason for this neglect is that I am not a citizen of a First World country who wants to challenge my fellow citizens to change their minds about this matter. My concerns lie elsewhere, as the rest of the book shows. I am writing as a human being with a firm conviction that every other human being has a moral obligation to prevent poverty occurring or to eradicate poverty already existing, wherever it might be.

Another reason for deliberately leaving this issue aside is that it has been debated thoroughly by philosophers of First World countries in the recent past. Examples are found in the work of Amartya Sen (2009), Martha Nussbaum (1995, 2000), Thomas Pogge (2002), Andreas Follesdal and Thomas Pogge (2005), Garret Cullity (2004) and Peter Unger (1996). These contributions are made mostly from the perspective of the moral responsibility individual well-off First World citizens have towards the poor people living in Third World countries. Note how Cullity (2004: 1) formulates the focus of his book:

> How much ought you and I to be doing about other people's desperate need? We are part of the minority of the world's population able to command enough resources to enjoy a life of ease, comfort and privilege. How much of those

resources ought we to be using to help the many people who suffer from extreme material want? . . . the question that applies to each of us individually . . . How much should I be doing to help the poor?

Similarly, note how David Braybrooke (2003: 301) articulates the problem directly as the issue of the moral responsibility of individual rich First World citizens towards poor Third World people. In his case he explicitly ponders aid given outside the realm of governments:

> What personal responsibilities do we, people living in rich countries, have for relieving miseries in the less fortunate countries? (301) I shall concentrate on people considering contributions to private charitable organizations. (303)

I do not intend to contribute to further illumination of these debates, as my focus lies elsewhere. I do, though, argue for a universal ethical obligation to aid people suffering from poverty. I base this obligation on arguments such as that (1) poverty violates the human dignity of its victims, (2) poverty causes an array of harms to human beings and, (3) it is in the self-interest of individuals and society to eradicate poverty to enable the well-being of human communities of every scale.

Given my belief in this universal ethical obligation I think it necessary to set out in detail the characteristics of poverty even if some of these may seem obvious or excessive to First World readers. The motivation for this meticulous unpacking of what poverty is, is that it is precisely this kind of 'obviousness' that cause such readers to react sometimes too glibly to the issue of eradicating poverty instead of engaging with all its complexities head-on. My argument is that poverty is a many-faceted phenomenon consisting of tightly interwoven characteristics that play out in a complexity of manners depending on the unique circumstances in individual situations. In the context of eradicating poverty, this nuanced nature forces the kind of unpacking of its features attempted in the book.

Before anything else, we must ask whether we have a moral responsibility to become involved in some way or another to eradicate poverty. This issue will be explored next.

Part 1

The Complexity of Poverty as a Moral Issue

1 • Are We One Another's Keepers Across the Globe?

Sometimes it seems as if most people care deeply about the fate of the world's poor people. Pop stars present concerts for the benefit of the poor and thousands of the world's well-off people attend these concerts, buy the recordings and applaud musicians who succeed to focus the world's attention on the plight of poor people everywhere. Some governments in First World countries have impressive aid packages for poor countries that run into billions of dollars. Many regional and global organizations have made the eradication of desperate poverty in underdeveloped countries their top priority. They have invested in the best scientific research to understand the dynamics of societies where poverty seemingly cannot be eradicated. They have formulated plans and policies that can hopefully accomplish the impossible. Even at those rare events where leaders of most countries in the world gather, poverty has been treated as one of the most urgent problems in the world that requires attention and action from every citizen on our planet.

Yet, poverty persists. Billions of people still suffer the wide array of consequences that poverty brings despite the good intentions expressed by the millions of people mentioned above. Millions of the poor people on earth die prematurely and suffer unnecessary health problems. Many millions more have inadequate opportunities to develop their human potential. So many poor people experience feelings of being deprived of the good things in life that our human skill and ingenuity can conjure up from the vast treasures available to us as resources.

Why does desperate poverty persist on such a massive scale in our world? Why can the good intentions of millions and large amounts of money not eradicate the kind of poverty that sucks life from literally billions of people? There are many good reasons why poverty is such a difficult problem to deal with effectively. Part of this book offers a theory that can help us explain why poverty is such a complex affair that is so difficult to uproot. In this chapter I focus on one reason only: the intransigence of millions of well-off individuals who refuse to make poverty priority enough to eliminate it from human societies.

Why are so many well-off people so comfortable with their wealth and so little worried about the desperate poverty of millions? Why do so many well-to-do persons claim their money for themselves and refuse to give money, time, resources, skill and expertise that could rescue desperately poor individuals from their fate? Why do they – we – neglect the poor if 'the extent to which we neglect the needy' can easily and with wide consensus be described as 'a serious moral failing' (Temkin, 2004: 365)?

Perhaps one reason is the overwhelming scale of poverty. What can an individual do that will make any meaningful difference to the lot of the world's billions of poor people? Although this sense of being up against overwhelming odds might be a reason for inaction, I want to explore another possible reason for the inaction of the world's well-off citizens in the face of the plight of the poor: an individualism that justifies any existing inequalities.

Many well-off citizens firmly believe that they deserve their good fortune. They have a right to their good income as they have worked for it. For this reason they can use their money to provide for their own needs for food, shelter and clothing. They can also justifiably use the money they have earned through their talents and hard work to satisfy their most fanciful wants, such as acquiring a luxurious car with state-of-the-art technology, going on an expensive holiday in an exotic location, having dinner at an exclusive restaurant or buying front row tickets for a concert or sports match full of superstars.

How could this way of thinking be wrong? If people do lawful work for which society pays a just reward, why should they not spend their lawfully deserved income as they see fit? Surely no one has the right to interfere with their liberty to spend their income according to their judgement?

I first want to undermine the individualism of this position by pointing out the extent to which any individual is dependent on and forms part of a network of people. Such networks are interconnected to various other networks of people throughout the world. I argue that individual merit is only possible as a result of an individual's deep dependence and reliance on many different networks of people who enable or facilitate what individuals do. If individuals can only function within various interconnected networks consisting of rich and poor people, educated and uneducated people, local and overseas people, then we will have to rethink our relationships with and responsibilities towards people everywhere.

Let me explain my view on the interconnectedness of individuals in networks by means of an imagined example that is true to life. Suppose we look at a CEO of a manufacturing business in a developed First World country. Such people often regard themselves as 'self-made' people who got to their privileged positions on their own steam. However, as babies they were dependent on care takers for everything: food, clothing, hygiene, income, care, love and so on. As children they relied on parents and guardians for income, food, shelter, clothing, educational opportunities, emotional nurturance and moral guidance. The roles of teachers and friends in their web of interconnected individuals are deeply significant as well. Similarly, the contributions of fellow citizens whose taxes paid teachers, constructed roads, built schools, developed parks and paid for sports fields cannot be denied, not to mention the efforts of the people who performed all these services. In the same way the work of the people who established the school and nurtured its traditions, as well as the large numbers of people responsible for the curricula and the knowledge found therein must be acknowledged as contributors to the success of our CEO. Obviously we cannot ignore the functions of cleaners and refuse removers whose work ensured that our CEO was not unnecessarily exposed to materials or organisms that could negatively affect his health.

At this point our imaginary CEO will have to acknowledge that his development from a child into an educated adult was heavily dependent on a whole range of individuals who belonged to different networks of people, some forming his personal world of home, circle of friends, school or home town. Others are further removed, such as fellow citizens of a local government, fellow citizens of a country responsible for an educational system or creators of scientific knowledge scattered through various countries of the world. Without these various inputs of different people from several networks our CEO would never have developed physically, emotionally, socially, intellectually or professionally. His success not only depended on his particular talents, but especially on being enabled by numerous other individuals to use the opportunities made available through the individual and collective efforts of other humans interfacing with his world and impacting on his life.

'But,' our CEO says, 'since my development into adulthood I have lived my own life. I have utilized opportunities through knowledge, insight, skill and hard work. I thus deserve my income as reward for smart and productive labour.' Perhaps our CEO would sing a different tune if we asked him to operate his business in the middle of the Sahara desert. All of a sudden our CEO would realize how much he is dependent on suppliers of water, electricity, raw materials, equipment, space, labour and services to run his manufacturing business, or how much he relies on customers to sustain the viability of his business.

Perhaps some detail of his reliance on others might prove useful. Our CEO depends on both raw and refined materials for his manufacturing operation. Some raw materials come from underdeveloped countries, where unskilled labourers perform most of the physical labour needed for extraction of such raw materials. The success and profitability of our CEO's business thus may depend on the reliable and cost-effective delivery of raw materials from mines in an underdeveloped country, based largely on the physical labour of unskilled workers. Don't forget that in addition to all the forms of dependence and reliance mentioned earlier, our CEO now also depends on a huge number of networks to provide him with consumer products to sustain his health, to move from one place to the next, to manufacture his wares, to find entertainment and so on. His jet-setting, for example, is only made possible through numerous networks of humans involved with matters as diverse as the production of scientific technology to issues as mundane as cleaning airport buildings and keeping birds off landing strips.

If it is true that our CEO is no self-made man, but that his entrepreneurial success depends on the inputs, contributions and interactions of a wide variety of individuals tied into several interfacing networks, does he then owe any individuals in these mutually influential networks any moral obligation? Does he have any responsibility to turn mutually influential relationships into mutually beneficial ones? Suppose the unskilled mine workers on whom he relies for raw materials get paid wages on which they cannot properly support a family, should he intervene? Does his responsibility towards others end when he pays them for their products and services?

There are two obvious reasons why our CEO seemingly ought to be concerned with the well-being of all the people with whom he shares some kind of interconnected web of relations. One reason is that he cannot operate his business nor take proper care of himself without the inputs and contributions of others with whom he is interconnected, however remote those interconnections might be. He simply cannot operate his business in the middle of the Sahara desert. He depends and relies too heavily on networked partners to provide him with products and services of all kinds to not care about their well-being. His own enlightened self-interest dictates that his multiple webs of interconnected partners must enjoy a minimum well-being to enable them to continue playing their roles in his life. Although these roles are of varying importance to him, he relies and depends on them for his continued survival, success and flourishing.

Perhaps our CEO might object at this point. He could argue that he is not able to care about people that far removed from him through physical distance. Through evolution humans evolved to be aware of and in touch with fellow humans within the normal range of our senses, like eyesight and hearing. Moral concern thus ends where normal human interaction with fellow humans is not possible anymore. To be concerned about people whom you have never seen is just too much to ask. To take the interests into account of millions of people who live far away and are totally out of sight is too taxing. Seeing suffering with your own eyes in your own life world is far more engaging and touches your moral sentiments more deeply than getting to know about suffering far off indirectly through the media (see Cullity, 2004: 21). As a result many well-off humans all over the world, Fabre says (2007: 96), 'allow distant strangers to live under conditions of deprivation which we would not tolerate at home'.

Is this objection valid in an era where instant communication puts us in contact with people from all over the globe? Larry Temkin (2004: 381), for example, claims that people can no longer 'confidently claim that they are not responsible for the situation in other countries . . . as our causal powers have expanded, so, too, have the demands of morality and justice'.

The other reason why our CEO ought to be concerned with the well-being of all the people with whom he shares some kind of interconnected relational web is linked to his self-interest to have a good public image. Our CEO cannot publicly be seen to act as someone who dominates all people he deals with, or as someone who exploits business associates in a ruthless way. Our CEO would not want a reputation as someone who deliberately extracts his wealth through abusing the weaknesses or vulnerabilities of others. In our contemporary world with its glaring media spotlights ready to focus on any whiff of scandal, he would be hesitant to behave secretly in these ways as well. If he thus feels pressure to display a hint of fairness in his business dealings, he will have to consider the interests of those individuals with whom he interacts within his numerous webs of interconnected persons. Again, his self-interest dictates that he must be seen to treat people fairly.

If we transpose the simplified example of our CEO to the complex interactions and interwoven webs of interconnected relationships between communities, countries and continents on many more levels than just trade, such as politics, science, technology, entertainment, sport and communication, we can easily imagine that our well-being as humans on earth have become so deeply linked that we cannot ignore one another's well-being any more. The significance of our webs of interconnected interactions show clearly in the fragility of local to intercontinental transport systems to fuel shortages and terror threats. It also manifests in the vulnerability of economic systems to failures of supporting systems or shortages of core resources that occur continents apart.

Thus, we can care somewhat about other people if we talk about our self-interest and public image at individual or collective level, but can we talk about *ethics*? Is it enough that we determine the nature of our interaction with other human beings only by taking them into account as far as they affect our self-interest? Should we merely consider other people's interests if they affect our livelihoods or if our public image might be tarnished if we treat other people inappropriately?

Throughout history some humans have been concerned about their impact on other human beings. Most sets of ethical values known to us attempt to take other people's interests and well-being into account to some extent. Thus, choices about how to live one's life are informed by what we judge a suitable balance between our own interests and the interests of those whom we affect. The kind of impact we allow our actions to have on others says a lot about the quality of human life we set ourselves out to accomplish. Blackburn (2001: 1) says we are 'ethical animals' that find our 'standards of behaviour' in our ethical values that give us our 'ideas about how to live'.

It is characteristic of our species that we have no innate instruction manual or instinct that determines how to live our lives or interact with others. We are born into communities where we are taught appropriate behaviour towards others and are exposed to various options of what meaningful human living might be. As we grow up, we question, interrogate, modify and revise available options as we select and appropriate parts of our culture in the process of designing and building a life of our own.

What are the matters that we take into account and the issues we resolve when we decide our ethics, that is, the guidelines for how we ought to interact with other people or the impact we might legitimately have on their lives? Let us join our imaginary CEO on his quest to develop an ethical life. He has now become aware of his impact on other people in addition to his variety of interactions with a diverse number of people: he is now aware of the way his actions influence and affect what happens to others and how his choices have consequences for the well-being of many people. He knows that those impacts are sometimes negative and sometimes positive. For example, he knows that the lack of adequate safety measures in his manufacturing plant can significantly harm a worker through injuries to his or her body. He knows that his attempts at saving costs through less frequent maintenance of his vehicles might lead to accidents that cause injuries to people's bodies or damage to their vehicles. The consequences of serious bodily injuries to workers could mean that those people suffer mental distress and reduced opportunities to engage in productive work that enables them to care properly for their families. Loss of income can have a knock-on effect on the accident victim's children whose chances are now diminished to develop their full potential through engaging in activities that require costly education or training. Thus, besides the physical pain brought about through bodily injury, our CEO's negligence may cause significant emotional distress in the worker's family. This family must now deal with the consequences that the impairment of physical functions necessary for gainful employment has on their lives that leaves the children with a smaller range of options available for their personal development into competent, mature adults.

In other cases the CEO finds it difficult to decide whether the negative impact of his actions should be avoided or endured. Suppose he has the good intention to mine sand dunes in a developing country to provide employment for a struggling poor community of thousands of jobless people. His project will benefit hundreds of families in the short term by providing jobs with good income. The project will advantage the children with much better educational opportunities in the longer term. Unfortunately, the environmental impact of this development will cause significant destruction of a unique ecosystem and endanger the continued existence of several rare species. The mining will also spoil the scenic qualities of a relatively intact wilderness area that will diminish the ecotourism potential of the area.

Our CEO now discovers that some human actions have multiple effects and consequences, of which some have a negative impact for some interest groups whilst others have a positive impact that increases the well-being of other interest groups. Now he will have to learn to weigh the impact and consequences of his proposed mining project so that he can be clear whether he can justify proceeding with the mine or not. He intends to use his entrepreneurial skills to alleviate the rampant poverty within this jobless community and realizes that his failure to do anything will continue the suffering resulting from large-scale unemployment in the community. However, if his intended job creation plans are to continue, he will have to find ways to resolve the conflict between the positive and negative outcomes in a way that will be fair to the interests of everyone involved, the fragile ecosystem included.[1]

Suppose our CEO successfully explores all possibilities of how to redesign the mining development to limit the negative impact it might have on the fragile ecosystem. He thus invests in the mining project, now to be accompanied by an ecotourism project as well. The ecotourism project will offer further opportunities for locals to utilize the natural resources of their immediate environment for their benefit.

Our CEO pats himself on the shoulder as he experiences deep satisfaction about his accomplishments through such projects. Not only has he employed his talents to engage in meaningful work through which he could properly care for his family, but his work had a positive impact on the life of an impoverished community. Not only could he help reduce their suffering that resulted from a lack of jobs and income, but he could also promote their well-being and enhance their flourishing through the consequences brought about by his project that enabled them to use their natural resources productively and wisely.

The rosy picture of the turnaround made by our morally enlightened CEO intends to illustrate that humans choose a set of ethical values to avoid negative impact on other people and to enable and enhance positive impact on them. We have an impact on other people through our words and deeds, as well as the consequences thereof. A negative impact comes from the ways we harm, injure or hurt people to cause harm, suffering, degradation or destruction. Negative impact also results from our refusal to take action to avoid harm or suffering to someone, or our unwillingness to become involved to make someone else's life better. Positive impact results from how we help, promote or benefit people to increase their well-being, pleasure or happiness.

Sometimes we find it easy to distinguish between the positive and negative impact we have on other people. To take a knife and slash open someone's intestines without reason is without a doubt negative. To provide water to an unknown traveller dying from thirst in a desert is positive. However, to distinguish good from bad, positive from negative can sometimes be very complex.

If human beings come without instruction manuals or instincts so that we have to find out for ourselves how to behave fittingly, our choice of ethics to determine what we judge as positive or negative impact on other humans is a shared matter, a social affair. Somehow we must try to reach some kind of agreement amongst ourselves as to what we regard as positive or negative impact. Imagine if all of us had conflicting views about this matter. I would treat you in ways that you experience as negative without any shared values to resolve the matter. You would thus clash with me about what is to be judged negative and what not. For this reason agreement on what constitutes actions with negative or positive outcomes for fellow human beings plays a major role to facilitate social cooperation in human society. Robert Nozick (2001: 240) argued that the function of ethics is to 'coordinate our actions with those of others to mutual benefit', as evolution may have shaped us to 'enjoy (and prefer) achieving our goals through interpersonal coordination and cooperative activity' (2001: 245).

Social cooperation means that we can work together without harming or destroying one another. It means that we can live together and share a geographical area without engaging in destructive conflict that will undermine or diminish our opportunities to become the kind of human beings each chooses to be. Social cooperation does not only mean that we avoid negative impact that harms, injures, wounds, spoils or causes pain to one another. Social cooperation also means that we fulfil roles and functions and share burdens and risks to enable one another to protect and preserve what we judge valuable, or to enable ourselves and others to survive life's vicissitudes and to achieve the flourishing of our talents and potential as much as we are capable of.

Humans have endless conflicts about the positive and negative outcomes they desire or refuse for their lives. Perhaps our CEO can help simplify the matter for us again. Suppose our CEO is so convinced that he knows what gives meaning to human life that he insists that the workers at the mine use their bread to symbolize communion with the CEO's God, yes, the CEO puts pressure on his workers to accept his religion. They revolt, as they prefer to offer portions of their bread to their ancestors. This conflict is clearly about how we make sense of the universe, what kind of beings we judge to be real, how we give meaning to our existence and what power we allow other human beings over us. The workers have freedom to legitimately resist his suggestions, as they demand autonomy to make such choices for themselves.

Suppose now that our CEO turns into a dictator that takes over the town and uses his private security company as soldiers to enslave the workers. He provides them insufficient food rations consisting of grass pellets and water only. Through violent repression he exploits their labour power whilst they gradually lose their physical strength as a result of their inadequate diet. Their inadequate diet will soon have consequences on their bodies. Their loss of weight and the physical symptoms of their lack of essential nutrients will show. Furthermore, their frustration, resentment and passive resistance to their loss of liberty and autonomy will be expressed in their faces. Almost any outsider will acknowledge that such food is harmful to human health and such domination and enslavement will frustrate and infuriate human beings of whatever kind.

If it is true that human beings clearly know that certain things are bad for members of their kind, what are those things? Most human beings do not want to die a premature death or experience bad health. We don't want to go without food or water, or not have clothes or shelter to protect us against the elements. Besides these kinds of harm to our bodies, we also prefer to avoid harm to our psychological health and prefer to engage in emotionally nurturing relationships. Humans generally dislike unnecessary mental distress and emotional pain.

Furthermore, most humans prefer not to be completely isolated from other human beings or the natural environment. When we do live in close contact with other humans – as we mostly do – we prefer not to be in continual conflict or to have destructive relationships. Exclusion and isolation from human company are also undesirable if it results from unemployment and an inability to be self-reliant. Unemployment and dependence on other people have negative effects on a person's sense of self-worth and self-respect.

Thus, if these are matters with negative impact that almost all humans avoid, then their opposites are the positive things most humans want for themselves. Most people want (1) bodily and psychological health, (2) food, water and shelter, (3) healthy, loving, nurturing relationships that provide security, (4) independent decision making about core aspects of one's own life and (5) meaningful, useful roles in society. These matters are prerequisites for choosing and constructing a life every person judges best for themselves.

What I hope to have shown thus far is the following:

1. human beings today function in interconnected networks that stretch across national borders;
2. our words and deeds, or lack thereof, have a negative or positive impact on other humans with whom we are connected within any of the multiple networks we are engaged in;
3. we know that many basic human words and deeds cause negative or positive impacts on the lives of human beings;
4. we benefit if the nodes in our networks, that is our fellow humans with whom we interact even though only remotely, function reasonably well. Their lack of well-being can have negative effects on our lives. Thus, our self-interest to maintain and enhance our well-being requires us to ensure the minimal well-being of all those people with whom we are networked;
5. we must justify to ourselves and to anyone affected by our words and deeds why we allow the negative impact of our words and deeds and

their consequences to negatively influence their lives. Or, we must justify why we allow our lack of appropriate words and deeds to let suffering persist;

6. we must be aware that the scope and nature of our decision making can have a deep influence on the world around us, just as we are subject to the decision making of other people in a variety of settings;

7. we know sufficiently well what positive things human beings want in their lives and what negative things we all would prefer to escape.

In the light of these seven statements, we can argue that each of us is accountable for our impact, through our actions or lack thereof, on other people's lives, wherever they are. Does this mean we must do something to eradicate the poverty of those with whom we are in some or other network relationship? To answer this question we must first determine what poverty is and why it is morally wrong that any human being is exposed to such a condition. As a first step to answer this question, I will present a definition of poverty in the next chapter that emphasizes its harm to the humanity of its sufferers.

2 • Defining Poverty as Distinctively Human[1]

There are lots of things one can say about poverty without fear of contradiction. Poverty is arguably the biggest problem facing humans today[2] and the greatest cause of suffering on earth.[3] Poverty is responsible for more preventable deaths than anything else.[4] We, human beings on earth, have all the knowledge and resources available we need to eradicate poverty everywhere.[5] Never before has poverty been so high on the agenda of so many governments and international bodies. The world has never before witnessed so many heads of state and governments publicly commit themselves to eradicate poverty.[6] Despite all this, poverty still persists as a massive problem affecting hundreds of millions of human beings across the globe.[7]

Most of us can identify human beings suffering from poverty easily, but find it slightly more difficult to understand poverty properly. Note the following remarks by a poor Kenyan man about the visibility of his poverty:

> Don't ask me what poverty is because you have met it outside my house. Look at the house and count the number of holes. Look at my utensils and the clothes that I am wearing. Look at everything and write what you see. What you see is poverty. (quoted in Narayan et al., 2000a: 30)

In this respect poverty resembles the common cold. Most humans can easily and accurately observe when a fellow human suffers from the common cold, as the symptoms are clearly visible and identifiable. A further resemblance between poverty and the common cold that will emerge later on is that both phenomena can be caused by a variety of factors. As the common cold is caused by a virus that constantly mutates so poverty results from one or more causes drawn from a wide-ranging set of factors.

In this chapter I aim to deepen our understanding of poverty by interpreting the conventional definitions of poverty in a new light.[8] I start with a defence of a claim that poverty is a concept uniquely applicable to humans. I then present a critical discussion of the distinction between absolute and relative poverty. I argue that a revision of this distinction can provide us general standards applicable to humans everywhere.

Perhaps some readers want to object at the starting point, arguing that middle-class academic researchers should not define and identify a condition of which they have no experience or intimate knowledge. They should rather allow poor people the audience to voice their own definition of a condition they suffer publicly and often embarrassingly so. Does this objection have a point? Such an objection contains controversial assumptions. One assumption borders on solipsism that suggests that one 'has to be one to know one'. Another assumption is that people experiencing a particular condition necessarily have the ability to best describe that condition accurately and insightfully.[9] Both these assumptions would invalidate large parts of the work of the human sciences.

There is a valid point in the objection though. Although one does not have to be one to know one, it is vital to listen closely to people with personal, close-up experience of poverty. For this reason attempts at a 'bottom-up' definition of poverty work, though perhaps not for the exact reasons underlying the aforementioned objection. In the process of constructing such definitions, researchers deliberately select people with special characteristics, that is, those who have experienced severe poverty. They sometimes use social workers or aid workers thoroughly familiar with more serious cases of poverty as informants.[10] More importantly, the researchers interpret the experiences reported and construct a definition from them, transposing poor people's self-descriptions into the typical theoretical constructs employed in the human sciences.

Thus, in practice, this kind of definition rests on the idea that a definition of poverty must be developed in dialogue between the discourses of the human sciences and the self-reported experiences of those who are poor, or who are in close contact with poor people.[11] If understood in this way, I agree with the point that underlies the aforementioned objection. Our academic understanding of concepts must be developed in dialogue with people affected by poverty and cohere with people's everyday experiences of the phenomena they wish to portray. Furthermore, our theoretical definition of concepts needs to be tested for the illuminating value it has in clarifying the nature of poor people's experiences.[12]

|

In recent United Nations Development Programme Reports (UNDP, 1997; UNDP, 2000), the authors use the term 'human poverty'. Why add the adjective 'human' to the concept of poverty? Is it possible that other living beings like plants and animals can also suffer from, or live in, poverty? Can we speak of 'animal poverty' or 'plants suffering poverty'? Let us test this proposal by means of an example. Imagine an elephant in a small zoo. The zoo has inadequate financial resources. The elephant is in a cramped cage with no trees, shrubs or grass. No other elephants are in sight. For more than three years the elephant has not had enough food and water. As a result the animal is in a bad physical condition, easily susceptible to disease and has many sores on its body. The elephant also seems psychologically depressed, communicating its negative emotional state by means of enfeebled body language and mournful sounds.

Anyone seeing the elephant in this state realizes that it might soon die. The condition and circumstances of the elephant roughly correspond with those of a human being suffering from severe poverty. The elephant might be judged to be suffering from neglect and its keepers thought to be cruel, but would we describe the elephant as poor, or suffering from poverty? The concepts poor and poverty are not usually applied in this way when talking of an animal, except when we exclaim in a pitiful voice, 'Oh, poor elephant!' In this case we use 'poor' metaphorically to express the bad condition and pitiful state of the animal.

In contrast to our description of the elephant, in the case of a human being without the minimum necessaries to sustain physical health we describe the person as suffering from absolute poverty. This implies that human beings in whichever part of the world are judged poor if they do not have adequate economic capacities to ensure access to food, shelter, clothing, security and medical care needed to maintain their physical health. Why then do we distinguish in this way, calling humans poor but not elephants?

One might suggest the crucial difference is the relationships the elephant and human have to other human beings. The elephant is being enslaved and imprisoned in a cage by a member of a more powerful species that is not taking proper care of the animal. The human does not have such a relationship of enslavement or imprisonment with other humans and thus could be described as free to autonomously determine his or her own life.

However, the example might be misleading if read in this way. Suppose we find this elephant in a similar emaciated condition where it roams freely, without restrictions imposed by humans, on the African savannah during a massive drought. Again, I am sure, we will not describe the elephant as living in poverty, or suffering from it. We might say that the elephant suffers as a result of drought, or that the elephant is a victim of a natural disaster. When we exclaim, 'Poor creature!' we are not describing its situation in terms of poverty, but using the word 'poor' metaphorically to express our compassion with its suffering. Thus, poverty is a concept uniquely applied to humans. If this is true, does the concept of poverty express something particularly important about what it means to be human?

Perhaps another feature of the concept of poverty can get us closer to unravelling the meaning of poverty as a concept applied uniquely to humans. Poverty is not only used as a descriptive concept, that is, to describe a certain human condition, but also in a normative way to comment on, or evaluate, human lives. Pete Alcock (1993: 6) defends such a view that the concept of poverty not only has normative and descriptive functions, but also contains an implicit imperative to act to relieve or eradicate someone's poverty. Jo Roll (1992: 7, 8) similarly claims that poverty denotes 'a kind of avoidable suffering' that implies onlookers 'cannot just stand by and watch; they must take action'. I suspect Alcock and Roll are onto something important, but overstate their point. If they are correct, the world would not have had millions of poor people on all continents. People would have heeded the implicit call to action in the word they use to describe and evaluate the misery and hardship of so many fellow human beings. Alcock and Roll may be correct, though, if we weaken their claim to that of saying that the concept of poverty has a strong evaluative component. Perhaps the judgement by Gordon, Pantazis and Townsend that poverty is not only a scientific concept, but also a 'moral concept' (2000: 91) is closer to the truth. Srinivasan's remark that 'Hardly anyone would choose to be poor' neatly illustrates this evaluative component in the concept of poverty (1994: 241).

The claim that the concept of poverty has an evaluative aspect can be defended as follows. When describing a human being as living in poverty, we normatively evaluate that person's life and judge it to be unworthy of how humans ought to live. To live in poverty, or to suffer poverty, exposes the victim to a lifestyle judged to be below the minimum standard appropriate to humans. Thus, to describe someone as poor is the result of a normative judgement that a specific human being has inadequate economic resources available to live a life that conforms to the minimum standards a group of humans have implicitly agreed upon as minimally adequate for themselves.[13] This idea squares better with one of Alcock's other remarks (1993: 9) that people living in poverty 'by definition' find themselves in 'an undesirable or negative situation (unacceptable state of affairs)'.

Let us test this idea by means of an example. Suppose Smith is an environmental activist. He wants to stage a personal protest against the consumerist lifestyle in First World countries that he thinks is responsible for the consumption of energy resources that causes global warming. Instead of building a house like everyone else, he digs an underground chamber for his family to live in, without using any conventional building materials or household appliances. The soil in his chosen location is stable enough not to pose any threat of collapsing. He decorates the interior with natural materials that he removes from nature without doing any visible harm. Smith does not use any source of energy that contributes to an increase in greenhouse gases. He thus relies on a few simple candles for lighting and chooses devices for cooking that utilize solar power. No indoor heating is needed, as the temperature below ground is stable at normal room temperature. The family cultivates most of their food in a small garden and they own only a few items of necessary clothing. Through this lifestyle they want to demonstrate to others how small the ecological footprint of a human family can be.

The family's standards of personal hygiene are lower than the rest of society due to their minimal use of water, consumer products and household appliances. Their clothing appears rather dirty and neglected for similar reasons. Their physical health is good, as their garden produces an adequate supply of nutritious food. Smith earns a lot of money in his job as accountant, which he mostly donates to environmental activist groups. Smith and his family are judged by their community as being weird and wacky. They are shunned by many as a result of their appearance, hygiene and unconventional lifestyle. They do not have any close friends whom they entertain in their underground chamber.

Are Smith and his family poor? We could hardly call them poor if they have chosen this lifestyle and have enough economic resources to live a perfectly 'normal' life. Although the family cannot be called poor, they do violate our sense of what constitutes 'normal *human* living' in current society. They do not comply with the standards of living judged to be appropriate for humans in our society. Yet they cannot properly be called 'poor', as they have voluntarily chosen to live with a minimum of economic resources and the consequences that choice has.

In contrast, if McArthur were to follow exactly the same lifestyle as Smith with the exception that both she and her partner are unemployed with no income, their family would surely be described as poor. McArthur and her family simply do not have the economic resources to choose any other lifestyle and therefore their condition of poverty is not voluntary.

Jenkins is a different case, though. Jenkins lives exactly as Smith does or, more accurately, 5,000 years ago he lived exactly as Smith does now. Jenkins, one of the leaders in his tribe, was very proud of his underground chamber with separate rooms for every family member. His enormous physical strength and endurance enabled him to build a house underground envied by others in the village. His use of beautiful stones collected from the top of the mountain and tree trunks dragged from the dangerous forest were regarded as innovative decorations.

Although long ago Jenkins lived exactly the same life as McArthur does now, Jenkins cannot be judged to have been poor. McArthur, though, is poor. In terms of his society's standards of what constitutes an appropriate lifestyle for human beings, Jenkins excelled. The society in which McArthur lives gives a different, more demanding, content to the standards of what constitutes a minimally acceptable, appropriate lifestyle for human beings. McArthur fails to live up to these more demanding standards due to her poverty, her lack of economic capacities. Smith, though, is a different case. He rejects these societal standards as inappropriate to adopt as lifestyle for so many humans on a fragile planet with limited resources. Smith is not poor, as he has freely chosen to live according to different standards. Despite having more than enough economic capacities to fulfil societal requirements, his project is to challenge the standards his society uses to determine poverty levels. By doing this, he wants to lower consumption patterns in favour of safeguarding the earth's fragile resources.

These examples can be extended further to bring out the idea that every society has standards for what is regarded as suitable styles of human living made possible through the use and exchange of economic resources. Suppose Thompson is too poor to afford accommodation. The best he can do is to sleep in an old dilapidated pigsty at the farm where he works. He has nowhere to hang his clothes, no bathroom or kitchen and feels too embarrassed to invite any friends or family to visit. In most human societies his 'home' would be considered unfit for human habitation.

Imagine Thompson explores the farm and finds a cave used by thousands of bats. He decides the cave provides better accommodation, as it is bigger and has more privacy from prying human eyes. He meets an old acquaintance, Thomas, in town and blurts out that he lives in a cave. Thomas is unfamiliar with Thompson's present circumstances, but remembers Thompson as an adventurer from school days. Thomas eagerly wants to visit the cave, while Thompson is too embarrassed to stop him. At the cave Thomas learns that Thompson is not an exploring researcher observing fascinating animal behaviour, but someone too poor to afford better living conditions. Will Thomas still be excited about Thompson's chosen abode/dwelling? Having taken in the full situation, will Thomas reckon that his old acquaintance, or any human being for that matter, should live like that?

What is appropriate accommodation for humans at a particular time and place? To judge that involves the following.[14] The kind of shelter fit for human use depends on the materials, skills and technologies available to people in a society, combined with the climate and the particular purposes for which they use housing. Almost all other living beings can be 'left outside' to find shelter for themselves if they wish, but we judge members of our species differently. We expect fellow humans to have access to housing adequate enough to shelter them against the elements, to provide adequate space for everyone living there, to serve as workshop for household activities and provide privacy for those activities judged to be of concern to individual household members only.

Obviously the exact ways different societies have set their standards have varied enormously through history and culture. But, nevertheless, it seems as if every society has some kind of determinate standards for appropriate accommodation. Igloos, tents, huts, caves, paper-houses, mansions, flats – whatever materials, technologies, skills or functional ideas were combined, they were judged to set up the kind of shelter needed by members of our species in the particular circumstances of a specific society. Those without the defined minimum standard would have been assisted to find something appropriate, unless they were considered to be outside the human community. Those humans who are ostracized or marginalized for whatever reason – as poor people mostly are – are left to their own devices.

I have thus far argued that the concept of poverty is an evaluative concept used by human societies to set minimum standards for those aspects of lifestyles acquirable through economic capacities.[15] Such lifestyles are judged appropriate for human beings in the context of the society's available knowledge, ideas, resources and circumstances. How have social scientists used the concepts of absolute and relative poverty to set such standards? Can the use of these concepts be improved by the argument that the concept of poverty signals a standard of living that is below what is judged to be appropriately human in a specific society? In the next section I will argue for revised definitions of the concepts of absolute and relative poverty, based on the idea that it is significant that we apply the concept poverty only to a certain condition suffered by humans.

II

In his groundbreaking research, B. Seebohm Rowntree (1901) gave a definition of poverty that went unchallenged for almost half a century. This definition requires critical scrutiny, as slightly modified versions persist in contemporary use of the idea of absolute poverty. After discussing the most influential definitions, I will defend a revised definition of absolute poverty.

Rowntree takes families as unit of investigation. He defines families as poor if their income, total earnings or 'minimum necessary expenditure' cannot obtain or provide 'the minimum necessaries for the maintenance of merely physical efficiency' for a family of their size (1901: viii, 87). He explains this idea as 'the minimum of food, clothing and shelter needful for the maintenance of mere physical health' (87).

The income needed for the minimum necessaries will vary with both the size of a family, as well as with the food required 'by the severity of their work' (Rowntree, 1901: 97). Acknowledging these variations, Rowntree investigates which kinds of foods and how much thereof would be adequate to maintain physical health (viii). He also notes what workers would have to pay for these foods (103). Thus, what might initially have seemed to be an inflexible universal standard applicable to every family in an identical way, Rowntree adapts to a standard tailored to the size of the families and the markets they have access to.

Rowntree's slight softening of the application of his austere minimum standard for determining poverty is undone by some of his other assumptions. He applies the standard on the strong assumption that poor families have good knowledge of the most nutritious foods and where to buy at the best prices. He knew they did not have that kind of knowledge (1901: 105). He furthermore assumed that poor families used all their available earnings for purposes of maintaining 'merely physical efficiency' (viii). If people had adequate income to afford the minimum necessaries for maintenance of physical health, but could not do so as a result of using part of their available income for other purposes, Rowntree described them as suffering from secondary poverty (ibid.). These people are poor because part of their earnings was 'absorbed by other expenditure, either useful or wasteful' (ibid.).

Rowntree defines primary poverty as a condition that occurs when a family's full income, combined with sophisticated consumer skills, cannot enable them to provide for a family of their size and with their levels of activity the minimum food, shelter and clothing to be physically healthy.

The strength of this definition is the provision of a threshold below which poor people's bodies will begin to suffer ill health of some or other kind. Despite the flaws in his attempted expert judgement to work out the details of an adequate diet and the over-optimistic assumptions about the skills and knowledge of poor consumers, Rowntree's definition provides a basis for the idea of absolute poverty that is generally accepted today. It might be difficult to spell out the exact nutritional requirements for each person with their bodily activities[16] and to determine the cost of such an adequate diet in different localities, regions, countries and continents. Nevertheless, it stands to reason that people without adequate food, shelter and clothing will suffer some or other form of bodily harm, even if only loss of weight and increased susceptibility to disease.

Rowntree's definition lives on in modified and adapted versions that now define absolute poverty. All these versions assume that human beings require similar things to maintain their physical health, such as a basic minimum of nutritious food, shelter to protect against the elements, proper clothing for diverse climatic conditions, security and medical care. Although the nature and cost of these provisions differ from society to society, a baseline applicable to all humans can be set: a person is absolutely poor if they do not have sufficient economic capacities to ward off a decline in physical health.[17] The decline can be measured in different ways in all humans: loss of weight due to lack of enough food, weight gain as result of lack of resources to procure food providing adequate nutrition, increased susceptibility to disease, etc.[18]

I propose to reject the use of the word 'absolute' in favour of the word 'extreme'. The choice of absolute as qualifier for poverty is motivated by the idea that this definition provides a universal measure of poverty that can be applied across all societies. The other definition of poverty often used is qualified by the concept 'relative', with the intention to show that this manifestation of poverty in the lives of its victims can only be understood in relation to what other fellow citizens in the same society have, not in comparison to human beings everywhere.

Although I want to retain most of the core ideas behind the two generally accepted definitions of poverty, that is, absolute and relative poverty, I want to change the two qualifiers. I rather want to refer to absolute poverty as extreme poverty and to relative poverty as intermediate poverty. The word 'extreme' places the emphasis on the degree of poverty involved, not whether it is a universal measure or not. To call poverty extreme means to focus on the fact that in a specific case we find poverty present in an exceedingly high degree, sometimes to the utmost degree possible. Similarly, the use of the word 'intermediate' emphasizes the degree of poverty that falls in between the extreme kind of poverty and no poverty at all, a distinction that will become clear later in the chapter.

The reason for my rejection of the words absolute and relative as demarcations for the distinction between two kinds of poverty are twofold. First, I intend to define both extreme and intermediate poverty in such a way that not only universal measures applicable across all societies are present in each, but also relative elements that can only be judged properly by looking at the societal context in which a specific case of poverty occurs. Note how Ruth Lister (2004: 28) argues that 'even supposedly absolute definitions of poverty involve an element of relativity'. She makes the point that 'universal absolute needs' can only 'be satisfied in particular historical and cultural contexts' (36). Secondly, the use of the words extreme and intermediate indicates the degree of seriousness of a specific case of poverty in terms of the harmful consequences for the well-being of humans afflicted by it. To typify two versions of a condition – universally acknowledged as harmful to humans – by the degree of harm it causes seems better than using a questionable distinction between one version supposedly being universally recognizable and applicable across all societies and the other not. If one examines closely all distinctions between absolute and relative poverty offered thus far, they all have a distinction between the severity of the two kinds of poverty partially embodied. Furthermore, the use of the seriousness of the harmful consequences as criterion for distinguishing between two kinds of poverty fits in with the evaluative nature of the concept referred to earlier.

Note the use of the concept economic capacities instead of economic resources. Rowntree assumed that poor people would be streetwise consumers able to buy valuable products in the most economical way, knowing that few of them can in fact do so. Although his assumption is too stringent a requirement to expect most consumers to fulfil, let alone only the poor ones, Rowntree touches on an important issue. Different people usually do not have the same skills in using economic resources. For this reason the concept economic capacities is more acceptable for use in this definition. Amartya Sen (1984) alerted us to the importance of our 'conversion capacity', that is, our capacities to utilize resources efficiently or not.[19] Using capacities instead of resources can avoid embodying an assumption in the definition of extreme poverty that ordinary consumers possess skills of smart economizing on scarce and valuable resources. I thus use the idea of economic capacities to refer both to resources as well the ability to utilize resources 'to provide adequately for themselves' (Alcock, 1993: 61). If we include capacities in the definition of poverty we can make reasonable allowance for the small failings and non-malicious wastage that ordinary people frequently incur in their daily consumer activities.

In his classical study of pauperism, Charles Booth (1892) exemplifies the kind of generous and humane attitude toward poor people that I want to endorse in the process of determining the extreme poverty line. Note how he identifies with the very human shortcomings and failings of poor people whom he has studied:

> they, like all of us, are nothing much to boast of morally and are far from wise. They quarrel with their bread and butter; they throw away their chances; they spend when they should save; they most of them drink and many of them get drunk; they marry imprudently; they spoil their children; they buy finery; they borrow money and lend it; they trust their lodgers and commit inconceivable follies of many kinds. (Booth, 1892: 45)

Booth assumes that in these matters poor people are 'like all of us'. We all have such human failings in our consumer behaviour. Many non-poor people waste resources and do stupid things with their money, but they are shielded from slipping into poverty by their adequate share of economic resources. If their share of economic resources were close to the poverty line, they would have been poor as well.

Not all contemporary definitions of absolute poverty are sufficiently precise. Take, for example, the definition adopted in *The Copenhagen Declaration and Programme of Action* (1995: 57). Absolute poverty is formulated as 'a condition characterized by severe deprivation of basic human needs, including food, safe drinking water, sanitation facilities, health, shelter, education and information. It depends not only on income but also on access to social services.'

Although many people have an intuitive understanding of what the definition wants to convey, it is difficult to figure out what exactly 'severe deprivation of basic human needs' means or to determine when precisely someone reaches that point. To operationalize this idea with the aim of developing a measurable baseline or poverty line can be very difficult, even granted that any attempt at ranking people in this way 'will always contain a measurement error and, if a poverty line is used, there will always be a number of misclassified individuals' (Halleröd, 2000: 171).[20] The definition used by the World Bank is hardly more precise. This definition says that 'the inability to attain a minimal standard of living, interpreted to include not only consumption of food, clothing and shelter, but also access to education, health services, clean water and so on' (Squire, 1993: 377; World Bank, 1990: 26). What exactly does minimal standard of living imply for each of the categories mentioned, when applied to specific societies?

I want to claim that the alternative definition of extreme poverty I propose is more precise and better able to be operationalized into a baseline. We can measure gradual deterioration of physical health in human beings in various ways, such as intake of nutritious foods, weight loss, stunted growth, susceptibility to disease and so on. Note the contextual elements in this definition. What is available as food, clothing, shelter and medical care differ from society to society, whether such societies are differentiated by culture, history, development, etc. Similarly, individual variations are obvious, as people's nutritional and medical requirements especially are not the same. An approach that one size fits all will not work when implementing this criterion, as it must be adapted to suit individual and societal variations. Nevertheless, the universal elements can be applied more or less accurately for measuring exactly when an individual in a specific society reaches the point that poverty, defined as a lack of economic capacities, leads to a deterioration of physical health.

Alcock (1993: 58) raises an objection to a definition of extreme poverty that implies a sufferer 'does not have enough to live on'. He judges this formulation 'a contradiction in terms' and asks the rhetorical question: 'how do those without enough to live on, live?' Alcock exploits an imprecise formulation about serious human misery. His rhetorical question fades if confronted with the more precise definition given above. People without adequate food, clothing, shelter, security and medical care suffer at least a gradual, if not sudden, decline in physical health. People living in extreme poverty can stay alive for a long time whilst their physical condition and health continue to deteriorate. At some point their living in extreme poverty meshes into destitution, a condition characterized by extreme hardship and miserable desperation.[21] Scenes of emaciated human beings barely alive in their destitution are common in some parts of the world. To see human beings in this condition usually shock and overwhelm human observers.

Although the definition of extreme poverty provides a universally applicable baseline of poverty, I want to claim that using only this baseline as measure of poverty strips human beings of their humanity (see Jones, 1990). This baseline assumes implicitly that such people, with economic capacities that barely enable them to maintain physical health, are living lives compatible with their status as human beings. The baseline implies that as humans these people need not be participants in the social life of a community, need no educational empowerment, requires no recreational entertainment, nor do they have any personal or communal events to celebrate with others. To live a life excluded from generally accepted social activities that normal human communities engage in is to live a subhuman life, that is, a life in which core activities typical of the human species are impossible to do. In addition to the misery of struggling with insufficient economic capacities, people just above the extreme poverty line suffer the humiliation of being incapable of living lives judged as fulfilling their society's minimal requirements to qualify as human.

The shortcomings in Rowntree's definition identified above lead us to the alternative and wider definition of poverty. How? One shortcoming of Rowntree's definition emerges from the following question. Can we really judge people as 'not poor' if they only have the minimum food, clothing and shelter to protect their physical health? If all the family's earnings can just cover their expenses for these minimum necessaries, they still have no transport, they cannot buy gifts for special occasions such as birthdays, celebrations and festive days, they have no access to any entertainment that costs money, they cannot invite friends over for tea, and so on. Furthermore, they are required to show much self-discipline in their consumption so as never to buy newspapers, magazines, sweets or anything else that does not secure physical health. They cannot entertain friends, go to shows or be spectators at sporting events. To have one's freedoms curtailed in such a way and to display such frugality can be very demanding. Not able to participate in normal social activities and practices of one's society means Rowntree's non-poor people become excluded as participants in the generally accepted social activities of a normal society. Peter Townsend (1954, 1979) formulated these objections and the major alternative definition of poverty to address the shortcomings of Rowntree's definition.

III

Thus far I have argued that the strict absolutist definitions of poverty with their exclusive focus on the minimum requirements for mere physical survival and maintenance of physical health can be perceived as inhuman if presented as the only definition of poverty. The definition of extreme poverty is useful for setting a baseline for a particularly severe kind of poverty, but needs to be supplemented by a second kind of definition.

There is surely more to a decent, dignified human life than mere physical survival and health? For this reason I will next explore the wider definition of poverty proposed by human scientists who classify people as poor if they cannot participate in the social activities of their community.

In response to Rowntree's influential research, Townsend (1954, 1979) formulated an alternative, wider definition of poverty. He develops his definition as response to Rowntree's definition. Townsend (1954: 132) judges the standards set by Rowntree as not related well enough to the 'budgets and customs of life of working people'. He also disagrees with the austere ways in which Rowntree proposed poor people ought to have spent their money. Townsend (1954: 133) accuses researchers like Rowntree of expecting poor people to act 'like skilled dieticians with marked tendencies towards puritanism' in their choice of food products. To spend their money according to such expectations, poor people would need 'virtues of self-denial, skill and knowledge not possessed by any other class of society' (1954: 133). Townsend therefore formulates a broader definition of poverty. His definition of relative poverty takes as a starting point the idea that poverty must be understood relative to 'the accepted modes of behaviour in the communities in which they live', as these are influenced 'by the practices adopted by the society as a whole' (1954: 134). He defines relative poverty as follows:

> Individuals, families and groups in the population . . . lack the resources to obtain the types of diet, participate in the activities and have the living conditions and amenities which are customary, or are at least widely encouraged and approved, in the societies to which they belong. (1979: 31)

When people's command of resources slips so low, Townsend maintains, 'they are, in effect, excluded from ordinary living patterns, customs and activities' (ibid.). A relative definition of poverty judges that people are poor if they do not have sufficient resources to participate in the style of life of the communities of which they form part (see Townsend, 1979: 54–88). If people do not have the resources to share, or participate, in the 'customs, activities and diets' commonly approved by their society and embodied in its style of living, they are classified as being poor (Townsend, 1979: 60, 88).

This definition has two attractive features. One is the focus on how poverty, as lack of economic capacities, can have the consequence that poor people cannot participate in the activities of their broader social context. Their poverty thus leads to social exclusion. Another attractive feature is the way that poverty is defined relative to the standard of living within a specific society. Poverty in a hunter-gatherer society must be understood and measured differently from poverty in a modern, industrial democracy. These two attractive features of Townsend's definition also contain two weaknesses. One weakness is Townsend's woolly description of what comprises social participation. Can we define a non-arbitrary list of social activities as part of the society's standard of human living that people ought to participate in? Townsend uses words like 'types of custom and social activity', 'diets' and 'home, environmental and work conditions' to closer delineate what styles of living involve. These words depict a rather comprehensive set of human activities that most people only partially engage in. Is it possible to narrow down the general abstract requirement of social participation?

Although a lot of important research has been done on poverty since Townsend formulated his views on relative poverty, no one has convincingly addressed the issues raised above. The milestone event of 117 heads of state or government who met in Copenhagen in March 1995 and made 'the conquest of poverty, the goal of full employment and the fostering of stable, safe and just societies their overriding objectives' did not produce a much better definition of relative poverty. In addition to their definition of absolute poverty discussed above, the Copenhagen Declaration's definition of 'overall poverty' is articulated by Gordon (2000: 52) as 'not having those things that society thinks are basic necessities and, in addition, not being able to do the things that most people take for granted'. This definition is hardly anymore detailed or specific than Townsend's version. The same goes for the Council of Europe's definitions of 1975, as modified by the European Community in 1984: poor people are those individuals or families 'whose resources (material, cultural, or social) are so small as to exclude them from a minimum acceptable way of life in the member state in which they live' (quoted by Gordon, 2002: 58).

A second weakness is the correct, but incomplete, emphasis on the relative nature of this kind of poverty. Can this kind of poverty that causes social exclusion only be defined in terms of the social conditions of the society to which the individual belongs? Is Halleröd (2000: 167) correct in saying that 'what is deemed as "severe deprivation" will always depend on the ordinary lifestyle and way of consumption that prevails in a society'? Is it not possible to embody a universal element in this definition, to formulate a set of generic social activities that humans throughout the ages have engaged in? Will it then be possible to judge a society's level of poverty or riches by determining the spectrum of such activities available and by measuring the extent to which its members are enabled to participate? Imagine a society where a lack of economic capacities is responsible for the particularly narrow spectrum of such activities the society offers and for the low level of participation of members in those limited activities. Surely this society would qualify as poor in terms of a universal standard applicable to all human societies?

One of the few philosophers who thought seriously about poverty comes a lot closer to reconciling a more universal definition of poverty with Townsend's definition of relative poverty. John D. Jones acknowledges that styles of living are determined by a specific society 'within the determinate historical situation in which they live' (Jones, 1990: 67). The crucial move that Jones makes is to link this idea of 'a mode of life customary in their society' with the idea that such a life is one judged by society to be 'minimally fit and appropriate for people and thus minimally required for an appropriate realization of human dignity' (67).[22] This move by Jones gives us access to the possibility of universal definitions of poverty applicable to all human societies.

I have already defined extreme poverty as the lack of economic capacities that endangers a person's health. I now propose the idea of intermediate poverty that falls in between extreme poverty and not being poor at all. Whereas extreme poverty is demarcated by threats to a person's health as a result of insufficient economic capacities, intermediate poverty is demarcated by the loss of human dignity a person suffers as a result of their inability to engage in typically human activities defined as necessary for a normal, decent human life as specified by their society. The universal element in this definition is the loss of dignity as a result of not being able to engage in a set of social activities judged to be constitutive of what it means to be human in that society, while the contextual elements are found in the nature and possibilities of human life as found in the particular society a person lives in.

The contextual elements in the definition of intermediate poverty are clear. Not all societies have the same kind or styles of festivities and celebrations, nor similar kinds of recreation or participation in shared activities, nor do such activities require the same kind of means to enable one's participation. Similarly, individuals do not have the same need or interest to engage in exactly the same set of social activities and thus exhibit wide variations in what they choose and how often they participate. Nevertheless, we can determine reasonably accurately when people's lack of economic capacities makes it impossible for them to even consider such participation.

Note that intermediate poverty is the first stage of poverty and extreme poverty is a further worsening of a person's condition. People who suffer from extreme poverty thus also suffer fully from all the harms, effects and consequences of intermediate poverty.

Intermediate poverty could thus be defined as a lack of sufficient economic capacities to engage in a set of basic, fundamental human social activities that defines what it means to live a life worthy of a human being in a particular time and place.[23] This definition makes sense of the experience reported by World Bank researchers who were struck by both the universality and the specificity of people's experiences with poverty all over the world: 'As we moved more deeply into analyses of poor people's experiences with poverty, we were struck repeatedly by the paradox of the location and social group specificity of poverty and yet the commonality of the human experience of poverty across countries' (Narayan et al., 2000a: 3).

The possibility now exists for defining a broad, universal set of social activities that indicates the standard for what it means to live a life worthy of a human being, although any particular community gives expression to such activities in their own culturally unique way. I want to claim that most human communities known throughout history would have engaged in the following set of activities in their own culturally defined way, if they had sufficient economic resources to do so. The principal activities in human communities are those that secure adequate food, clothing, shelter, security and medical care to ensure the survival of the group. Most other social activities focus on fostering social cooperation and enhancing social solidarity, crucial for survival and prerequisites for achievement of a rich and diverse cultural life. Typical activities include governance of diverse aspects of the community's shared life to maintain social order, education to train and equip others to fulfil useful tasks, initiation ceremonies for welcoming new participants in diverse social practices, thanksgiving events for expressing gratitude for services rendered in smaller or larger contexts, celebration of significant events on smaller (family) and larger (society) scale and entertainment to amuse and amaze others through expressing rare individual and team talents and skills.

The rationale for this set of human activities is that they seem to encapsulate the set of activities human communities have engaged in throughout known history. Engaging in a configuration of such activities expresses our humanity. Put differently, to qualify as human, communities should be economically able to enact their versions of such activities.[24] Any normally functioning human community ought to have the economic capacities to generate and sustain their own interpretation and expression of such activities. If this is true, we have a universal, albeit an approximate, standard to determine the level of poverty or riches of a particular society. Why do I qualify the universal standard as being approximate, that is, as a measure that can be reasonably accurate, but not exact and precise? The way that individuals, families and communities of varying sizes choose to design and implement their life plans, the values they profess and live and the possibilities available within geographical locations and historical circumstances will vary and deeply influence their lifestyles. Note how state-of-the art knowledge and science, climate, natural resources, human values, acquired skills and societal determinants of life chances influence the ways we concretize and actualize these universals.

Let us explore this idea. Society X has been poor for many decades and in addition has suffered severe droughts over the past few years. Agriculture is the main source of income. Although they share their minimal resources with one another, many have died as a result of not having enough food to eat. Virtually all of them are living in extreme poverty. They do not have resources to feed themselves properly, let alone any reserves that they can use for celebrating birthdays, religious festivals or public holidays. Although they can still entertain one another through telling stories, they had to close their radio station and cannot afford any theatre productions. Many of them are so bogged down by the problems of their society and have so little energy as a result of their diet that is low in nutritious foods that they do not participate in such entertainment activities anymore. On visiting such a community, people from non-poor countries would typically exclaim: 'This is not the way humans should live!'

Society X is similar to many known societies throughout the world. Such societies are poor as a whole, because they do not have the economic resources to set up, run and maintain the most basic social activities one expects to find in any human society. Anyone concerned about the well-being of fellow human beings ought to be deeply worried about a society where everyone falls below the poverty line.

IV

In this chapter I have developed the following ideas. (1) Poverty is a concept uniquely applied to humans to indicate when a specific person has fallen below the standard of life thought appropriate for someone in that culture, (2) extreme poverty means that a person does not have adequate economic capacities to provide adequate food, clothing, shelter, security and medical care to maintain their physical health, (3) intermediate poverty means that although people have adequate economic capacities to provide adequate food, clothing, shelter, security and medical care to maintain their physical health, they cannot participate in any other activities regarded as indicative of being human in that society.

To be poor thus means to suffer as a result of all the consequences of not having enough economic capacities. Poor people experience the humiliation of not being able to live fully human lives as specified by their society. Poverty entails the desolation of realizing that others do not demonstrate care that you experience poverty in all its fullness, while they furthermore deny any responsibility in the genesis of your situation, as well as their responsibility for improving your lot. Many morally sensitive people experience moral outrage that humans are allowed to suffer such deplorable conditions. Others are reluctant to acknowledge the full impact of poverty on fellow human beings and they avoid the discomfort and challenge of recognizing the inhumane situation of poor people.

If one has a concern for people living in extreme poverty, should one have similar concerns for everyone living in poverty, albeit only of the intermediate kind? Should we be similarly worried about people who live in a society where no person is poor at all, but whose economic capacities are moderately to vastly unequal to those of their fellow citizens? Should all such inequalities be of similar moral concern to us as the contrast between rich and poor citizens? These issues that deal with the topic why the inequality of poverty is morally wrong and deserves our primary moral concern will be discussed next.

3 • Why the Inequality of Poverty is Morally Wrong

I

Defining poverty as a concept uniquely applicable to humans has thus far helped us understand poverty as a condition that causes its victims to live lives in which they cannot fully participate in the range of activities expressive of their nature as human beings and they may even fail to be able to maintain their physical health. They are excluded from full participation as human members of society.

The issue I wish to address next is whether the description of inequality between humans in a particular society by means of the dichotomous set of concepts rich and poor is distinctively human as well. I argue that it is the case and that further issues arise from acknowledging this aspect of our social life. I focus on the moral significance of the overlaps between poverty and inequality. I then argue that the eradication of poverty – one specific kind of inequality – must be our first priority because of the specific kinds of harms it inflicts on humans.

Suppose it is true that the concept of poverty cannot be properly applied to animals. Do we nevertheless find similar inequalities between animals that share a territory like those we express through the kind of inequality denoted by the distinction between rich and poor humans? Let us consider the following example. We discover a group of fifteen emaciated elephants on the lush sprawling plains of the protected African wilderness. To explain their condition is a mystery. Good summer rains have turned the landscape into all shades of green. There is no shortage of food and water. The mystery is solved when we notice a much larger group of elephants, approximately fifty, showing considerable aggression towards the small group. The elephants of the larger group are in much better shape, fat actually, and they have guards to force the small group to utilize only a few barren hills in the middle of the plains. The large group has decided they want to protect the plains from other animals for their own use. They plan to store grazing for the dry winter months ahead.

This kind of behaviour by animals is rare, if it occurs at all. Perhaps in some species dominant animals mark and guard their territory and try to keep others out. However, they cannot patrol all the boundaries of their territory at once and there usually are sufficient food resources available to the others so as not to dramatically affect their physical condition. Animals do not have the abilities of humans to preserve resources or convert them into valuable artefacts symbolizing riches, or to store resources and riches on a vast scale like humans can.[1] These abilities enable some individual humans to gather resources far outstripping the combined resources of thousands and often millions of other human beings. Animals also do not have the institutions and guards that enable such protected storage of resources in converted form. Planning in advance for events in the distant future is also something more uniquely human. These extraordinary human abilities, shared only weakly by some animal species, make vast inequalities possible, which we describe in the set of dichotomous concepts rich and poor.

In this chapter I claim that the inequalities expressed in the distinction between rich and poor are unique human phenomena. They show how humans choose to accept and condone such inequalities that deny poor people their human dignity and threaten their health. If we can legitimately claim that sharp inequalities between living beings that share similar circumstances and conditions are something that occurs almost exclusively amongst humans, how does this fact change our perspective on these inequalities? Does it mean that humans have unique capacities to inflict harmful consequences on one another through the collective choices we make about the distribution of material resources? The answer seems to be yes.

To answer the questions raised above, we must do several things. We must look at poverty from a perspective that highlights the distinction between rich and poor that expresses the inequalities between people who share the same village, town, city, province, country, continent and world. Then we must explore to what extent the concepts poverty and riches cover the same ground as inequality. Next I will determine whether all inequalities between citizens are worth our equal concern. If not, as I will claim, we must ask when does inequality become a matter that needs our urgent attention. My claim is that the inequalities that overlap with the distinction between rich and poor are ones that are morally particularly serious.

II

Social scientists investigating poverty formulate strong empirical hypotheses about the suspected interlinked relationships between rich and poor people in a particular society. The truth of these hypotheses depends on the contingent empirical support available in the case of particular societies. The patterns of relationships with significant empirical support observed thus far are as follows. Despite enormous growth in wealth during the twentieth century, vast numbers of people still live in either extreme or intermediate poverty throughout the world. The victims experience 'the poverty that afflicted the few, or at least the minority, in many (usually industrialized) countries and the poverty that afflicted all but the few in other countries' (John Kenneth Galbraith, paraphrased in Townsend and Gordon, 2002: 415).

The distribution of resources within and between countries is judged to be 'extraordinarily unequal' (World Bank, 2001: 3). Millions of those desperately poor die as a result of starvation. Preventable death, ill health, hunger, slum conditions, tattered clothes and limited options for self-development persist despite the fact that enough wealth is available to eliminate poverty throughout the world. The reason for this persistence is the vast amounts of riches concentrated in certain countries and in possession of powerful individuals.[2] For this reason, researchers claim, poverty can only be eliminated at the cost of the rich,[3] who will have to sacrifice at least part of their control over vast resources and modify their often extravagant lifestyles.[4] In a recent survey in the UK 58 per cent of respondents indicated that they believe 'inequality persists because it benefits the rich and powerful' (Orton and Rowlingson, 2007: 39). An even more devastating finding comes from a major recent UK study where the researchers state the following:

> A fraction of the wealth of just a proportion of the richest would be enough, if transferred perfectly, to tip all those who were materially poor above any conventional poverty line.

> Poverty tends to rise as the proportion of wealth held by the best-off increases – but that does not necessarily imply more wealthy households – just that wealthier households have become wealthier still. (Dorling et al., 2007: 84)

Similar remarks about the link in the UK between the poverty of many and the riches of the few are made by Callinicos (2000: 103) when he says that the inequalities in the UK are so deep and unjust 'that the situation can begin to be remedied only by dramatic transfers from the rich to the poor'.

These remarks already suggest an inextricable link between poverty and riches. In the light of this possible link, some researchers question the wisdom of allowing economic and political institutions, policies and practices that produce outcomes where millions of people cannot satisfy even their most basic needs to stay alive, whilst others have such quantities of resources to satisfy even their most frivolous wishes.[5] Questioning these outcomes becomes a lot more serious when scientists can provide solid empirical evidence that the vast riches of some economically powerful individuals and groups rest on their exploitation of those who are economically and politically much weaker.[6] This implies that the institutions, laws, rules, conventions and practices operative in a society allow some to derive unfair benefits from the toil and labour of others. For example, empirical evidence often shows that some employed people, referred to as the working poor, are paid a pittance, enabling their employers to sell cheaper products and services to maximize their market share and increase profits.[7]

What exactly is the moral concern here? At issue is that people who live interconnected, shared lives have such widely diverging life chances and enjoy such different opportunities to optimize their potential. Furthermore, some citizens cannot live out their hopes and dreams to any reasonably similar degree as those who are so much more advantaged. No wonder a renowned poverty researcher claims that 'where socio-economic realities are wide' society not only tends to 'pay lip-service to the principle of equal worth and human dignity', it actually becomes a fiction (Lister, 2004: 121). Poor citizens are furthermore exposed to a wide-ranging series of harms and indignities not faced by these people better equipped with economic capacities. The question thus arises whether these inequalities are fair, especially if these inequalities most often prove not to be caused by those suffering from them.

For such reasons, many social scientists see poverty and riches as two sides of the same coin.[8] As some are rich and others are poor as a result of a specific distribution of society's finite resources, many researchers propose that an understanding of poverty will also provide an understanding of riches.[9] R. H. Tawney articulated the supposed intertwinement of poverty and riches as follows, 'What thoughtful rich people call the problem of poverty, thoughtful poor people call with equal justice the problem of riches' (quoted in Roll, 1992: 17; and Alcock, 1993: xi).

Let us assume, for the sake of argument, that these empirical claims about the interrelationship between rich and poor are no more than acceptable hypotheses with more or less empirical confirmation. Despite being provisional claims, these statements direct our attention to the possible interdependence and interaction between rich and poor in society. Can we see something of this supposedly empirically confirmed relationship between rich and poor manifested in the meaning of the conceptual distinction between the terms rich and poor?

Poverty is part of a set of dichotomous concepts, where 'rich' defines a good condition desired by most people and 'poor' a miserable condition chosen only by a very few for other purposes, mostly religious. What light can a definition of the concept riches cast on the meaning of the concept of poverty?

In everyday language the concept riches refers to a condition of having a lot of money or possessions or, more generally, having abundant means considered valuable in society. Riches thus refer to valuable means and possessions of individuals, families, groups or countries. People are described as rich when they are amply provided with money or possessions. People who have large quantities of money or possessions are considered people with abundant means to fulfil their plans, projects, purposes or dreams. They have more power than other people to produce the outcomes most congenial to their plans, purposes and wishes. Diener and Biswas-Diener (2002: 121) argue that a 'multiplicity of positive variables . . . co-vary with income', as riches can be related to 'many positive outcomes in life'. Rich people have the resources to influence and direct other people's lives. The words 'abundant', 'amply provided with' and 'large quantities' suggest that people are rich in comparison with other members of their society or other members of comparable societies. They seemingly have more than others do, or possess valuable things in excess of the degree to which others possess them.

When we apply the concept rich to particular actions or things, other dimensions of its meaning emerge that elaborate the meaning described above. When we talk of a mine rich in iron ore, we mean that this mine contains large amounts of valuable resources. A rich imagination produces many creative, new ideas. A rich country abounds in natural, material or human resources that yield many things judged valuable. Similarly, rich soil can produce good crops because the soil abounds in qualities conducive to the production of good crops. Riches furthermore refer to qualities of great value that things or persons have in abundance. Examples include references to a person who is richly talented, the riches of our language or to a country's riches in petroleum.

An important dimension of the meaning of the concept rich is that things or persons so described possess something precious that is of great worth or value. Take the following examples. A rich voice is full and rounded, abounding in sweetness and harmony. Rich food has choice ingredients and therefore particularly strong stimulative or nourishing effects. A rich interpretation of a musical work describes a highly developed or cultivated performance demonstrating superior skill, knowledge and insight.

Note the following caveat. All the examples of the metaphoric uses of the concepts 'rich' and 'poor' already suggest that a worthwhile life consists of much more than merely income and wealth! Riches play an important role to improve only some aspects of subjective well-being. Diener and Biswas-Diener (2002: 129–30) point out that many aspects of subjective well-being cannot be improved by riches. This point is reflected in the metaphoric uses of riches above, which demonstrates that many good things in life that can be characterized as rich have nothing to do with money or wealth. Furthermore, the phenomenon of declining marginal utility means that an increase in riches makes a much bigger difference to a poor person's life. If one would double the income of a poor worker it would have a huge impact on the person's life who can now better afford to satisfy the household's basic needs. A doubling of the income of a rich person would not make that much of a difference to a person's life who could already easily satisfy basic needs and non-necessary wants.

Thus, the main dimensions of the meaning of the concept of riches are as follows. The concepts 'riches' and 'rich' refer to people who might (1) have large amounts of valuable resources, be amply provided with or have a lot of money or possessions and possess precious things considered to be of great worth, (2) command abundant means considered to be valuable in a society and can use those means to exercise power over others. The concepts also refer to activities or performances that (3) have qualities of great value and (4) yield or produce things considered to be of great worth.

In stark contrast to the above definition of the concepts rich and riches, the concept poverty has thus far first been defined as extreme poverty, which means that a person does not have sufficient economic capacities to provide adequate food, clothing, shelter, security and medical care to maintain their physical health. In everyday language this means people do not have enough means to procure even the necessaries of life. Such people cannot secure their survival and are dependent on others for help. Gifts, community assistance, allowances, governmental aid or charitable relief stand between their bare subsistence and ill-health or even death.

Poverty has furthermore been defined as intermediate poverty, which means that although people have sufficient economic capacities to provide adequate food, clothing, shelter, security and medical care to maintain their physical health, they cannot participate in any other activities regarded as indicative of being human in that society. In this case people are unable to afford participation in characteristic aspects of human life, that is, they are people without sufficient money, wealth or material possessions to afford anything more than the barest necessities to keep themselves physically alive and well.

In everyday language the concepts poverty and poor are used with several meanings related to those in the definitions above. These related uses are mostly metaphoric applications and focus our attention on individual acts or performances, rather than being descriptions of the lives of individuals or groups. Nevertheless, these uses further clarify the dominant meaning of the concepts poverty and poor. One example is the meaning of poor as lacking an essential property, for example, when someone speaks of spiritual poverty, or poor soil. The soil has a deficiency in the desired qualities and thus yields little and is described as unproductive, inferior and of little value. In the case of soil, the desired properties needed for a good crop are scanty and inadequate. Growing crops in that soil does not go well, but rather badly. The soil cannot be used with any success. The words used to explain the meaning of 'poor' and 'poverty' in this context clarify the ordinary language understanding of the condition of poverty as a situation where people lack means, experience deficiencies in the provision of their needs and have access to scant or inadequate resources.

The above meanings assigned to the concept poverty show why poverty can often be described as privation. Privation is a condition where humans lack access to attributes or qualities they ought to possess for living lives that qualify as worthy for members of their species. It can also refer to a state where humans lack essentials needed for decent living according to an acceptable standard.

People in such unfortunate circumstances deserve some kind of sympathy, compassion or pity. This is reflected in the use of the concept poor as referring to people who deserve pity, who are unfortunate, unhappy, miserable and in need of people sharing their negative feelings. For example, one could speak of the poor fellow who was killed in a car accident, regardless of this fellow's socio-economic status. In this use the focus is on the person afflicted by unfortunate circumstances, who suffered an unfortunate calamity, who deserves to be pitied. Again, this use clarifies the dominant use of the concepts poor and poverty. Poor people are often pitied, seen as miserable and unhappy and regarded as unfortunate to suffer from desperate circumstances.

Everyday use of the concepts poor and poverty also suggests that poor people are sometimes to blame for their poverty. The concept poor is often used to refer to a performance unworthy of a person's position or ability. The cricket player played a poor shot that cost him his wicket, or the ballet dancer gave a poor performance of the lead role of Swan Lake. It could be that both stars gave performances far below their ability, or that they do not have the ability to perform according to the standards required of top performers in their field. This clarifies the condition of poverty by pointing to some people's inability to provide adequate means for their survival, or their below-standard performance – for whatever reason – that fails to deliver the required goods. If these ideas are linked with the earlier definition, one could argue that poor people are forced by their condition to live a life below the minimum standards their society has set for a minimally decent human life.

The insignificance and low position of poor people are also reflected in the everyday use of the concepts poor and poverty. Sometimes we speak of someone as a poor creature, or refer to a person's view as a poor opinion. This can mean that person and opinion are despicable, insignificant, humble, lowly or of little consequence. Sometimes people refer to themselves, their performances, belongings or what they offer to others as being poor. In such cases they are either modest or apologetic, attempting to depreciate themselves, what they have or offer to others. Again this clarifies the human condition of poverty by pointing to the low position of poor people in society as people who seemingly have a meagre or no contribution to make and who apparently have no substantial positive influence on the well-being of society. As a result many people look down on them. For similar reasons many poor people resist identifying themselves as poor. To identify themselves thus would be a negative portrayal of oneself as someone who cannot reach societal standards, a person with a pitiable problem in need of help. Poor people trying to live with dignity in a society prejudiced against them might not voluntarily want to adopt 'poor' as a self-description (Alcock, 1993: 208).

The main dimensions of the meaning of the concept of poverty are thus as follows. The concepts poverty and poor refer to people who (1) have insufficient economic means to procure the necessaries of life or inadequate resources to participate in human social activities, (2) lack essential properties, have deficiencies in desired resources or have access only to inadequate or scant resources, (3) have a low position in society without substantial influence, (4) sometimes perform unworthy of their position or ability and (5) make a seemingly small or no contribution to society.

A comparison between the meanings of the concepts poverty and riches reveals the following. The meanings of rich and riches turn on positive terms such as precious, valuable, luxurious, prosperous, worth, contribution and abundance. Rich people are described in similar positive terms, signalling the admiration they often receive. The focus is on their power to command a large share of valuable resources available in society or to use such resources to secure outcomes they prefer. In the case of poverty the focus is on negative terms such as inadequate, insufficient, deficient and unworthy. Social scientists typically use the following terms in their descriptions of poverty, 'deprivation',[10] 'exclusion',[11] 'insufficient', 'lack', 'dependent',[12] 'unable to',[13] 'loss of assets',[14] 'too little', 'shortage',[15] 'disabilities',[16] 'incapacities'[17] and 'fall below'. In contrast to the positive terms that unpack the meaning of riches denoting valuable qualities and characteristics in demand by many, the negative terms associated with poverty suggest something very different, at the very least that poverty in this sense is not something easily chosen by anyone, unless they have compelling reasons for doing so. What exactly does this suggestion amount to?

If one understands poverty in contrast to riches by pointing out what poor people cannot do compared with those who are rich, the following picture emerges. This picture shows why poverty is such a serious moral issue. Poverty as lack of economic capacities makes it difficult for its victims to develop and deploy their abilities to engage in social life as rich people do, disables people from giving their full input in employment, diminishes their range of activities as full members of society and restrains them from utilizing opportunities they would otherwise qualify for as rich people can easily do. For poor people a lack of economic capacities implies some things cannot be acquired, some activities cannot be engaged in, because the prerequisites are not there, the enabling circumstances to make something of their lives are absent. They just don't have what rich people do. The things, support, circumstances and resources to acquire what is necessary to engage in a fully human life are not accessible to support their life's project. They are disabled in their quest to live a life worthy of humans as defined by society. They cannot empower themselves sufficiently to exploit the opportunities available to them as human beings seeking to live lives comparable to those of their rich fellow citizens. If these are possible effects of poverty on its sufferers, it deserves moral outrage for taking away opportunities for making a decent living and for depriving people of life chances approximately the same as others have for making and implementing meaningful choices.

Note that in a constitutional democracy, for example, the objective set of liberties assigned to each citizen still belongs to poor people, but they cannot grasp those liberties and act in terms of them as rich people easily can. The opportunities available to their peers are still open for them to exploit, but they cannot due to a lack of resources to facilitate engagement. They are not enabled nor empowered by means of what economic capacities can provide to utilize many liberties and opportunities. Thus, within a society with many liberties and opportunities available to all citizens, poor people must decline participation or be satisfied with limited engagement only. Tantalizing options cannot be considered, exciting opportunities cannot be grabbed, spectacular events cannot be experienced and attractive activities cannot be taken up, all because of a dearth of economic capacities. There is almost something cruel about this: society offers a range of interesting things to do, be or acquire, but the poor person cannot make use of them, cannot participate nor acquire any because they do not have the requisite economic capacities. In contrast, rich people can choose from a vastly wider range of human activities, so wide that rich people can never dream of engaging in all. We humans have these massive inequalities between people in the same geographical area where both rich and poor are exposed to similar living conditions. Why do these inequalities become morally serious and deserve our urgent, undivided attention?

III

Poverty has thus far been defined as intermediate poverty, that is, as a condition that causes its victims to live lives in which they cannot fully participate in the range of activities expressive of their nature as human beings, and also as extreme poverty, which in addition means that people may even fail to be able to maintain their physical health as a result of their lack of economic capacities.

Let us suppose this definition of poverty works and it is therefore possible to specify a universal standard to determine when a particular society is poor, then the relationship between poverty and inequality can be depicted as follows.[18] In the first case we can depict inequality in a society where everyone is poor. In graph 1, for example, we can visualize the poverty of society X. If the set of 10 equal values of 10 represent the poverty line for society X, then all of society X's members fall below the line, albeit with unequal economic resources. Society X has an unequal distribution of resources, with everyone living in poverty, although some much more so than others. In this society there is nothing but poverty, although the conditions of the poor people are unequal. In this society poverty overlaps with inequality.

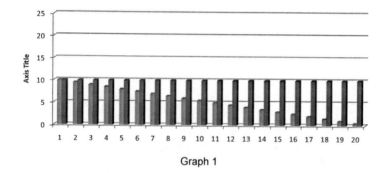

Graph 1

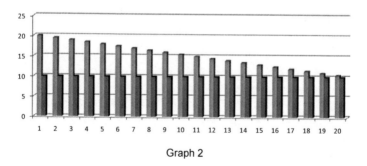

Graph 2

In the second example we have inequality in a society with no poverty at all. We could easily imagine a society with a similar poverty line, set at the value of 10. In this society, let's call it society Y (see graph 2), everybody is better off than the minimum required by the poverty line for that society. Although society Y has no poverty, there is considerable inequality amongst its members. Society Y is thus an unequal society with no poverty, although some command much more economic resources than others. If one compares society Y with society X, it is clear that society Y is a much richer society. Members of society Y are all above the poverty line, while no one achieves that in society X. In society Y there is no poverty, although inequality persists.

Next we can portray inequality in a society where half of its members are poor. In the third society with a poverty line set at the same level of 10, society Z (see graph 3), poverty and inequality intersect. The inequality of society Z is such that nine members get less than the poverty line for their society requires, while the rest are either on the line or above it. A strictly egalitarian distribution of resources in this case would make everyone's share equal, at exactly the level of the poverty line. Society Z is an unequal society in which almost half of its members suffer from poverty, whilst at least some are not poor, that is, some of those better off are much richer than members below the poverty line.

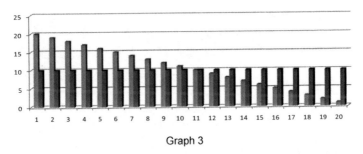

Graph 3

Sometimes inequality in society manifests with half the population poor and the other half not, while those living in poverty can be split between the people living in extreme poverty and those living in intermediate poverty. If we distinguish between extreme and intermediate poverty in society Z, we could have a graph like the one below (graph 4). In a strongly inegalitarian society like society Z, at least five members of the society fall on or below the extreme poverty line. Similarly, at least five members fall on or below the intermediate poverty line, but not on or below the extreme poverty line. Ten members of the society are above both poverty lines.

Imagine that the Redistribution Party comes to power in society Z with the promise to bring about greater equality. Society Za reflects the distribution of income five years after the Redistribution Party came to power

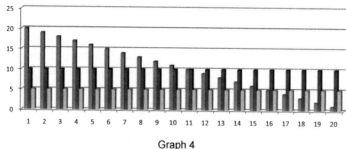

Graph 4

in society Z (see graph 5). The Redistribution Party had as its goal the reduction of inequalities. The party had major success with that, but nevertheless failed to reduce the number of people living in poverty, as exactly the same number of people are still below the intermediate poverty line. Nevertheless, overall reduction of the inequalities has led to a reduction of the levels of poverty suffered by poor people, as five members have moved significantly beyond the extreme poverty threshold. All poor people are now intermediately poor, with no one below the extreme poverty line.

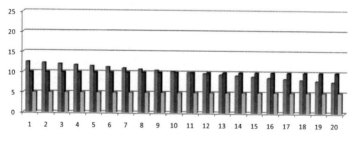

Graph 5

The last example shows that part of measurements to determine whether a particular society is rich or poor is to judge and compare the levels of poverty among the individual members of society. One can thus determine who is extremely poor and thus does not have enough food, water, clothes and shelter and who is intermediately poor, that is which people have enough resources to cover their basic needs but cannot participate in the normal range of human social activities and loving, nurturing relationships that provide security that is only available if one has sufficient economic resources.

Different measures can be employed to determine these poverty levels in a society. Empirical investigations can reveal the number of members of a society that have the resources to participate fully in those social activities as practised by their community and the number who cannot. We can also measure the degree to which those described as poor cannot participate in generally practised human social activities. Such indicators show the scope and depth of their exclusion from human activities others experience as normal for human beings like them to engage in.

From the above depiction of the relationship between poverty and inequality it is clear that not all cases of inequality are cases where there is a clear contrast between rich and poor. In some cases of inequality there are no poor people and in other cases of inequality there are no rich people. Thus, cases where virtually all people in a society can be classified as poor need our urgent attention, as all people would be suffering the indignity and consequences of poverty. Furthermore, not all cases of inequality between rich and poor can be classified as equally bad. Cases of inequality where some people are extremely poor are worse than cases where people are only intermediately poor, as extremely poor people cannot fulfil their basic needs for food, water, shelter, clothing and medical care as intermediately poor people can.

IV

The contrast between the unequal lives of rich and poor citizens can be staggeringly big and comprehensive. When do these inequalities require our urgent moral attention and possible intervention? In the light of the discussions above, I want to draw the following conclusions:

1. The problem of inequality between rich and poor citizens is a very specific problem amongst the broader issues regarding inequality of any kind between human beings. Why?
    a) People who are intermediately poor experience a loss of human dignity not suffered by rich people, because they cannot engage in activities their society judges expressive of their nature as human beings.
    b) People who are extremely poor, in addition to being intermediately poor, do furthermore not have sufficient economic capacities to ward off a decline of their physical health, as rich people can.

c) Note also the serious nature of the specific harms poverty inflicts on human beings.

2. Socio-economic inequalities between people with different incomes who are not poor at all are morally different from the inequality between rich people and people suffering from intermediate or extreme poverty.

a) In comparison to the case of people suffering from intermediate poverty rich people do not suffer a loss of human dignity due to a lack of economic capacities.

b) In comparison to the case of people suffering from extreme poverty rich people do not have a serious threat to their personal health as suffered by people living in extreme poverty. Such serious harms, as loss of dignity and serious threats to their health, will thus not befall those who are non-poor or rich due to their adequate supply of economic capacities.

3. A comparison between the meanings of the concepts poverty and riches in ordinary language revealed the following.

a) The meanings of rich and riches turn on positive terms such as precious, valuable, luxurious, prosperous, worth, contribution and abundance. Rich people are described in similar positive terms, signalling the admiration they often receive. The focus is on their power to command a large share of valuable resources available in society or to use such resources to secure outcomes they prefer.

b) In the case of poverty the focus is on negative terms such as inadequate, insufficient, deficient and unworthy. Social scientists typically use the following terms in their descriptions of poverty: 'deprivation', 'exclusion', 'insufficient', 'lack', 'dependent', 'unable to', 'loss of assets', 'too little', 'shortage', 'disabilities', 'incapacities' and 'fall below'.

c) In contrast to the positive terms that unpack the meaning of riches denoting valuable qualities and characteristics in demand by many, the negative terms associated with poverty suggest something very different, at the very least that poverty in this sense is not something ever easily chosen by anyone, unless they have compelling reasons.

d) By allowing this kind of inequality, we tacitly approve the existence of two classes of humans categorized in terms of dichotomies such as powerful – powerless and advantaged – disadvantaged.

The rich experience huge benefits due to their access to abundant
economic resources whilst the poor are deeply negatively affected
by their deficient, scant access to economic resources.

e) Do we have any adequate justification acceptable to everyone for
this major disparity in which one group experience a loss of their
human dignity, severely diminished participation in core social
activities, unnecessary health problems and less than satisfactory
estimation of their worth as humans from their peers while the
other group, all things being equal, avoid those things because
they have sufficient economic resources? (Obviously they might
experience some of those things, but then for reasons other than
a lack of economic resources.)

f) If rich people have such effective power as measured against the
poor, this asymmetry of power imposes moral obligations on them
to engage in reasonable behaviour towards the poor (see Sen, 2009:
205–6). It might be considered reasonable to work towards eliminating the harmful consequences that poverty inflicts on its victims,
like violating their human dignity, threatening their health or depriving them of adequate social participation.

4. The degree of inequality between rich and poor is morally significant
as well.

a) The more desperate and extreme the cases of poverty are, the more
they violate people's human dignity and harm their life chances
by threatening their health.

b) The more people have abundant riches of economic capacities,
the more possibilities for their life chances are enriched and the
better their options are for developing capacities and exercising
power.

5. When inequality collapses into a mere distinction between people
suffering from extreme poverty and intermediate poverty with no
rich people in sight, the moral significance changes again. Now the
moral obligation falls on sufferers to help one another with their
meagre capacities, as well as on well-to-do non-poor outsiders with
sufficient means to assist in eradicating poverty.

6. When inequality manifests as a distinction between people none of
whom can be classified as being poor in any way, the moral significance
of the inequality must be found in other reasons than a loss of dignity

or a serious threat to one's health. Meaningful differentials in power and privilege that enable domination or make possible unfair starting places in life immediately springs to mind as examples.

The inequality most deserving of our attention is the one between rich people and extremely poor people, as the level of harmful consequences show the greatest difference between these two groups. The second kind of inequality deserving our moral concern is between rich people and intermediately poor people, as the harmful consequence of the loss of human dignity separates these two groups. The socio-economic inequalities between non-poor people require a different kind of reasoning to show why they are morally serious, but in any case they have less priority than the two mentioned inequalities above, because lesser harm is seemingly at stake.

Thus far I have established that poverty violates the human dignity of its sufferers and threatens their health. In contrast wealth enables its holders possibilities of engaging many tantalizing, enriching opportunities for growth, development and enjoyment. To talk about poverty in such a general way is inadequate, as the full extent of the harm it can possibly inflict on humans can only be seen in the diverse details of many poor people's continuous everyday struggles. I show how some of these possible details play out in the lives of individuals in the next chapter.

4 • Poverty Violates Fundamental Human Values[1]

Although poverty devastates the lives of millions of people everywhere in the world, especially in developing countries, many non-poor people ignore their plight. Why should all non-poor people in the world take poverty seriously? Why should they care about a 'recognised evil' (Gordon et al., 2000: 81) negatively affecting the lives of others around them? Why did the 117 heads of state and government sign a declaration that calls for 'urgent actions' to address the 'glaring contradiction' of the 'expansion of prosperity for some, unfortunately accompanied by an expansion of unspeakable poverty for others' (Copenhagen Declaration, 1995: 5)? Why should anyone care that 25,000 children die every day (United Nations, 2009: 1) as a result of a preventable human condition such as poverty?

Why does poverty pose a moral challenge to all non-poor people? If some people face much greater risks of losing their lives than others as a result of avoidable circumstances, surely it calls for urgent moral action? Preventable death, for example, is one of the effects of poverty. Poor people can die for several more reasons than non-poor people, such as a lack of food, diminished resistance to disease as a result of inadequate diet, deficient or no medical care and exposure to cold weather as a result of insufficient clothing or decrepit shelter. Preventable death is by far not the only effect of poverty. If some people suffer from stunted physical or mental growth, lack of education and possess much less opportunities for personal growth and development, then surely questions must be asked as to why some people are exposed to such circumstances and others not, especially if those circumstances are most often avoidable through some kind of human action?

Poverty no doubt causes immense suffering to millions of people worldwide. Poverty has become a major social-political issue. Throughout the world millions of people are suffering from poverty and its crippling effects: 'Fifty-six percent of the world's population is currently poor: 1.2 billion live on less than $1 a day and 2.8 billion live on $2 a day' (Narayan et al., 2000a: 265). Poverty has been called 'the world's most ruthless killer and the greatest cause of suffering on earth' (Gordon, 2002: 74).

Many people also judge that there is no real progress to eliminate poverty on a global scale. Bill Jordan (1996: 1), for example, refers to the 'deterioration in the living standards of the worst-off members of all kinds of societies' as one of the 'most striking features of the past two decades'. Even worse, Alex Callinicos (2000: 1) suggests that the increase in wealth is a factor linked to poverty: 'Rich beyond the wildest imaginings of earlier generations, the world enters the twenty-first century heaving with poverty and inequality.'

In this chapter I want to substantiate the claim that poverty presents one of the most urgent moral challenges facing humanity, as poverty violates moral values about what constitutes a minimally decent human life broadly shared throughout the world. How can such a claim be substantiated? One has to judge the harmful impact of poverty on individuals and show that the moral repugnance of these effects on human beings makes it obligatory that eradicating poverty should be high on the agenda of all people. I want to show how devastating the effects of poverty can be for individual human beings and why poverty is such an affront to a person's dignity. My focus is mainly on the moral unacceptability of poverty's harms to individuals' lives and not on the similarly serious effects on societies. I judge the impact of the harms poverty inflicts on poor people's lives by evaluating them in terms of moral values widely shared throughout human societies. These values seem sufficiently uncontroversial not to need any special defence.

Why is it important to highlight the harms that poor people experience? I choose a holistic approach that portrays the wide range of dimensions complexly assembled in every case of poverty in a profile that expresses a comprehensive grip of the multidimensional nature of poverty. In this way I can highlight the diverse range of harmful impacts poverty might have on people's lives. This profile provides the proper background for a deep understanding of a seriously troubling condition that will be an appropriate illumination of the salient issues for moral evaluation. This approach is in line with Gasper's argument (2004: 15) that there is a danger when theorizing in ethics that one can focus too much on the good of human flourishing that one then neglects a very important focus on 'analysing and counteracting the bad'.

This chapter will enable us to get the perspective of victims of poverty so that we can critically assess the negative consequences they believe poverty causes in their lives (Allen, 2001: 348). Through evaluating poor people's claims carefully, I draw the conclusion that poverty is a great evil. My conclusion can be defended through my examination of poor people's 'actual experiences of poverty' and my own 'feelings of sympathy and imaginative identification' (Hampshire, 2000: 80). Through an in-depth understanding of the harms that poverty causes in people's lives I will furthermore meaningfully devise appropriate values of ethics and justice (later in the book) to eradicate poverty and prevent such detrimental experiences for all people in future (Allen, 2001: 340).

Someone might object that I ignore the positive outcomes poverty produces when people take up poverty's challenge and succeed against all odds to make their lives meaningful. The fact that I focus on the negative impact of poverty on people means just that: I am directing attention to the harm poverty does to individual people. I am not denying the positive characteristics some poor people develop and display in dealing with these harmful effects. Poverty damages the lives of individuals. As in all cases of hardship or trauma, the damage that poverty does can elicit resilience, stimulate positive growth and develop valuable qualities in people. I do not deny that poverty can have these positive effects on people, nor that poor people often have exemplary ways of dealing with poverty, or that people can give deep meaning to their experience of poverty.

Although some people suffer deeply from poverty, they are not necessarily victims. Some are victims, but others show resilience by making clever plans in their efforts to survive (May, 1998b: 18). As individuals or groups, poor people 'develop complex and innovative strategies to survive poverty and adversity' (UNDP, 1997: 61). That the narratives of poor people's lives are often 'a testimony to their resilience, their struggle against hopelessness, their determination to accumulate assets and their will to live for their families – particularly their children' (Narayan and Petesch, 2002: 1) does not detract from the harms poverty inflict on them, nor does it avert the terrible consequences poverty has on people who cannot successfully ward off its ravages. The bottom line is that poor people try their best 'to cope with poverty, to resist it and escape it' (UNDP, 1997: 62). My focus is on what they are so desperately trying to avoid.

Thus, the fact remains: through its diverse effects the impact of poverty does lots of harm to its sufferers, albeit in varying degrees. The consequences of poverty on the lives of people vary and these variations are determined by factors such as the duration of poverty, its severity, the history and personal characteristics of its victims and the level of social cooperation within the community they are part of. Poverty might not be the sole cause of certain effects, though it often acts in concert with other causes. Poverty often triggers behaviour by providing the spark that sets things off, or poverty exacerbates existing problems. Although poverty researchers can point to clear links between poverty and certain negative effects on people and bad consequences for their lives, the exact link between poverty and such effects and consequences can only be determined empirically in each individual case (see Halleröd, 2000: 171).

In what follows, I want to sketch a profile of the negative impact poverty has on individual human lives. I will first give a general moral assessment of poverty, showing it to be a violation of poor people's dignity as human beings. I will then provide a detailed analysis of the specific, separate moral challenges that poverty engenders. In this sketch, I do not claim that all poor individuals are similarly affected by poverty's harmful impact. I merely show the negative effects that poverty has on some people of all races, creeds, languages, genders, ages and origins throughout the world. My purpose is not to assign blame or ascribe responsibility for the negative effects of poverty. I depict the possible negative consequences that poverty can have on its sufferers. According to Daniel Little, 'poverty is a unique bad in its concentrated and destructive effects on the realization of the full human capacities of the poor' (2003: 32). These sometimes devastating consequences constitute a series of moral challenges deserving everyone's serious consideration.

The Fundamental Issue: Poverty Violates Individual Human Dignity

I claim that merely to suffer from poverty constitutes one serious blow to a person's dignity, as it signifies a lifestyle below that judged appropriate for human beings in a particular society. Furthermore, if one's fellow citizens ignore your condition and allow you to continue suffering from poverty it strikes another blow to a poor person's dignity, as they are excluded from care apposite to beings of their kind. The truth of these claims is shown in the fact that poor people so often resist being described as 'poor'.

I have already presented the case that poverty is a concept that is almost uniquely applied to humans. Poverty refers to a condition where a lack of economic capacities causes its human victims to live lives where they cannot fully participate in the range of activities expressive of their nature as human beings. Sometimes poor people may not even be able to maintain their physical health (see Halleröd, 2000: 167). To describe someone as poor thus indicates when a person has fallen below the standard of life thought appropriate for a human being in a specific society. Little (2003: 23) correctly argues that 'among the diminishments imposed by poverty are enduring assaults to human dignity over the whole of a human life'.

We can reasonably assume that poverty results from the choices humans make about the distribution of income, wealth and opportunities in their society and from the social forces they allow space to operate to produce unequal distributions. If this is true, we can say that the levels of poverty and riches in society are the collective responsibility of its citizens.

If poverty is indeed a condition that results from collective choices made by fellow citizens, then it is something that can be changed. Poverty is thus a remediable condition that continues to exist by the grace of the political decisions of citizens who allow it to be. Whilst poverty reflects a condition in which human beings live lives below those their fellow citizens think appropriate for humans, it also shows that non-poor citizens do not care enough about victims of poverty to change the social order to prevent, ameliorate or eradicate a condition that degrades fellow citizens.

If some humans are forced through a lack of economic capacities to live a life judged by their peers as below the standards set for humans in their society, such humans experience their human dignity violated. Ruth Lister (2004: 100) states that for many poor people it is 'the lack of respect and loss of dignity that result from "living in contempt of your fellow citizens" that can make poverty so difficult to bear'. If, as mentioned above, their fellow citizens do not care about the degrading condition they face, poor people suffer the humiliation of being valued not worthy to be cared for. They are not regarded as human beings who ought to be treated with a certain minimum level of respect for their rights and concern for their well-being. In this case they experience their human dignity denied. This lack of care shown by fellow citizens adds another blow to their dignity, as they are not shown the consideration proper to humans in similar degrading circumstances.

Note how poor people react to their human dignity being denied in these ways. For example, people in Bulgaria refer correctly to 'the humiliation and loss of status that accompanies a fall into poverty' (Narayan and Petesch, 2002: 242). No wonder that many poor people resist being identified as poor (see Lister, 2004: 114). Some poor people try to 'conceal their poverty to avoid humiliation and shame' (Narayan et al., 2000b: 38). Others refuse to admit that being poor means by definition 'to occupy an undesirable or negative situation' and thus do not want to identify themselves 'in such a negative, exclusionary and even stigmatizing fashion' (Alcock, 1993: 9). Many poor people use their cultural identity and their membership of smaller social groups to help them continue 'to believe in their own humanity, despite inhuman conditions' (Narayan et al., 2000a: 4, 5).

Some poor people go so far as to refuse to take up available aid, so as to 'maintain their independence or to avoid the shame of pleading poverty' (Townsend, 1979: 849). Their resistance to being depicted as 'poor' or to describe themselves as living in poverty is a brave attempt to keep their human dignity intact. Observe how poor people also try to protect their dignity through the kind of funeral they save for. Worldwide poor people invest some of their meagre resources in burial societies. Narayan et al. (2000a: 149) interpret this investment as 'a testament to the high priority that poor people assign to ensuring that at least in death they are respected and accorded dignity according to local rites'.

Despite these attempts at concealing or denying that one is poor, it is not that easy to accomplish. Poverty is publicly observable in most cases. Poverty is easy to recognize, especially when poor people are encountered in their home environment. Poor people are thus faced with threats to their dignity that poverty challenges them to deal with.

The details: poverty's harms to individual lives

How does poverty harm people's individual lives? In what follows I present common trends found amongst poor people everywhere. I rely on comprehensive social science reports on the poverty of people in different parts of the world to identify the most often recurring patterns of harm in poor people's lives all over the world. I use evidence from these social science studies to support the profile of recurring patterns of harm that I present.

Poverty harms people's physical well-being

In modern cultures lots of resources are invested to improve preventative, curative and palliative medical care. In these cultures we morally reject any unnecessary, preventable suffering to the bodies and health of human beings. Poverty, however, harms the bodies and health of human beings in many ways, especially in more severe cases.

Poor people without sufficient economic capacities to provide properly for their basic needs might easily suffer the consequences of an inadequate diet. Studies of poor people's diets confirm that although only a small percentage of the poor do not have enough food to eat, most cannot afford a healthy and balanced diet (Wilson and Ramphele, 1989: 100; Murray, 1932: 126). While some poor people can manage to include proteins and vegetables in their daily food intake, very poor people's diets are severely deficient in basic foods needed for a healthy body (Wilson and Ramphele, 1989: 100). In 1901 J. Seebohm Rowntree (1901: 303) made the following remark, which is still true today. He said that he did not intend 'to imply that labourers and their families are chronically hungry, but that the food which they eat . . . does not contain the nutrients necessary for normal physical efficiency'. Not all cases of inadequate diets are caused by a lack of economic resources; sometimes poor people are ignorant about what a proper diet ought to consist of (Murray, 1932: 127).

Thus, in many cases poor people simply do not have enough good food to eat. An inadequate diet can lead to further harm. Not enough food or an inadequate diet furthermore often leads to malnutrition, with negative effects on the bodies of poor people. Researchers note how strikingly often they encounter poor health as a result of malnourishment among poor people (May, 1998b: 118). Malnourished people are constantly tired, both physically and mentally (Murray, 1932: 47). Their ability to concentrate, work productively and resist disease is significantly reduced as a result of malnourishment (ibid.). Note how poor agricultural workers in Bangladesh describe their experience of 'a vicious cycle' in which 'inadequate food leads to weakness, reduced energy to work and illness, which in turn reduces income and the spiral continues' (Narayan and Petesch, 2002: 119). In this respect poverty resembles a lack or deficiency. Many poor people lack food, that is, they are without proper food for a healthy diet, or they have too little of it. They have deficiencies in their diet, that is, they have a shortage of adequate nutrition necessary for a healthy human body.

There is no doubt about the links between inadequate food intake, malnutrition, inadequate sanitation and many of the diseases poor people suffer from (Wilson and Ramphele, 1989: 120; Kabir et al., 2000: 707). The World Bank puts it simply, 'the incidence of many illnesses . . . is higher for poor people, while their access to health care is typically less' (World Bank, 2001: 27). Many poor people, especially children, die from diseases that are triggered by malnourishment (Wilson and Ramphele, 1989: 100). The consequences of illness and disease for a poor household can be severe. Narayan et al. (2000a: 53) state that poor people 'dread serious illness within the family' more than anything else, as illness destroys a productive household member's labour power and income. Illness in a poor family has direct effects such as 'reduced income, increased insecurity of employment and increased expenditure', which may deeply affect and strain relations between household members (Kabir et al., 2000: 710).

Sometimes poor people suffer more from specific diseases related to the circumstances that they live in. Gastroenteritis, for example, is regarded as an illness related directly to poverty. The incidence, prevalence and severity of gastroenteritis, especially for children, are regarded as reasonably indicative of the socio-economic status of a community (Wilson and Ramphele, 1989: 112). The correlation between the socio-economic status of a community and the incidence of deaths resulting from gastroenteritis is striking in one South African study during apartheid (ibid.). Gastro-enteritis was the most common cause of death in the 'coloured' (mixed race) community (176 per 100,000), the second most common cause in the black community (86 per 100,000) and almost insignificant in the case of the privileged white community (4 per 100,000) (ibid.).

Note how poor people in Malawi are vulnerable to disease due to the following health risks that their kind of poverty exposes them to, that is, 'hunger, strenuous labour, extreme weather, leaky shelters, contaminated waters, poor sanitation, promiscuity and unprotected sex' (Narayan and Petesch, 2002: 65). These health risks lead to frequent 'outbreaks of diseases such as cholera, schistosomiasis and malaria, together with the killer scourge HIV/AIDS'. These poor Malawian people are deeply affected by the consequences of the health risks that they experience as many are 'orphaned, widowed and disabled' (ibid.). Not only do they suffer psychological trauma through the loss of significant others, they incur the costs of disease and a funeral, as well as the loss of someone who might have contributed to the household income.

Sometimes an epidemic affects poor people more than others. The UNDP highlights the interaction between poverty and an epidemic such as HIV/AIDS. On the one hand, they say, poverty offers 'a fertile breeding ground for the epidemic's spread'. On the other hand, once the illness starts spreading through poor communities, it sets off a 'cascade of economic and social disintegration and impoverishment' (UNDP, 1997: 67). When families are affected by a terminal illness such as HIV/AIDS, the consequences 'can be catastrophic for the family' (ibid.). The family might lose a member that provides a crucial source of income and the cost of medical care 'rapidly eats up the family's financial resources' (ibid.).

Lack of sufficient income to provide for urgent needs affects poor people's ability to have access to proper medical care to ensure the health of their bodies. Most societies believe any member ought to have access to basic medical care available in their society in times of physical need. Being unable to afford doctors in private practice, some poor people have to rely on public health services. They often do not even use these services, as the location of the public health facility might be too far away for them to travel, the reduced rates they have to pay might still be more than they can afford and the hours that public health services are open might not be accessible to working poor people (May, 1998b: 60, 61). As a result many poor people make use of traditional healers, herbalists or self-medication instead (May, 1998b: 118). Although good for some medical conditions, these alternative treatments are not necessarily effective for all.

Poverty is at times akin to disease or infection. Like disease, poverty leads to discomfort or a disturbance of health. Poverty can cause crucial human functions to derange and thus negatively affect various parts of people's lives. Like infection, poverty has primary manifestations, like malnutrition, that produce knock-on effects that can be transmitted throughout other areas of a person's life where further injuries or harms result.

Poverty-related diseases are not the only source of harm to the bodies of poor people. Ill health can also be caused by dangerous or bad working conditions that often accompany low paying jobs (May, 1998b: 118). Poor people often qualify only for jobs that are considered 'physically risky' in which 'cases of debilitating and fatal injuries, assaults, illnesses and psychological abuse abound' (Narayan et al., 2000a). Again the lack of opportunities for proper education is interwoven with the restricted set of options many poor people have for gainful employment.

Some poor people are responsible for harming their own bodies. The widespread abuse of alcohol is a prime example. Poverty exacerbates alcohol abuse in certain poor communities and poor men abuse alcohol a lot more than women do. In the Kyrgyz Republic poor people comment that 'rising crime and alcoholism are consequences of the deteriorating economy' (Narayan and Petesch, 2002: 281, 282).

Poverty harms people's mental well-being

Life in the twenty-first century is stressful enough for most people trying to cope with its everyday hassles. We morally reject any attempts to make life unnecessarily more complicated for people than it already is. However, people without sufficient food to eat, who do not have enough water for household use, or do not have an adequate income, are at risk of disease and violence, and who do dangerous or boring, repetitive work for low wages experience considerably more stress than others without such problems. Lack of economic capacities thus exacerbates stress in human beings. This aspect of poverty resembles an infectious spread of something bad throughout different dimensions of a person's life.

Researchers consistently find high levels of stress and feelings of frustration and anxiety among poor people (May, 1998b: 50; May, 1998a: 41). Lister says depression and psychological distress 'are all too common among those in poverty' (Lister, 2004: 125). Worries about income, food, school fees, violence, keeping warm during winter and the well-being of family members can negatively affect the mental state of many poor people. Research suggests that some poor people often dread the future, 'knowing that a crisis may descend at any time, not knowing whether one will cope' (World Bank, 2001: 135).

Sometimes the uncertainties of whether they will have an income and how much it will be gnaw at many poor people's peace of mind. Peter Townsend (1979: 56, 57) notes that for poor people the amount of resources they have available for their household needs often change 'in the long term, over the entire life-cycle, but also in the short term, from month to month and even week to week'. Furthermore, many people who are on the verge of becoming poor 'regard some of the resources flowing to them, or available to them, as undependable' (Townsend 1979: 57).

Poverty can thus be characterized as an ill or hardship. As an ill it reduces a person's quality of life and becomes injurious to someone's health. The result often is that people experience their lives as miserable, troublesome or wretched. As hardship poverty is a series of painful challenges people find difficult to bear. Poverty inflicts harsh conditions on people that they find tough to endure.

Poverty harms people's interpersonal/family relationships

Human relationships of all kinds are crucial to develop the strong social aspects of our nature as human beings. We morally require human beings to engage in mutually beneficial relationships of different kinds. Poverty can have a devastating impact on such relationships. The dangerous mix of stress about inadequate resources for need satisfaction and the negative self-image formed from many poor people's feelings of personal powerlessness can wreak havoc on interpersonal and social relationships.

One example of poverty's negative effect on social relationships can be seen in the report by Narayan et al. (2000a: 44, 45) that some poor people often define poverty as 'violation of social norms'. Part of the explanation for this definition of poverty amongst poor people is that the definition expresses their inability to be equal participants in social events, as they cannot always 'reciprocate with gifts or participate in community events'. Their inability to participate and reciprocate as equals has harmful consequences that range from 'humiliation, loss of honor and psychological distress, to social marginalization and exclusion from important social networks' (Narayan et al., 2000a: 44, 45).

Family (household) relationships often suffer the most through poverty. Researchers frequently refer to fractured or unstable families with broken relationships, especially where fathers and husbands are absent or children live apart from their parents (May, 1998a: 4, 30; Terreblanche, 1977: 67, 76). Rural men and women often migrate to urban centres of economic activity in order to find jobs, while leaving their children behind in the care of family members such as older children, grandparents or uncles and aunts. Parents from urban areas often send their children to family in rural areas because of lack of space, time and resources to take care of their children themselves (May, 1998b: 78). Poverty thus creates conditions that make it extremely difficult for many people to engage in deep, meaningful relationships with their loved ones, thus another fundamental human need becomes more difficult to fulfil. Reports from poor people in Ghana illustrate this point clearly where researchers indicate that feelings of 'being neglected or abandoned by family also emerge in many other discussions about what it means to be poor' (Narayan and Petesch, 2002: 21).

Again the knock-on effects of poverty are clear. Like an infection these effects of the shortage of economic capacities spread much wider throughout a person's life than merely affecting the availability and quality of food, shelter, clothing, medical care and participation in loving relationships providing security and other social activities.

In patriarchal marriages women take full responsibility for managing and executing household duties, while men make decisions concerning household income. Poor women's unpaid work of household maintenance takes up most of their time and energy, leaving them exhausted. Consequently they are unable to take proper care of their children, to engage in activities to generate income or to utilize opportunities for education or self-improvement (May, 1998b: 80). Such women do not have sufficient time 'to rest, reflect, enjoy social life, take part in community activities, or spend time in spiritual activities' (Narayan et al., 2000b: 34). These women thus do not get fair equality of opportunity to make lives of their own as men do. It is striking that even unemployed men with little to do will not assist women in domestic duties to ensure the maintenance or survival of the household (May, 1998b: 102).

Patriarchal gender relations can thus become particularly strained when families suffer from poverty. Sometimes poverty places enormous strain on poor people's marriages, for example, when unemployed male partners have to deal with female partners who become the household's sole breadwinners. In their desperation to make ends meet, these women try to find paid employment even though 'only degrading or low-paying work is available to them'. Poor people in 'very diverse settings' note that this kind of stress caused by a female breadwinner in a patriarchal relationship 'frequently triggers increasing family conflicts, rising alcohol abuse among men and heightened domestic violence against women' (Narayan and Petesch, 2002: 9. See also Narayan et al., 2000b: 110).

While some poor households can deal with such a crisis, many others cannot. Sometimes such relationships (marriages) disintegrate, as men find it difficult to accept 'their "failure" to earn adequate incomes under harsh economic circumstances' (Narayan et al., 2000a: 6). These men find it hard to deal with a partner who has become the main breadwinner. Many male partners in patriarchal relationships cannot deal with their partner's new role nor accept that this new role 'necessitates a redistribution of power within the household' (ibid.).

In general, most contemporary societies morally require protection for weaker and vulnerable people, not exposure to violence. Interpersonal violence causes injuries to people's bodies and destroys trust between relationship partners. In many poor communities women and children are more at risk from interpersonal violence than in other communities. The UNDP (1997: 31) judges that among the 'worst threats of violence are those against women'. Many women in poor communities, according to responses in a survey and judging by cases reported to police services, suffer more from rape than women from more affluent areas (Wilson and Ramphele, 1989: 153; May, 1998a: 130).

Violence against women in the domestic sphere often results from conflicts over food or money and the risk of such violence increases with rising levels of poverty and male unemployment (May, 1998a: 131). Poor women are often trapped in abusive relationships where they endure violence as they depend on the abusive male for money, food and shelter (ibid.). Many women see no way out of abusive relationships as they have nowhere else to go. The UNDP estimates that one-third of married women in developing countries 'are battered by their husbands during their lifetime' (1997: 31). Researchers for the World Bank make the link between poverty and domestic violence even more explicit when they claim that although domestic violence affects both rich and poor women alike, 'the incidence is often higher in poor households' (2001: 137).

Poverty often does not affect all members of a household equally. We simply cannot assume that 'all resources entering a household are pooled and used equally by its individual members' (Townsend, 1979: 178). Therefore, in a household, so Narayan et al. claim, 'individuals both cooperate and compete for resources' (2000a: 175). The distribution of meagre resources within a poor household often becomes a source of serious conflict, as some family members contest the fairness of both the procedure of distributing resources and the outcomes of such distribution. The scarcity of resources to address multiple needs raises the stakes involved in the distribution thereof within the household. Decision making about and management of scarce resources often lead to destructive conflicts in poor households, or exacerbate existing ones.

The result of conflict about the distribution of resources within households 'may not be equitable and may leave many women living below the standards enjoyed by their partners' (Alcock, 1993: 137). For this reason women often challenge men's waste of precious resources on alcohol (wine and beer), tobacco and other women (May, 1998b: 48). Conflicts between male and female partners concerning decision making about resources are often resolved through violence or the threat thereof. Violence is often an important means of control that some men use against women, and functions as a deterrent for women to press their claims for an equitable division of household resources against these men or in cases of money required for child support (May, 1998b: 54). Reports from poor communities in Ghana state bluntly how these conflicts play out by causing 'turmoil and violence in gender relations' that find expression through 'dissatisfaction, quarrels and beatings' (Narayan and Petesch, 2002: 41).

The background of these conflicts lies in the fact that men often tie their self-worth strongly to their earning capacity and thus to their ability to take care of their family (see Narayan et al., 2000a: 175). For this reason some men develop negative emotions, such as feeling 'powerless, redundant and burdensome' when they cannot contribute to household income and 'may react violently'. Thus, their inability to provide adequately for their families spills over into worsening interpersonal relationships. Some men react to their loss of the role as breadwinner by 'collapsing into drugs, alcohol, depression, wife-beating or by walking away' (Narayan et al., 2000a: 203). For these reasons, poor women are thus more exposed to domestic violence than rich women (World Bank, 2001: 137).

The relation between poverty and some women's increased exposure to domestic violence must be explored further, as women in all socio-economic categories face abuse by their partners. Poverty merely exacerbates this common human problem. In Argentina researchers found clear links between male aggression, unemployment and poverty. For some men unemployment 'has been a blow to their authority and self-esteem' (Narayan and Petesch, 2002: 340, 341). Some men are adapting, especially those who find new roles helping their families and communities, but many others seem to be withdrawing into antisocial and even abusive behaviours. Poor men often express themselves clearly about 'the frustration, anger and humiliation that stem from a diminished traditional male role and the misery of joblessness' (Narayan and Petesch, 2002: 343). Male aggression resulting from poverty can also be seen in Russia, where in 'virtually all the communities visited, men and women report that quarrels about money are now more frequent and the increased stress on couples is contributing to divorce' (Narayan and Petesch, 2002: 325).

The impact of poverty on families can disadvantage women in other ways as well. Risks of sexual abuse and pressures of sexual harassment often lead to teenage pregnancies and early marriages which rob women of valuable opportunities for education and put a heavy strain on limited resources available to a poor family (May, 1998b: 59). A further disadvantage for poor women comes from their own family's attitude towards their education. Poor families still often argue over not investing in the education of female children who are going to marry into another family and render their services there. For them it makes more sense to invest in the male children who will generate income for the benefit of their own family (May, 1998b: 59).

That many poor women have negative perceptions of men should thus come as no surprise. They perceive men as a drain on their resources that expose them to the risks of emotional, sexual and violent abuse. Men are furthermore perceived as interfering with women's time and decision making about household matters (May, 1998b: 111). Men also sometimes deny women opportunities to develop and enjoy their lives in ways similar to the opportunities they claim for themselves.

At times one gets the impression that in some cases the deep emotional impact of being poor leads to self-mutilation. What do I mean? The combined emotional experience of having to cope with less than enough means to live one's life, the awareness that one's life is below the minimum standard for humans and the resulting emotional response to the knowledge that your life does not measure up to standards the majority of other people fulfil, sometimes leads to self-destructive behaviour.

Poor parents and their children

The moral sensitivities in many contemporary societies require children to be educated by their parents and treated decently so as to ensure that they have opportunities for optimal development as human beings. Children often suffer many of the consequences of poverty on poor families. They are often part of unstable and fractured families, or live apart from one or both their parents. They are often raised by people other than their parents. They are thus deprived of the tender, loving care parents are supposed to provide.

Lack of resources within households implies that children are often malnourished, poorly dressed and without money for educational requirements (May, 1998a: 30). Children are often forced to work to generate income and so are deprived of educational opportunities, despite the fact that parents might recognize the value of education as a method to escape poverty (Narayan et al., 2000b: 241).

The inability to continuously be a parent to one's children constitutes one form of neglect besides others. Poor people often don't have the time or energy for proper parenting. When poor parents live with their children, they often do not have the energy to be involved in their children's lives to give spiritual, moral, emotional or educational guidance (Terreblanche, 1977: 76). Although the parents might be physically present, they are emotionally or psychologically absent from their children's lives. Often the only way they are involved is either by getting rid of their frustrations through their children or by enforcing overly strict and cruel discipline. Tired parents sometimes discipline children through cruel physical abuse, as they are too tired to take proper care of children through more appropriate verbal communication (ibid.).

Frustration can be expressed through various forms of abuse and discipline is often arbitrarily enforced and accompanied with severe corporal punishment (ibid.). At times some poor adults vent their anger and release their negative emotions of failure, frustration and powerlessness through abusive and violent behaviour towards children (ibid.). A poor mother in

Armenia provides an example of expressing frustration through corporal punishment when she says, 'They reproach me for beating my children. But what should I do when they cry when they are hungry? I beat them to make them stop crying' (Narayan et al., 2000a: 238).

Children are often victims of interpersonal violence in poor communities (May, 1998b: 18). From a young age many children's bodies bear the scars of the inability of some adults to cope with too few resources. Note the fate of many poor children in Brazil (see Narayan and Petesch, 2002: 375). They are portrayed as the most powerless members of a very poor society who nevertheless 'suffer most from the violence that permeates their homes and streets'. Many poor parents who know their children's safety is at risk express frustration that they 'cannot shelter them from physical and sexual abuse in their homes and from violence and drugs in their communities'. Note how severe interpersonal violence has become in this poor community, as described by one of its members: 'Here there is battering all over the place. Women hit men, men hit women and both hit children' (ibid.).

Researchers use strong language to refer to these aspects of some poor children's lives. These children in poor households are seen to be 'massively vulnerable to violence of many kinds' and are said to face 'appalling conditions' (May, 1998a: 30). Although these conditions already include deprivation of basic necessities of life, the additional abuse of poor children 'in all forms, is pervasive' (May, 1998b: 18). Abuse includes physical violence, sexual abuse, rape and being forced into prostitution (May, 1998a: 30). Besides being subject to violence from relatives, some poor children are exposed to many negative experiences, such as violence against women and substance abuse. They cannot fail to observe such behaviour in the cramped conditions of overcrowded homes and residential areas. The impact of these negative experiences on their early childhood leaves scars that can hardly be erased in later years (Terreblanche, 1977: 76).

In many poor communities we find parents who have contradictory relationships with their children. On the one hand some parents place their children's well-being at risk by either requiring them to work from an early age or by venting their anger and frustration caused by poverty on their children. For some poor families, the need to 'provide additional income takes precedence over education' (Narayan et al., 2000a: 239). In the process, poor parents sometimes force their children 'into the most risky forms of employment', sometimes even prostitution (ibid.). On the other hand, poor people are often good parents. Through all their suffering, poor parents from everywhere 'keep coming back to their deep longing for a better future for their children. *Whatever happens, they say, let the children be all right*' (Narayan and Petesch, 2002: 1).

Poor people have stunted development

In virtually all societies humans want babies to develop into healthy adults, capable of playing a role that suits the talents that they were born with. Children ought to have opportunities and resources to transform themselves into adults who become full members of society, share responsibilities and contribute their share to the quality of life available for everyone. That poor children's physical and intellectual development could be stunted and retarded in various ways is almost too obvious to mention, yet neglected enough by non-poor people that it must be mentioned explicitly.

Any person's development is linked closely to economic capacities and publicly provided opportunities that make education and training possible. The things that a specific person can do or not do – their capabilities, in the term used by Nussbaum (1995) and Sen (2009) – depend on 'specific, effectively resourced capacities which they can deploy in actual circumstances' (O'Neill, 2001: 189). To what extent does the lack of economic resources diminish poor people's capabilities to do things they need to do for themselves?

Even the quality of parental upbringing at least partially presupposes adequate economic resources. In most societies people have strong moral views on the need for children to have enough food and a proper education. If growing poor children with developing bodies do not have adequate nutritious food, surely their development and growth will be stunted, as pointed out earlier about poor people generally.

Poor people furthermore often find it difficult to acquire resources to provide schooling to their children, if adequate public provision is unavailable, inadequate or costly. The World Bank (2001: 27) states that in some poor countries, 'most children from the poorest households have no schooling at all'. In some poor societies children are required to earn money by working like adults and this happens most often 'at the expense of schooling' (World Bank, 1990: 31). For example, in Bangladesh child labour often implies that both boys and girls 'perform domestic and agricultural labour and their workload is described as heavy and sometimes even as harmful or deadly' (Narayan and Petesch, 2002: 125). Most poor young people acknowledge the value of education and its significance in finding employment. They therefore express 'despair over the obstacles to obtaining education, especially secondary school fees' (ibid.: 65).

Fees aside, do educators sufficiently take into account the disadvantages poor children face? Some have neither access to computers nor to libraries, or even electric lights to study at night. Some do not have books or desks for study purposes or do not have transport to school. Lack of proper clothes to wear might lead to humiliation or disease. Lack of access to knowledgeable adults to assist with learning also affects many poor children. Such disadvantages can deeply affect the success rate of many poor children.

Like children adults also need to sharpen their skills and increase their knowledge. To survive in contemporary fast-changing societies, most workers need to engage in continuous education, upgrade their skills and acquire flexibility to adapt to new work conditions. Failure to do so often results in unemployment. Lack of economic capacities makes it impossible for many poor people to personally develop their employability. Often the low-level jobs of some poor people do not include any form of education or training. Often citizens furthermore do not have equal and fair opportunities to be appointed to jobs or they do not have or ever had the means to gain 'the skills needed for performance of these positions' (Little, 2003: 44).

The link between poverty and the inadequate personal development of individuals is clear. Gunnar Myrdal (1970: 197) points out that in Pakistan, 'the ignorance of the masses stands as a complex of serious inhibitions and obstacles for economic development' that can keep people poor with no prospect of improvement. Myrdal's judgement is reinforced by the World Bank that concludes that many poor people lack so-called 'human capital' because everywhere poor people have less educational qualifications than the general population that they form part of (1990: 31). Many Nigerians, for example, know that job opportunities are 'directly proportional to one's level of education'. For this reason poor Nigerians 'specifically blame their lack of education as a major factor in their inability to escape poverty' (Narayan and Petesch, 2002: 100).

In these cases poverty is similar to oppression. If oppression amounts to people not being given opportunities to develop their talents and exercise their capacities where appropriate in their social environment, then some effects of poverty are virtually identical to oppressive social treatment.

As human beings we all form part of a broader society, in which governments at different levels provide services that require our involvement as prerequisite for enjoying their benefits. Part of our social development is to learn how to be informed about public services and how to become enabled to access them. Poor people often do not have opportunities to acquire such knowledge about the workings of their society nor to develop the competency to utilize them. They thus suffer from social illiteracy. Social illiteracy means not having information about how your society works, not knowing what services and goods you qualify for and being ignorant about ways to influence policy makers and public officials to legislate in your interest and do things for your benefit.

This kind of illiteracy implies that many poor people are often ignorant about assistance they are entitled to request, do not know which officials are in positions to provide them assistance and do not understand how to lobby for aid. Townsend notes that there are 'severe problems in acquainting potential applicants with information about the conditions of benefit' (1979: 849). Many poor people are often unaware of policies developed for their benefit, they do not know how to let those policies work for them and they do not understand how to influence a government to take their interests seriously (May, 1998b: 124). As a result available aid and assistance often do not reach them. The comfort that their situation is being addressed by governments or non-governmental organizations, albeit incompletely, never consoles them either.

Poverty increases people's vulnerability

People's vulnerability depends on whether they can deal with the negative effects of life's shocks and changes and if they can recover from those effects (May, 1998b: 3). Poor people's normal human vulnerability is increased by their lack of resources and income. Note that poverty can make some people more vulnerable than others to life's normal shocks: 'For those with little, small shocks have big effects on wellbeing' (Narayan et al., 2000b: 176).

The World Bank calls vulnerability 'a constant companion' and a 'constant feature' of poverty (2001: 36, 77). Many poor individuals, families, communities or regions are threatened by slowly occurring changes over a long term, such as drought or an economic recession. Drastic changes or shocks, that is, 'an unexpected event that leads to economic and social crisis' (Kabir et al., 2000: 709), such as floods or the death of productive family members, can be even more devastating. The World Bank says that this kind of threat, 'an unfavourable turn of events, especially an unexpected one, can be catastrophic' (1990: 34). Changes in the seasons occurring in normal annual cycles that threaten harvests can further increase poor people's vulnerabilities (May, 1998b: 3).

These effects of poverty are similar to the impact of the AIDS virus on people's immune systems. In the same way that the AIDS virus reduces the resistance and immunity of a human body to effectively fight disease, so poverty diminishes the capacities and options available for poor people to respond effectively to life's shocks and changes. As a result many poor people are often reduced to dependency, which means that they must rely on other people for support to cope with life's basic challenges. They become unable to do without assistance that gives them access to basic necessities required to cope with the demands of everyday living.

The inabilities of poor people to procure sufficient resources to satisfy their basic needs thus make them vulnerable to life's shocks and changes (May, 1998b: 3). If their health is good and they have a decent education, they might have at least some resources to use in a recovery process. In general, most human communities help vulnerable people to deal with and recover from troubling, traumatic situations that they face. A further asset that some poor people might have available is the strength of the social networks that they have established prior to such changes. Not only does the strength of those networks matter, but also the extent to which the people forming those networks have both the capacity and willingness to assist them (ibid.). However, such help and assistance are often not forthcoming for many poor people, for whatever reason. The absence of state or communal support increases vulnerability when no mechanisms are put in place to 'reduce or mitigate the risks that poor people face' (World Bank, 2001: 37).

Poor people have problems with employment

A major cause of poverty is unemployment. The effects of unemployment are amplified in cases where people have no social or family support. Some very poor communities are characterized by the virtual absence of people who are formally employed (May, 1998a: 75). To be unemployed does not necessarily imply that people are unskilled or uneducated.

Although many poor people are unskilled, some have skills that are not in demand by the current economy. Even highly skilled people can become unemployed during times of economic recession, if employment opportunities shrink and companies start downsizing. For these reasons many poor people all over the world realize their need to develop their employability by learning new skills for gainful employment (Narayan et al., 2000b: 245).

However, not all poor people can be classified as unemployed and unable to find suitable jobs. Poor people are often full-time employees and evidence of the 'problem of the working poor are still widespread today' (Alcock, 1993: 13). In a major survey of poverty in the UK, Townsend found that a 'majority of people living in or on the margins of poverty are dependent for their main source of income upon earnings' (1979: xxx). Many poor people are employed full time, but the nature and remuneration of their jobs contribute to their poverty. The stark truth is that some employed people simply do not earn wages that are sufficient to provide for the basic needs of themselves and their dependants (May, 1998a: 4; Wilson and Ramphele, 1989: 54). A recent survey in the UK completed during 2004 and 2006 indicates that 2.8 million working people are classified to be among the poor (Palmer, McInnes and Kenway, 2007: 36).

Some lower status jobs have no prospects of increased salaries or status attached to them (Terreblanche, 1977: 79). Townsend (1979: 650) found that low pay is associated with negative aspects such as 'poor working conditions, small period of entitlement to notice, unsocial working hours and lack of fringe benefits'. Many of the inadequately paid jobs are furthermore done by poor people in dangerous conditions (Wilson and Ramphele, 1989: 72). Such jobs involve heavy physical effort, carry health risks and expose people to injuries or death (May, 1998b: 80).

Not all people can be classified either as full-time employees or as being unemployed. Townsend (1979: 615) judges that there are not only 'two broad states of employment and unemployment', but a 'hierarchy of states from whole-time secure employment to continuous unemployment'. Some forms of employment often do not provide the security of being permanent, as workers might be employed on a seasonal, temporary or casual basis (May, 1998b: 45; Townsend, 1979: 589). These kinds of employment rarely provide workers with adequate income.

Poor people are often inadequately qualified to be considered for better jobs. One reason might be that those people do not – and did not –

value education as a means to land a better job (Willcocks, 1932: 19). This reason might be less common today than decades ago. Another less common reason that nevertheless persists in some parts of the world is that some female children are denied an education as they are to marry into another family (May, 1998b: 59). A more common reason for many poor people's lack of employability is that they often find access to education difficult, as the costs involved are too high, the distance too far to travel or the quality of facilities or teachers available to them inadequate (May, 1998a: 34; Wilson and Ramphele, 1989: 144).

Poverty erodes people's moral values

Poverty erodes people's moral values as desperation to make a living gives them an incentive to be immoral. They are too poor to be moral. If you need to lie or steal for you and your dependants to survive hunger and desolation, can you afford not to? For example, in Bulgaria a poor person expresses this alternative as follows: 'Many people steal – you can't starve to death' (Narayan and Petesch, 2002: 254). Some Roma Bulgarians acknowledge openly that they steal, but try to soften the moral violation with the justification that 'theft is a solution to discrimination in employment and lack of work' (ibid.). In a sense they rationally weigh their options and choose the one that they judge will have the least harmful effects.

As poor people's bodies are often their only asset, they try to protect its value through stealing when faced with constant hunger, especially their children's hunger (Narayan et al., 2000b: 92). Some poor people may argue that morally acceptable methods of earning a living did not work for them, they followed the rules of society to no avail, therefore they are in a position where making a living through immoral means becomes a serious option (Willcocks, 1932: 78). They do not have the material means to continue living a moral life (Terreblanche, 1977: 70). In this way poverty becomes an instigator of moral decay (Willcocks, 1932: 78).

Moral decay starts when some desperately poor people are dishonest or tell lies in order to make a quick profit, to present a falsely good impression to prospective employers or to get aid from government or relief organizations that they do not qualify for (Willcocks, 1932: 78). Moral decay goes further when some poor people decide to enter the 'underground economy' by engaging in illegal trading of goods such as alcohol, diamonds, drugs or sex (ibid.: 83, 85; Wilson and Ramphele, 1989: 156). Others make stealing a career and steal food, cars, household goods, farm animals, water or become poachers that steal wildlife on farms or in conservation areas (Wilson and Ramphele, 1989: 156; Willcocks, 1932: 83, 84). Many poor people confided to World Bank researchers that desperation and hunger sometimes led them to 'anti-social and illegal activities', that included 'to steal, drink, take drugs, sell sex, abandon their children, commit suicide, or trade in children' (Narayan et al., 2000b: 60).

Once people's moral decay sets off by contravening fundamental moral values for the sake of survival, the issue is whether they will stop in time before becoming serious criminals inflicting much greater harm on other people. If immoral behaviour leads to financial success, social power and peer approval it may become so much more difficult to return to a moral lifestyle rather than slipping ever deeper into immoral and criminal behaviour. For this reason, poor communities are often beset by serious problems of crime, from petty stealing to assault, rape and murder (Terreblanche, 1977: 63). Crime is often regarded as one of the 'most tangible social consequences' of poverty (Wilson and Ramphele, 1989: 152).

Poor communities pay a high price for criminal activities in their midst. High levels of crime by some of their own members have devastating social effects. Poor people may suffer individual losses when some of the few material assets they own are stolen. So crime further disempowers them from engaging in entrepreneurial activities aimed at improving their lives (May, 1998a: 256; May, 1998b: 18). Their quality of life can be reduced by high levels of fear and distrust in their community, which also erodes social cohesion and cooperation (May, 1998a: 257). As a result of illegal activities, Narayan et al. state that 'the household and often the wider community must face the fear and anxiety that these means of coping bring in their wake' (2000b: 60).

Criminal behaviour creates insecurity among many poor people who are already insecure because of their lack of sufficient economic capacities. When these feelings of insecurity combine with the frustrations most poor people experience in their desperate circumstances, they often lead to various forms of abuse and violent crimes. It is significant to note that most poor communities suffer more than other communities from interpersonal crimes, such as assault, rape and child abuse, than from property crimes (May, 1998a: 130). A consequence of a high crime rate in a community is that many investors, capable of creating employment opportunities or improving facilities and services, avoid those areas. Chances of reducing poverty are thus driven away.

Conclusion

In this chapter I argued in defence of the claim that the harmful impact of poverty on individuals directs urgent moral challenges to all non-poor people, as the existence of poverty in a society violates widely shared moral values. I first gave a general moral assessment of poverty, showing it to be a violation of poor people's dignity as human beings. I then provided a detailed analysis of the specific, separate harmful effects that poverty can have on individual lives. I pointed out that poverty often does serious harm to poor people's minds and bodies, their interpersonal and social relationships and their moral fibre.

A first response to the moral challenge of the harmful impact of poverty might be the following. Any human society must judge the eradication of poverty in its self-interest, as poverty drastically affects economic productivity by impairing many poor people's 'willingness and ability to work and to work intensively' (Myrdal, 1970: 54). Also, poverty increases the risk of immoral behaviour and crime.

However, are there also important moral reasons for taking poor people's plight seriously? With access to a full picture of the impact of the diverse harms that poverty can do to the lives of individual human beings, non-poor people are called to account for their response to the plight of poor people. Three moral challenges that follow from the above depiction of the impact of poverty on individuals are particularly relevant and urgent.

1. Why do so many non-poor people of the world sit back and allow fellow human beings to suffer from a condition causing such diverse kinds of harm? To give aid to people in need and to help people avoid significant harms to some aspect of their lives seem to be generally accepted moral injunctions. So why do we, as individuals and as collectives, so often avoid doing what is necessary to end the suffering of poor people? Why do we do nothing when individuals cry out as follows: 'Poverty is humiliation, the sense of being dependent and of being forced to accept rudeness, insults and indifference when we seek help'? (Narayan et al., 2000a: 30). Why do we not treat poor people as human beings, or as our fellow citizens, whom we publicly avow to be our moral equals, who should not be allowed to suffer in these ways?

2. Why do so many non-poor people exploit poor people and profit from their desperate situation? To exploit vulnerable people is judged to

be a serious moral offence, so why do so many non-poor people exploit the poor and so many others turn a blind eye?

3. The effects and consequences of poverty on individual lives show many overlaps and similarities with other conditions we know and deal with more effectively. If the consequences and effects of poverty show similarities with those of illness and disease, gross injustices, political domination and even anomie and anarchy, why do we not have institutions, resources and expertise to deal with poverty as effectively as we deal with these other conditions?

Someone might argue that the medical facilities and personnel, political and judicial institutions and social policies in contemporary constitutional democracies are designed to deal with various distinct aspects or dimensions of poverty that are analogous to the other conditions mentioned. Poverty might thus be the collective name for a syndrome of interrelated human conditions, but each is worthy of being called the kind of hardship it independently is (see Halleröd, 2000: 183).

Let's suppose that is true. Let us suppose further that liberal-democratic institutions, facilities providing medical care and disciplinary institutions such as schools and prisons are all designed to deal with one or more of the problematic conditions generated by poverty. The basic question then still remains: why do so many societies nevertheless have large numbers of poor people in their midst? If the right mechanisms, institutions and policies are in place to combat poverty and all the negative effects it entails, yet poverty persists on a significant, bothersome scale, how do we cross-check the sensitivity and workability of the precautions we have put in place? Why don't these institutions and policies eradicate poverty?

Perhaps we must remind ourselves of the essential economic core of the definition of poverty: it is a lack of economic capacities that brings a host of negative effects and consequences in its train. Why do the vast majority of contemporary societies not succeed in addressing the basic problem, that is, that hundreds of millions of people suffer as a result of a lack of economic capacities? To argue that the global community does not have enough resources to eradicate poverty is no defence anymore. We do have enough resources in our global community, as well as the know-how to get rid of poverty. The success of some north European societies stands as reminders of what is possible. Will we, however, find appropriate ways of sharing resources and know-how to relieve the suffering caused by poverty on a global scale?

We owe our fellow citizens suffering from poverty consistent, serious and competent reflection about these issues and workable answers to these challenges. It is the very least we are obliged to do if we recognize them as human beings, if we respect their human dignity and if we judge that they should not unnecessarily suffer harmful consequences brought about by an avoidable and remediable condition.

In this chapter I have shown how poverty can harm human beings through injuries on a more individual level, such as relationships, moral values, employment and increasing vulnerability to life's shocks. That is not where poverty's possible harms to people stop. In the next chapter I investigate the harms poverty does through negatively affecting the environments within which poor people live.

5 • Poverty's Impact on Human Environments[1]

At the dawn of the twenty-first century, people throughout the world are more conscious than ever before of the fragility of our planet and the ecosystems on which we depend for our livelihoods. More human beings attach value to a sound environment than ever before, as we and our children need the environment for our survival, health, recreation and general well-being. No human being can escape the deep environmental interdependency we share with human beings elsewhere in the world, as even some of the most local forms of environmental degradation can have global impact, if added to the billions of similar small events that occur every day.

In addition, the impact human beings have on one another and the influence our artificially constructed environments have on our development are well known. In diverse ways our growth and development can be obstructed, skewed or even derailed if the human company we have or the physical circumstances of our built environment have negative impacts on us. In the light of a deep concern for the environmental well-being of our planet and for the deep significance of social environments for human development, we have to look at the impact of poverty on the human environments we live in.

A definition of 'environment'

The highly influential World Commission on Environment and Development, chaired by Gro Harlem Brundtland, sets up a starkly simple argument about the relationship between human development and the environment. The report gives the following definitions of the two concepts (Brundtland, 1987: 3). It defines the environment as 'where we all live' and development as 'what we all do in attempting to improve our lot within that abode'. Can these definitions be so simple? In a sense, yes, if one acknowledges the complexities behind these deceptively simple definitions. For example, how must we understand the definition of the environment as 'where we all live'? Does this description refer to planet earth or to our physical houses? Perhaps the description refers to our being part of a country, a geographic region or a human community. If we define our environment as that which surrounds us, what do we need to include in a proper definition?

In this chapter I propose that we analyse the environment as our surroundings we are in contact with daily into three distinct aspects. These aspects are (1) the environment as a treasure chest of endless possibilities offered by natural resources that developed through millennia and are sustained largely without human ingenuity or intervention, (2) the humanly cultivated, constructed and built environment that aids us to locate, extract, convert and produce means for ensuring our survival and goods for enabling our flourishing and (3) the human environment consisting of people organized into communities of varying sizes with whom we interact daily.

Once I have defined and described these three aspects, I will apply them to the results of contemporary poverty research to make sense of all the possible links between poverty and our human environments. In our everyday lives we interact with worlds that consist of combinations of these three dimensions. We find ourselves daily within numerous smaller environments in which the natural resource world combines in interesting ways with the humanly constructed and humanly populated worlds. Let us now look at these three dimensions of the environment separately and explore how poverty can be linked to each.

Environment as a 'treasure chest of natural resources'

We can best appreciate the perspective of our natural environment as a 'treasure chest of natural resources' if we compare our planet with all other known planets and stars. Our planet is the only one we know of that has all the necessary conditions to enable a rich abundance of diverse life forms of varying complexity. Characteristic of our natural environment is that it came about without any significant human input or contribution. Nevertheless, we are totally dependent for our survival and flourishing on the resources provided by our natural environment: food, water, shelter, materials and almost everything else we need originally comes from a source within the natural environment. However, we humans have developed significant skill, insight, ingenuity and competence to use the offerings of the natural environment to make impressive lives for ourselves.

The Millennium Ecosystem Assessment Project (see Millennium Ecosystem Assessment, 2005) provides a valuable perspective on the links between humans and our natural environment. There is a common view that climates, soil types, vegetation and forms of animal life are all elements within one or more of the complex interactive webs of life defined as ecosystems. This view is developed further to bring into focus the various kinds of 'services' that ecosystems provide humans to enable our survival, well-being and flourishing. Ecosystems provide humans with clean water, food and materials for clothing, shelter, tools and manufacture. Besides these provisions of ecosystems, they regulate our climate and prevent floods, for example. Furthermore we use ecosystems for recreation and inspiration. They provide us business opportunities, present aesthetic landscapes, reveal awe-inspiring natural wonders, contain ancient traces of extinct life-forms and manifest expressions of forces beyond our comprehension and scope of action.

If all humans are dependent on ecosystems for the quality of life and the degree of well-being we can accomplish, we are accountable to one another for the ways in which we use these ecosystem services. We can hold one another responsible for at least the following things. The first matter we are accountable for is whether we make appropriate use of the ecosystem services available in our part of the world so as to be able to properly take care of ourselves and our dependants. The second thing we must account for is whether we fairly use scarce natural resources so that others are enabled to get similar opportunities to access such resources. We can also be held responsible for the ways we utilize ecosystem resources in sustainable ways or not. Our use of resources today will determine whether future generations will have similar opportunities to live lives of approximately the same quality as we can now. Finally, we can call one another to account for the effects our individual and collective actions have on the environment, that is, whether we degrade or pollute ecosystems, alter local, regional or global natural forces and thus spoil resources for other people living now, diminish their opportunities to build decent lives and even threaten their health and survival.

What would most humans generally regard as morally ideal relationships between humans and their natural environment? Hopefully most of us will endorse responsible use of the amazing possibilities locked in natural resources to enrich our lives. Responsible use implies the following. Through applying our minds we can develop the most appropriate scientific knowledge and technological skills to unlock the treasures available in natural resources. If we develop respect for the other values of natural environments, we can cultivate a deep appreciation of the diversity of life forms, explore recreational activities in nature, enjoy the beauty of the diversity of landscapes and find new perspective when contemplating the unique and irreplaceable character of natural phenomena that developed through millennia. These multiple relationships with natural environments ought to enable our survival and enhance the flourishing of our lives without damaging or spoiling the environment. We should also be able to benefit fairly from nature in these diverse ways without our ecological footprints depriving other people living now or in future from benefiting similarly from our natural environment.

Perhaps the most fundamental aspect of the relationship between poverty and the environment is the inability of many poor communities to access ecosystem services to provide them with a decent, human standard of living. There could literally be dozens of reasons why some poor people cannot appropriate what nature has on offer to them. It might be that the number of people in a specified geographic area exceeds the available capacities of ecosystems in that area. The poor people struggling to survive might not have the required knowledge, skills or training to adequately utilize whatever resources are available. A dominating government might be restricting people's access to natural resources or an oppressive regime might prevent people's access to knowledge and technology that can aid them to properly harness natural forces to their own benefit. A wealthy, domineering class might have privileged access to ecosystem services and might be converting those resources into wealth for themselves only. Whatever the reasons might be, the bottom line is simple: many poor people cannot adequately access and productively utilize potentially available ecosystem resources in their environment.

If this is true, it points us – the citizens of our world – to a serious problem. We are not a vulnerable species on earth anymore. We do not have to survive in a wilderness filled with dangerous animals and ferocious predators armed only with elementary stone tools. We have become the dominant species on earth that has conquered all wilderness areas. We have developed immensely powerful tools that can destroy our earthly abode with ease. Our skill, capacity and ingenuity to cultivate the earth to produce food and clothing are truly astonishing. Our abilities to extract materials and put them together intelligently to produce gadgets, instruments, vehicles and equipment to travel, heal, manufacture and relax are simply amazing. If we have these awesome creative and productive powers, why are so many people dying and suffering for lack of things that we can produce easily?

If it is true that there is a discrepancy between the basic needs of some poor people to live a decent human life and their ability to satisfy those needs through accessing and utilizing natural resources, then several consequences follow. Many poor people often place a lot of stress on their limited available environments through depleting natural resources and degrading the natural environment in their efforts to secure a minimal living. Furthermore, some poor people are often too powerless to resist becoming victims of other people's neglect and degradation of the environment. As a result of these matters, such poor people often become alienated from natural environments in several ways. These matters will be discussed in slightly more detail below.

All social scientific reports comment in detail on the daily struggles of many poor people to adequately access the ecosystem services in their environs. We as humans find it morally deplorable if members of our community do not have enough food to eat, proper clothes to wear or appropriate shelter to protect them against the elements. People who slip into poverty find it difficult to provide basic necessities for themselves and their dependants. Many poor people lack income or resources that can be used to buy or trade commodities needed for physical survival. Some poor people are unemployed and therefore have no income. Others earn wages that do not cover expenses for their basic needs (Wilson and Ramphele, 1989: 54). A lack of income means that people do not have money to buy enough food. In this context, reliance on other sources of income is crucial. Some people with little or no income have their incomes supplemented by remittances sent by family members who work as migrants elsewhere or by old-age pensions granted to elderly relatives (ibid.). If these sources are not available, some poor people may resort to borrowing money from family, friends, relatives, shop owners or employees (May, 1998b: 63). Women are more inclined to borrow money, as they are most in need and more often take responsibility for running the household. Borrowing money is a common practice that characterizes the lives of many poor people (ibid.).

Without an adequate disposable income many poor people are not able to acquire commodities necessary for survival, or they might have greater difficulties gaining access to them. Food is a good example. Many poor children do not have food to eat before leaving home for school in the mornings (Wilson and Ramphele, 1989: 147). Children – and adults – who go without enough food, or whose family cannot afford nutritious food to ensure a healthy diet, suffer from malnutrition and all its associated effects that cause poor performance at school and work. In most human societies we find it morally wrong that human beings should go without enough food to eat, as it exposes them to dangers of many kinds.

Access to water is another example of the problems some poor people face in satisfying their basic needs. To be without clean water, a basic necessity for nutrition and general health, is another moral taboo in most human societies. The absence of a dependable, accessible and affordable water supply can incur heavy costs on poor people. These costs include money, time, health and loss of economic opportunities. In urban areas where many poor people do not have access to piped water, they often pay up to thirty times more for water than other citizens pay local councils (May, 1998a: 217; Wilson and Ramphele, 1989: 48). In some rural areas women spend three hours per day on average to fetch water. In India water scarcity is 'the most frequently identified problem'. Researchers found that 'wells can be far from the homes of poor people and lower-caste people may be denied access'. In some villages there are 'government-installed water pumps and wells, but the equipment is often in disrepair or provides water irregularly' (Narayan and Petesch, 2002: 156). Carrying water over these long distances exposes their bodies to injury and places them at risk of assault and sexual harassment (Wilson and Ramphele, 1989: 48). A further health risk is the lack of proper hygiene due to insufficient water available for washing themselves, their clothes and kitchen utensils. Poor health and loss of time contributes to the inability to utilize opportunities to generate income, just as the lack of water inhibits opportunities to grow food for own use or marketing purposes (May, 1998a: 139).

Human beings need sources of energy to provide light, warmth and heat for preparing food. Many poor people often lack energy too. Sometimes they have access to electricity, but do not have enough income to pay for its sustained use (May, 1998a: 148). Often electricity is not even available as an option. Alternative fuels, such as paraffin and wood, are commonly used. Poor women often lose a lot of time collecting firewood, as well as being exposed to sexual assault (Wilson and Ramphele, 1989: 44; May, 1998b: 65). These fuels are dangerous, with both the risk of fire and exposure to dangerous fumes always present. The risk of fire is exacerbated in areas of high density housing such as shanty towns, where housing is constructed from highly flammable materials, such as wood and plastic (May, 1998a: 65). As a result of the high density of such areas, the absence of access roads and the general neglect of such areas by local councils, protection by emergency services (fire brigades) is not particularly effective.

If poverty is defined as lack of economic capacities to make a decent human living, then it stands to reason that some poor people will maximally exploit available environmental resources in their immediate environment in the hope of ensuring their physical survival (see Brundtland,

1987: 27). For this reason poor communities often cause environmental problems and in return low quality environmental resources often make the survival of poor human communities a desperate struggle (ibid.: 5). The UNDP (1997: 32) confirms that environmental degradation often leads to 'continued impoverishment'. In the light of this evidence Hollander bluntly calls poverty the 'real enemy' of the environment and the 'environmental villain' (Hollander, 2003: 2). I am doubtful whether Hollander's judgement is correct, as carbon emissions from rich (and poor) countries have the largest impact on our global biosphere by far. Also, the impact of poor people is most often not as severe as the impact from mining companies or large infrastructure developments such as roads and dams. Note how Little (2003: xv) gives a more balanced view when he says that 'conditions of poverty and rapid economic development alike intensify pressure on the environment'.

Hollander does not say that poor people degrade their immediate environments out of 'wilful neglect'. Some poor people degrade those environments 'only out of a need to survive', not for their comfort or pleasure. Nevertheless, their exploitative actions that overuse natural resources mean that sometimes some poor communities have to 'plunder their resources, pollute their environment and overcrowd their habitats' in order to secure survival (2003: 13). The Brundtland report justifiably concludes that human settlements where poverty is rife 'will always be prone to ecological and other catastrophes' (Brundtland, 1987: 5 and 43, 44).

The limited options for making a decent human living available to the poor often results in them degrading the immediate environment of their abode. The example of fuel as source of energy for poor communities illustrates the point. Using wood as fuel in densely populated rural areas in a dry country with sparse vegetation like South Africa often leads to environmental degradation. In a short space of time many rural areas lose their natural vegetation, implying that poor people find it all the more difficult to find wood to use as fuel. At the same time the damage to the ecology of the area harms its agricultural productive capacities and destroys its aesthetic appeal as recreational areas (Wilson and Ramphele, 1989: 44). Another example comes from India, where poor people 'go to the nearby forests to collect leaves, flowers, tamarind and other products to sell in the market'. The recent impact of humans on the forest ecosystem has meant that 'very high rates of deforestation have drastically reduced these livelihood alternatives' (Narayan and Petesch, 2002: 156).

David A. McDonald (1998) gives a vivid picture of the interaction between poverty and environmental degradation, drawn from examples in the urban areas of South Africa. Unplanned urban settlements can lead to 'serious environmental degradation' when houses 'sprout up in ecologically sensitive areas like river banks and sand dunes causing irreversible environmental damage'. When urbanites have to use fuels such as wood, coal or paraffin to supply energy, 'deforestation and erosion (occur) in the peri-urban areas'. The large-scale use of these fuels furthermore results in 'dangerously unhealthy levels of air pollution' (75).

Powerless poor people without significant influence on governmental policies and practices are often victims of environmental degradation committed by industries or local governments. According to McDonald almost one-third of urban people in South Africa live 'without adequate sewerage and sanitation'. A consequence of the absence of these services is that 'ground and surface water supplies in most metropolitan areas are heavily contaminated with bacterial and toxic waste' (75). Poor people often have no option but to live in heavily polluted areas where no one else would choose to live.

The Brundtland report comments how easily industries can get away with high levels of pollution if powerless poor people are their victims, 'because the people who bear the brunt of it are poor and unable to complain effectively' (Brundtland, 1987: 46). The neglect that they suffer from local governments often means that poor people bear the brunt of unsound waste disposal practices. In Ecuador, researchers found 'the problem of raw sewage' to be acute in poor areas. Poor people live 'along "black waters" filled not just with excrement, but also with the untreated effluents from the larger metropolitan area' (Narayan and Petesch, 2002: 405). The UNDP (1997: 32) refers to some poor people's 'aggravated health risks from pollution'.

Thus, many poor people do not have economic resources to live in areas other than those heavily polluted or environmentally degraded with so much less potential for satisfying their survival needs. Their ability to sustain their livelihoods and the health they need to do so are both diminished. Poor people living near the Amazon forest in Ecuador experience being victims of environmental degradation caused by others. They report that 'they eat far less fish, game and wild fruits and nuts than they used to'. They ascribe diminishing natural resources to the following factors, all indicating excessive human impact: 'the forest has receded and the rivers have become increasingly polluted since the arrival of roads, the oil industry and large numbers of non-indigenous colonists' (Narayan and Petesch, 2002: 399).

Most poor people experience some kind of alienation from pristine natural landscapes and environments. Many poor people experience themselves as being cut off from the natural aspects of the environment that still exist and flourish with minimal human intervention. These pristine natural environments typically display characteristics developed over centuries that were only affected by the almost minimal impacts of early humans through hunting, gathering and limited cultivation of the earth. Most poor people don't have the money to visit conservation areas where places of natural beauty, unique landscapes and irreplaceable plant and animal life are set aside for educational value, aesthetic enjoyment and spiritual upliftment. As a result a typical attitude common amongst modern urban dwellers may be reinforced among poor people as well, where people feel detached from the natural world except for their experience of their geographic area's climate.

In this case poverty leads to the exclusion of those poor people from the natural heritage of humanity. Their lack of economic resources shuts them out of places worth visiting and they are prevented from sharing the enrichment places of scenic beauty can offer.

If we take into account the impact of poverty on the natural environments where many poor people live and add that to the current human impact on all the earth's ecosystems that is driving massive pollution and degradation, global climate change and species extinction as a result of unprecedented human intervention in all habitats, then it becomes clear that the earth's ability to provide a home for humans is being seriously jeopardized.

'Environment' as the humanly cultivated, built and constructed environment

If we use the word 'environment' to name the humanly cultivated, built and constructed environment, then we refer to the environments created and built by human knowledge, skill, ingenuity and labour. These environments are designed and established through making use of natural resources by means of various processes of cultivation, design, processing, manufacture and production. We build houses, shopping malls, sport stadiums, concert halls, factories, roads, airports and educational institutions. We construct dams, nurseries, abattoirs, fields, gardens, fences, parks, zoos and game reserves. We cultivate plants, breed animals, build engines, design vehicles and create computers to enable good human living. In many countries of the world the degree of human intervention in the natural world is so extensive that it is difficult to find pristine landscapes with few signs of human presence.

The humanly cultivated, built and constructed environments offer us far more functions than merely empowering us to locate, extract, convert and produce means for ensuring our survival and enabling our flourishing. Other functions of these human designs and constructions include spaces for privacy, opportunities for recreation, places to engage in sport as participants or to observe as spectators, room for entertainment, buildings for shopping, specialized areas for healing in hospitals and clinics, areas for meditation and worship, commercial properties for trading, public spaces for observation in museums, zoos and art galleries, quiet places for browsing and reading in libraries and bookshops and many multi-purpose spaces that in addition serve the purpose of socializing with friends or loved ones.

We cannot survive on our planet without creating our own purpose-built environments. Most humans wish these human constructions to be both in harmony with natural landscapes and capable of fulfilling our human needs for living good lives. To live a good life is impossible without spaces for adequate shelter, sites for trade, places for recreation and socialization, pathways to travel and all the supporting elements of infrastructure to enable us to engage in our life projects of dealing with life's numerous challenges as best we can. Most people's sense of fairness would at least allow them to wish for others similar quality environments that would likewise fulfil their requirements for living worthwhile lives.

If one adds the idea of our environment as the humanly cultivated, built and constructed environment to the idea of the environment as the natural possibilities offered by various intersecting ecosystems, we see that many poor people's suburbs are mostly ugly places with little or no aesthetic appeal of any kind. In contrast to the 'leafy' upmarket neighbourhoods of the middle and upper classes, most poor suburbs throughout history have been overcrowded, polluted, under-serviced, often un-planned, with poor roads and inadequate public spaces. Green areas such as parks and beautiful gardens are mostly scarce in poor urban neighbourhoods. Small houses are lumped too close together without appropriate private spaces for families or proper public spaces for business, education, sport and recreation. The smart shopping malls, huge stadiums, beautiful gardens, cool clubs, graceful churches, handy agencies of financial institutions and other necessary services are seldom found in the poorest suburbs. In addition, local government services are often shabbily rendered to poor communities.

If poor people have difficulties in accessing ecosystem services to provide food, water and sources of energy for their own use, then access to adequate housing within the humanly built environment will be an issue too. This is confirmed in most social science studies on poverty. Already in 1901 Rowntree found that overcrowding 'is due to sheer inability on the part of the tenants to pay rent enough to secure adequate accommodation' (Rowntree, 1901: 176). In most societies today we value sufficient space for individual family members within properly enclosed areas that protect inhabitants from the elements, provide opportunities to engage in normal indoor human activities and enjoy appropriate privacy.

Most poor people have a lack of space. Overcrowding is common in poor homes, as is living in inadequately constructed houses that are often in desperate need of maintenance (May, 1998a: 4; Wilson and Ramphele, 1989: 124). For example, in India both 'rural and urban groups identify dilapidated housing as a widespread problem' (Narayan and Petesch, 2002: 159). The extent of people's poverty can often be observed in their minimal space for accommodation. For example, sometimes desperately poor migrant workers cannot even afford to rent a house or a room, but only a bed in large communal rooms, which they share with wives and children. This bed is called 'home' and dramatically presents the problems of overcrowding suffered by many poor people (Wilson and Ramphele, 1989: 124. See also Ramphele, 1993). In these cases poor people lose out significantly. Couples have no privacy, children have no place to play, storage room is minimal and it is uncomfortable, if not impossible, to entertain visitors (Wilson and Ramphele, 1989: 124). These are not optional functions most human societies assign to accommodation, but functions necessary for the maintenance of healthy personal and family life.

Perhaps the most embarrassing part comes with a focus on the personal, private spaces poor people have at their disposal. Most genuinely poor people live in homes that are too small to satisfactorily provide for their personal and privacy needs. In many cases too many people share a room for sleeping with the result that parents, children, family, friends or acquaintances do not have the required privacy for their personal lives.

In addition to the lack of space, poor people's homes are mostly not made of good quality building material and are not well enough maintained. The decorations and furnishings are often not up to acceptable standards either. In most cases of desperate poverty poor people's houses provide only the barest minimum protection against the elements, making the inhabitants far more vulnerable to a range of avoidable diseases than well-to-do people are.

Many poor people across the world have no access to what millions of people in different countries now regard as basic services for a household: electricity, flush toilets, running water and refuse removal. Again, these people are unnecessarily exposed to disease, are deprived of learning opportunities and live in a personal environment with more burdens and waste than the average middle-class person.

If one asks about the presence of the technological marvels of our age in the homes of poor people, we often find that a majority of desperately poor people don't have access to communications media (telephones, newspapers, magazines, television) that could have advanced informal learning and enabled contact with the outside world.

Many poor people are dependent on the cultivation of the environment through agriculture. They often have inadequate resources to farm with (May, 1998b: 104–5). Money for good quality seed or fertilizer is not available, nor for fencing or additional labour. Technological equipment to enable more productive labour, such as tractors for ploughing fields or trucks to transport produce to markets, are too expensive.

We can thus conclude that the average poor person can be judged to be severely deprived in terms of the amount and quality of household, urban and open public spaces available within their environment.

'Environment' as the humans we are surrounded by

We often refer to the people in someone's surroundings as being part of that person's environment. All human beings are surrounded by other people. The members of one's household, your family, friends, acquaintances and neighbours form some of the significant others in any person's life. Other important people with whom most humans are in direct daily contact are those you meet through educational institutions, work opportunities, business dealings, public bureaucracies, recreational venues or sports fields.

There is no doubt about the impact other people have on our lives. The knowledge and nurture others provide, the role models and heroes we emulate, the behaviour patterns and ideas we become accustomed to, the level of skill and resources displayed by many in our community and appropriated by us – all these fellow humans influence us with the lives they live before us and with us. They provide us with options and possibilities that we can adopt, modify, develop and explore. They enrich or impoverish our lives. Peet (1975: 568) argues for this point: individuals get all kinds of services, acquire information and establish connections 'from the social resource complex formed by the people and institutions within the daily-life environment' open to them. The influence of other people on our lives is so strong that Peet (1975: 569) judges that individuals carry 'the imprint' of their particular human environment. I must note that although this imprint strongly influences people, it never fully determines individuals, especially if a person's agency and autonomy develop sufficiently.

Most humans judge co-operative, empowering, supportive and friendly human environments as ideal for living a good life according to one's own lights. We want to live in human environments filled with considerate people who take other's interests into account and don't harm anyone unnecessarily. We wish to be part of a human environment where people benefit others if possible and share their knowledge, skills and wisdom graciously with their fellow citizens.

All human beings are surrounded by other people who thus constitute significant parts of their environment. Who are the people forming the immediate, direct human environments within which poor people find themselves? To what kind of people are the poor exposed? In so many poor communities all over the world, lots of poor people live and move in a world populated mostly only by other poor people. Children especially are prone to be bound inside poor communities compared with some of the employed adults who have jobs in the non-poor world. Even for the ones employed in the well-to-do areas, their primary areas of socialization and recreation remain the poor communities they hail from.

The impact of the human environment on poor people is most dramatic in the case of children. Any parents can be good role models for exemplary ethical behaviour to children and provide children with fun and laughter through humorous stories and light-hearted play. Any parents can fail their children through emotional absence or abuse, violent discipline or through failing to provide guidance by means of responsible parenting. Although poor parents are just as capable as anyone else of providing these things to their children, they struggle to provide other valuable goods to their children. Children in poor communities often lack interaction with knowledgeable, successful adults who can be inspiring role models. If one looks at the interests, hobbies, careers and organizations within well-to-do communities and compare them with what is available in poor communities, then the lack of economic capacities for survival and the dearth of opportunities for human flourishing show clearly in the absence of mutually enriching activities in poor communities. Furthermore, social science reports on poverty all refer to the negative impacts poor people often have on one another. In the next paragraphs, I will refer to the role of alcohol and violence, dependence and powerlessness, a so-called 'culture of poverty', a lack of social capital and social illiteracy as some of the negative impacts the human environment of many poor people have on them.

Humans have a strong need for safety and security in their environments. Alcohol abuse and interpersonal violence undermine a sense of security and personal safety within people's daily human environments. Alcohol abuse often occurs on a much larger scale in poor communities than others. In the context of scarce household resources, alcohol abuse easily leads to domestic or interpersonal violence and criminal behaviour amongst poor people themselves (Terreblanche, 1977: 64). The consequences of alcohol abuse, such as violence against vulnerable bodies and a drain on limited resources of poor households, are more devastating for poor people than for well-off people with more financial, social or emotional assets available as backup (Wilson and Ramphele, 1989: 159). Poor people often acknowledge their inability to deal with alcohol abuse, making it yet another example of the powerlessness of some to manage their lives satisfactorily (ibid.).

The use of violence is morally frowned upon as a method of dealing with conflict, except in extreme circumstances. Harming others through interpersonal violence occurs frequently among poor people and not only as a result of the abuse of alcohol. Poor people suffer more from interpersonal violence than the rich. A national survey in South Africa on people's experience of the most important crimes committed against them yielded telling results (May, 1998a: 130). Half of the poor people approached indicated assault as the most important crime that they experienced, while only 10 per cent of the rich had similar experiences. After assault, poor people thought child abuse and rape the most important crimes (May, 1998a: 130). Similar patterns of crime occur in Malawi's desperately poor communities, where researchers heard reports in every community they visited about 'theft, robbery, burglary, murders and other acts that pose physical threats to people's lives' (Narayan and Petesch, 2002: 69).

The UNDP describes a lack of personal security as something 'felt strongly in most poor communities', and says that most of the victims of rising levels of crime and violence are poor (1997: 31). Alcock (1993: 84, 85) reports that crime statistics in Britain have shown that 'the highest level of criminal activity and criminal threats are experienced amongst generally deprived groups living in deprived areas'. According to many poor people in another study, they feel particularly insecure when they leave their homes for work, as 'what few belongings they own are vulnerable to thieves because they live in shacks that cannot be secured' (Narayan and Petesch, 2002: 369).

The consequences of frequently occurring interpersonal violence are high levels of fear and distrust in a community that tears social bonds asunder, minimizes communal cooperation and diminishes space and opportunities for making full use of people's human and productive capacities (May, 1998a: 256–7). The UNDP judges that some poor people are doing themselves serious harm through these violent criminal actions. They conclude that the social assets of some poor communities 'can be eroded by stresses in social relations, however, especially from violence, alcoholism and other destructive behaviour' (1997: 63). These forms of violent crime and their consequences transgress even the most basic ethical values that any society sets for the flourishing of its members.

In most societies human beings live in interdependency with one another. We need multiple interactions with our human environment for optimal human functioning. We are comfortable with our being dependent on others for some services and independent in providing other things for ourselves. Thus, in most contemporary societies human beings morally frown on people who live in dependence on others while they possess the requisite capacities to make independent contributions to their own welfare. In some cases researchers define poverty in terms of lack of independence, or self-reliance. The independence of people can suffer in different ways as a result of poverty. Poor people's independence is restricted by the way that poverty curtails their ability to make decisions about their own lives for lack of resources they command and opportunities they are able to utilize. Poverty then refers to an inability to be self-reliant, that focuses our attention to the incapability of families to provide the minimum means for living a decent life for themselves. Poor people with strong feelings of powerlessness tend to become dependent on other people, the state or relief organizations for aid or to take care of them (Willcocks, 1932: 24, 172, 219). Many poor people are often aware of their powerlessness and the negative consequences thereof. Narayan et al. (2000a: 31) state that poor people are 'acutely aware of their lack of voice, power and independence that subjects them to exploitation' in their relations to all kinds of institutions and different kinds of people. Lister notes that poor people themselves 'identify lack of voice as critical to understanding their situation' (2004: 167). Some poor people in special circumstances experience powerlessness in unique ways, such as many farm workers who are wholly dependent on their employers for housing, water and transport. In some cases farm workers even depend on their employers for the provision of schools and entertainment (May, 1998b: 26).

Although aid might generally be thought to improve the lives of poor people, that is not always the case. Even aid given with good motives, though in wrong ways, might stifle initiative and self-reliance, whilst reinforcing the wrong kind of dependency (Wilson and Ramphele, 1989: 262; Willcocks, 1932: 87). Wrong ways of aiding poor people can create an attitude of entitlement that persists beyond their time of need, such that they deserve aid and have a right to it, regardless of whether they need aid or not (Grosskopf, 1932: 219). From these remarks it becomes clear why 'the way of giving' can be important and why some poor people develop 'resentment and humiliation' if treated as 'a problem to solve' (Baudot, 2000: 32).

In many contemporary societies the notion that everyone gets equal opportunities to make something of their lives regardless of their background is important. Most people severely affected by poverty can hardly share in these opportunities on offer in the broader society. Many poor people cannot visualize themselves as agents who actively work and strive to change at least some of their circumstances. They have lost belief in their ability to influence events and thus live with a consciousness of their own powerlessness and inability to influence or change anything (Terreblanche, 1977: 66; May, 1998b: 50; Wilson and Ramphele, 1989: 267).

Note how poor people in India, citizens in a parliamentary democracy, react when asked whether 'they can exert any influence over government institutions'. They indicate that they 'very often feel they have no effective channels to press for more or better government services' (Narayan and Petesch, 2002: 164). The UNDP describes powerlessness as 'a central source of poverty' (2000: 72). If you do not have the power to make your life comply with the minimum standards your society sets for human beings, how can you realistically experience yourself as someone with any kind of power or influence that can impact on your social world? Many poor people often experience themselves as powerless in the face of life's challenges and adversities (Terreblanche, 1977: 66; May, 1998a: 41; Willcocks, 1932: 69).

Lack of power is close to the heart of what poverty means to many poor people. Power means the ability to do something, to influence people, to have an impact on a community, to accomplish one's goals, to grab people's attention, to have freedom to explore different options or the ability to use ideas or resources to change people's lives. Poor people often experience themselves as powerless, as they find themselves with no strength or ability to do many of the things that they could legitimately want to, influence people to have a significant impact on the circles of human association they are involved in or change anyone's life positively through using capacities whose training require adequate economic resources.

Narayan et al. find it striking to note 'the extent to which dependency, lack of power and lack of voice emerge as core elements of poor people's definitions of poverty'(2000a: 64). This attitude of being powerless and ineffectual also concerns the events and histories of many poor people's own lives. These poor people often experience life as something happening to them and not as though they are co-makers of their own history (Wilson and Ramphele, 1989: 267).

People who experience sudden, short-term poverty 'are filled with disbelief and demoralization' and will often make 'comparative statements contrasting the better past with the intolerable present'. Those poor people who experience long-term poverty often exhibit 'almost fatalistic acceptance' of their situation (Narayan et al., 2000a: 42). As a result such poor people often show a lack of diligence, motivation or initiative (Terreblanche, 1977: 68; Willcocks, 1932: 51). Jones (1990: 193) uses insights from theories about learned helplessness to explain this attitude of some poor people. He explains that when people are 'consistently and massively frustrated in engaging in successful action in an environment, they lose the will to act in that environment'. For this reason he interprets the apathy of poor people as 'a predictable yet tragic response which makes successful action impossible' (ibid.).

Lack of essential resources for a decent life, feelings of powerlessness to do anything about it and dependence on others lead poor people to develop a negative self-image, experience strong feelings of inferiority and to resign themselves to their situation (Terreblanche, 1977: 68, 70; Albertyn, 1932: 19; Wilson and Ramphele, 1989: 267). Negative views of themselves due to their lowly position compared with others in society and their inability to change that give poor people feelings of fatalism, hopelessness and resignation (Terreblanche, 1977: 69; Albertyn, 1932: 19; Wilson and Ramphele, 1989: 267). They accept their situation and lose motivation or willingness to even attempt any changes.

Developing these feelings and attitudes can deeply entrap some people in poverty, as these feelings and attitudes mesh with poverty as a condition that results from 'economic, political and social processes that interact with each other in ways that exacerbate the deprivation in which poor people live' (World Bank, 2001: 1). Powerlessness combines with hopelessness and resignation and often results in some poor people's inability to take the long view (see Narayan et al., 2000b: 37). Their time horizons become short and they live a 'hand to mouth' existence not by choice but as 'an immensely frustrating necessity' (see ibid.).

In some specific cases of poverty that stretches over generations, a culture of poverty arises where several factors already mentioned combine to form a network of mutually reinforcing and interlocking barriers encircling people in poverty (Terreblanche, 1977: 79; see also Halleröd, 2000: 167). Some of these factors are articulated in a report about poor communities in Malawi where poor people report 'a large set of inter-related problems, including hunger, land shortages due to population growth, unemployment, lack of loan facilities, high commodity prices, poor roads, unsafe water, diseases and poor access to medical care and rising crime and theft' (Narayan and Petesch, 2002: 56). The researchers were struck by the fact that severe problems of poverty were exacerbated by the extent to which 'a confluence of these problems entangles every community visited' (ibid.).

Elsewhere researchers report the following results from discussion groups that strengthen the claim about interlocking factors entrenching poverty: 'Many of these disadvantages are described as interlinked and are illustrated by study participants as circular, with many impacts becoming causes and many causes becoming impacts, all feeding back into ever deepening cycles of destitution' (Narayan and Petesch, 2002: 71, 72).

Note the metaphors used to describe the experience of entrapment, itself a metaphor: being encircled, feeling trapped by the interlocking strands of a web, being imprisoned and living in bondage (see Narayan et al., 2000b: 236). These conditions 'interlock to create, perpetuate and deepen powerlessness and deprivation'. This interlocking makes it difficult for poor people to rid themselves of poverty. They therefore easily 'fall back into poverty after clawing their way out' (Narayan, 2000b: 236). A recent UK study refers to this kind of poverty as a 'theme across the literature' that depicts the 'profound, cumulative impact of long-term poverty' (Smith and Middleton, 2007: 31).

In cases like this one poverty resembles a syndrome, that is, poverty is like a disease or condition where one finds a characteristic combination or concurrence of symptoms. Van Kempen (1997) calls this phenomenon of interlocking factors entrapping a whole community in poverty a poverty pocket, where poverty rules the lives of inhabitants of a local geographical area. The claim is that within such areas, young people's behaviour is shaped by the role models they observe in members of their neighbourhood. The ways poor people in these poverty pockets behave and make livelihoods are defined as 'deviant' by non-poor people. This behaviour arises as 'locally accepted and internalized adaptations to the specific circumstances of the poverty-stricken local environment' (Van Kempen, 1997). These areas are often stigmatized by outsiders, which leads to discrimination against people living there. Van Kempen (1997) aptly refers to such neighbourhoods as 'communities of fate' rather than 'communities of choice', showing some poor people's lack of alternatives in choosing where their home will be. In addition, the expression shows these poor people's disability to better their lives.

This phenomenon of interlocking factors entrapping people in poverty is confirmed by other researchers. The World Bank judges that different aspects of poverty 'interact and reinforce one another in important ways' (2001: 15). The UNDP refers to 'downward spirals', where the degree of poverty deepens and affected poor people lose their few remaining assets. Such loss of assets 'transforms transient poverty into chronic poverty that can extend to the next generation' (1997: 64). In such cases these poor people can become virtually immune to re-habilitation (Terreblanche, 1977: 79). For successful rehabilitation to break the stranglehold of this entrapping network, a comprehensive strategy must address their circumstances, as well as the harms to their mental well-being (Willcocks, 1932: 176; Albertyn, 1932: 98).

Perhaps even more important as a negative aspect of poor people's social relations within their human environment is the inability of some to join organizations or even self-help initiatives due to their lack of resources such as time, energy and money (May, 1998b: 109). Again we observe the close similarity between poverty and disability, where the consequences of poverty resemble a condition that limits people's performance, or exposes their inability to fulfil functions judged as normal by other people. Although such organizations fulfil essentially 'a defensive and usually not a transformative function', that does 'little to move the poor out of poverty', they are nevertheless important coping mechanisms to ward off the ravages of poverty (Narayan et al., 2000a: 6). The World

Bank (2001: 20) refers to important sources of social capital that can reduce poor people's vulnerability through financial or emotional support when faced with risks and shocks, such as crime, violence, illness and natural disasters.

'Social capital' consists of groups such as 'family-based networks, occupation-based groups of mutual help, rotating savings and credit groups' (World Bank, 2001: 20). Some very poor people cannot even participate in such groups, as a result of their own lack of resources which makes them incapable of contributing anything to others. For example, when poor people have to cope with illness, their household might become 'a net drain on the other members of the network, always seeking assistance and contributing little in return' (Kabir et al., 2000: 714). In Russia researchers found that 'deepening poverty makes it difficult to keep up relations and reciprocate favours' (Narayan and Petesch, 2002: 324). In Nigeria researchers observed that while 'savings-credit co-operatives are widely valued, participants say they often exclude the poorest of the poor'. They cannot become members as a result of their inability to make regular financial contributions (Narayan and Petesch, 2002: 95). In such cases poor people's social isolation increases and they lose opportunities for mutually beneficial social cooperation (Willcocks, 1932: 37).

Through loss of normal social cooperation as a result of various conflicts, the use of violence and exclusions, poverty can often lead to a deterioration of traditional moral values. Note the following example. The much celebrated traditional African ethical value of Ubuntu, which implies sharing whatever little you have available with others, has been 'severely eroded' by poverty in many communities (May, 1998b: 85). This erosion implies a deterioration of familial and social ties that could have functioned as valuable assets, thus increasing vulnerability to the devastation that poverty can cause.

Part of living well within a human environment is that people need social contact with friends, acquaintances and other members of the groups to which they belong. Their psychological well-being in part depends on being recognized as equal human beings with dignity or acknowledgement of their role as valued members of society. One must note the often reported rude and dismissive ways in which many poor people are treated by the well-to-do. The well-off people who form part of poor people's human environment often do not aid or empower the poor, but aggravate poor people's already suffering lives. The dominant, influential and powerful members of society often ignore the poor people they encounter, or treat them with disrespect. Note the claim by a recent report of the United Nations that even in democratic and relatively well-governed countries, many 'poor people have to accept daily humiliations without protest' (United Nations 2009: 2).

Poor people are thus often isolated and alienated from the surrounding communities in their human environments. One reason is that poor people are often blamed for their poverty, which is perceived by non-poor people as a condition that the victims of poverty have brought on themselves (Alcock, 1993: 195, 198). Another reason is that non-poor people often look down at poor people with contempt and show no sympathy towards them (Grosskopf, 1932: 16). Non-poor people might feel ashamed of members of their own family, ethnic, linguistic, religious or national group who have become very poor and consequently ignore them with resentment (Grosskopf, 1932: 16). As a result poor people might be uncomfortable in the presence of non-poor members of society, unable to engage with them on a sociable level (May, 1998b: 38). In this case the exclusionary consequences of suffering from poverty manifest again. Poor people often experience exclusion when they are shut out of social interaction, thought to be unwelcome at family or neighbourhood celebrations, unable to share in paid entertainment or considered not part of any trendsetting groups.

Many poor people often feel themselves subjected to 'rudeness, humiliation, shame, inhumane treatment' by other members in their human environment (World Bank, 2001: 35). In their experience even public officials treat them inappropriately, as they experience a 'lack of civility and predictability' when interacting with governmental officials (ibid.). Some poor people have a clear perception of discrimination against them, based on their lack of economic capacities to live lives defined as suitable for humans in their particular society. No wonder that such poor people often feel humiliated and ashamed of their poverty as a result of others ignoring and neglecting them, describing themselves as follows, 'We are social outcasts . . . we are like refuse, like animals, like a rubbish bin' (Narayan et al., 2000b: 142).

Poor people's treatment by non-poor fellow citizens in their human environment forms a crucial part of the negative experiences associated with poverty. These interpersonal contacts often express widely held beliefs and attitudes towards the poor and merit more detailed exposition. John D. Jones quotes E. V. Walter who strongly states that poor people 'are vulnerable to bad experiences and they are targets for destructive actions, ill treatment, bad services and malevolent neglect' (1990:

103). Townsend (1979: 567) found in his study of poverty in Britain that many poor people are unfairly viewed by non-poor citizens as 'work-dodgers, welfare state scroungers, inadequate has-beens, or unfortunates who cannot survive the highly principled competitiveness of the market'.

Narayan and Petesch (2002: 12) found this kind of discrimination in human environments in all countries. They comment as follows:

> Of course, in every country, the mere fact of being poor is itself cause for being isolated, left out, looked down upon, alienated, pushed aside and ignored by those who are better off. This ostracism and voicelessness tie together poor people's experiences across very different contexts. The manifestations of this exclusion, however, are endlessly diverse.

Poor people in India are aware of the converse of the exclusionary treatment poor people often get, when they note the 'intangible dimensions' of well-being. They clearly observe how the well-to-do have 'influence over government officials and the ability to command attention in public ceremonies'. These poor people consider intangibles such as 'influence, honor and respect in society to be indicators of well-being' (Narayan and Petesch, 2002: 154).

Within the broader context of human environments, we believe every person ought to be treated justly and fairly, by treating them with appropriate respect and by taking their interests into account in public decision-making. Poor people are often the victims of injustice and exploitation by many official actors in their human environment. If people are deprived of political rights and thus excluded from participation in government as a result of some aspect of their group membership, those people stand a good chance of being impoverished through neglect or lack of power and influence.

The governments that form part of poor people's human environments often treat them scandalously. People are often poor because governments at local, regional and national levels deny them an equitable part of public resources. People thus impoverished are not part of the politicians' priorities for public spending. Excluded people's needs are ignored and they are allocated vastly unequal shares of government budgets. According to research done by the World Bank, some poor people have a strong sense of their own 'voicelessness and powerlessness in the institutions of state and society' and they 'feel acutely their lack of voice, power and independence' (2001: 34, 35). Some poor people are adamant that as a result they are subjected to exploitation 'at the hands of the institutions of state and society' (ibid.: 35).

Many poor people are part of the vulnerable groups excluded from government that receive less public services, benefits and facilities than those provided to politically powerful groups. The UNDP says that 'poorer communities often lack basic social services that are more plentifully available in richer communities' (1997: 63). Favoured groups benefit from the bias in public expenditure at the cost of excluded people, who are more and more impoverished through deliberate neglect. For example, in Nigeria poor people from sixteen study communities consistently report that, 'with the exception of a very few local entities, public, private and civic institutions are corrupt and exclude or abandon poor people' (Narayan and Petesch, 2002: 91). In India poor people similarly describe some government officials as 'corrupt, withholding information and directing benefits only to better-off groups in their communities and to those with influence' (Narayan and Petesch, 2002: 164).

In general most poor people all over the world experience the political institutions that constitute fundamental parts of their human environments as 'ineffective, inaccessible and disempowering' (Narayan et al., 2000a: 83). As a result these poor people often harbour feelings that they have been 'abandoned or forsaken by their governments' (Narayan et al., 2000b: 82). Local councils often neglect the residential areas of poor people, resulting in negative consequences. Services dealing with sanitation, refuse collection, roads and water drainage are often inadequate and badly maintained (Wilson and Ramphele, 1989: 132). Brundtland (1987: 17) refers to the living conditions of urban poor people in the developing world as 'mushrooming illegal settlements with primitive facilities, increased overcrowding and rampant disease linked to an unhealthy environment'. Badly maintained or no public services lead to environmental degradation in urban residential areas and health hazards for residents. Poor residential areas also often lack appropriate recreational facilities, such as swimming pools, playgrounds for children, sports fields, as well as shopping centres, post offices, public telephones and libraries (Wilson and Ramphele, 1989: 132).

People populating the business world that form part of poor people's human environment often also exploit poor people. The UNDP claims that 'many people have a vested interest in the perpetuation of poverty' (1997: 95). A typical example would be people with economic power, who 'may benefit from exploiting the pool of low-paid labour' (ibid.: 94). Within economic environments poor people are often badly treated. They are sometimes naive and unsophisticated consumers who are ignorant about the finer details of many kinds of business transactions. Many business people exploit these weaknesses to trap some poor people in bad debts or to let them incur monthly payments they cannot afford (Willcocks, 1932: 40). Through these exploitative business practices naive consumers with very few financial resources often lose their purchased items, as well as the money already used as down payments.

Note the ambiguous feelings about money-lenders in Bangladesh, where researchers report on the one hand that despite 'their exorbitant interest rates and ruthlessness in recovering loans', moneylenders are valued for the easy access to credit they offer poor people and the flexible lending terms they provide. On the other hand, many poor people feel that being dependent on moneylenders 'leaves them deeply vulnerable to losing any scarce assets they may have and to rising cycles of indebtedness' (Narayan and Petesch, 2002: 134). Some poor people can also suffer discrimination through business practices such as 'redlining'. Through this practice money-lenders refuse to lend money to poor people for buying a house if they live in specified areas, as they are judged to be risky clients (Van Kempen, 1997).

Conclusion

In this chapter I have explored some possible sides of the relationship between poverty and human environments. In the struggle for survival and the quest for flourishing human lives, humans find themselves within three distinguishable environments: the natural environment as treasure chest of possibilities, the humanly built and constructed environment to fulfil some of our numerous needs and wants and the humans surrounding us in various relationships in our daily lives.

These environments determine our access to empowering relationships, social networks, services, goods and opportunities. They have a particularly strong influence on our perceptions of human relationships, the quality of our social networks, our skills, knowledge and labour capacities, our impact on our surrounding worlds and our general well-being. This chapter has shown to what extent poverty as a lack of economic capacities has harmful consequences for human environments. If these ideas ring true, then exposure of poor people to as wide a range of enriching and empowering environments as possible must form part of a quest to rid them of poverty.

Besides poverty's possible negative impacts on the lives of poor individuals and their environs, it can also have a major impact on the function and well-being of larger social structures, such as the govern-ance functions of a political system. In the next chapter I show how poverty can threaten the core values that enable the flourishing of modern constitutional democracies.

6 • Poverty as Threat to Democratic Values[1]

Introduction

Already in 1901 B. Seebohm Rowntree made convincing arguments why the eradication of poverty is in the self-interest of societies. He argued that poverty implied that many workers will be less efficient than their abilities make possible and therefore poverty will impact on economic growth and societal development (Rowntree, 1901: 303). He further warned of possible disruptions and instability, saying that no country can be 'sound or stable' if it harbours large numbers of poor people he described as a 'mass of stunted life' (304). If many people are condemned to a struggle for existence so desperate 'as necessarily to cripple or destroy the higher parts of their nature', then it will have a major impact on how we give meaning to our shared existence as humans on earth (305).

The reluctance to eradicate poverty shown by citizens and governments of many modern constitutional democracies is puzzling. If poverty threatens societies in various ways, why would citizens in many countries with a strongly agreed upon system of democratic governance fail so painfully to find the commitment and appropriate action to eradicate poverty?

Rowntree makes the point that the eradication of poverty is in our best interest as it removes the bad consequences and negative effects of poverty from society. Allowing poverty in a society even threatens the meaningfulness of our shared living and thus the removal of poverty will improve also the meaning non-poor people find in life. If we take our democratic values seriously – and many of the individual moralities on offer in contemporary democracies – we have to do more to assist poor people to make better lives for themselves. Adherence to our own professed moral values requires much more action than most people are now willing to give.

Besides these self-interested reasons for eradicating poverty, the dire effects of poverty on people's lives significantly increase the suffering many people have to endure. Thus, if we care about the fate of our fellow human beings at all, we would be willing to address persistent poverty head-on. However, most of us don't.

In this chapter I want to investigate the discordance between poverty and democracy. I first briefly articulate the broad underlying values of modern constitutional democracies. Then I analyse the ways in which poverty violates the underlying values of democracy. Next I try to explain why poverty is still widespread in democracies, despite the multiple ways it violates democratic values. Finally I look at the implications of my findings in terms of the functions of democratic values in contemporary democracies.

A brief characterization of democratic values

I assume that the core values of modern constitutional democracies can be portrayed adequately, though not necessarily fully, in the three concepts that drove the French Revolution, liberty, equality and solidarity. I will give a brief characterization of these three concepts as background for my analysis of the discordance between poverty and democracy.

Liberty has the following place in modern constitutional democracies. Liberty, as the idea that citizens are free from unnecessarily imposed human constraints and free to act according to their lights, is embodied in a range of rights that protect various specific liberties held equally by all citizens. These rights enable citizens to choose different aspects of their lives in the light of their own judgement of what is good for them, subject to a condition that they do not violate similar rights possessed by their fellow citizens. Rights furthermore guarantee opportunities to participate in social and political activities according to their choice. Among their liberties they also have rights that protect them from any arbitrary, unjustified interference in their lives by state agents or fellow citizens.

These liberties make it possible for citizens to participate in activities of their choice and live the lives they see fit without unwarranted interference. Such liberties are empty in cases where a citizen cannot exercise a choice due to the lack of means to sustain life and health. For this reason citizens in most democracies are aware that their capacity to make use of their liberties is an important matter (see Sen, 1999). Therefore, governments in many democracies have a serious concern whether citizens have the requisite resources to enable them to engage in those actions regarded as ones minimally decent people usually do. Thus, whether citizens are able to participate in a range of activities appropriate to living a human life has become an issue inextricably linked with the question whether they have appropriate freedoms.

Most democracies have a very strong emphasis on the equality of its citizens. Ann Phillips (1999: 16) argues that debates about democracy 'are always, in part, discussions of what political equality means and how far it should be taken'. Although citizens are unequal in so many different ways, they are judged to be equally human in distinction from animals, plants, machines or rocks. Democrats often refer to the dignity or worth that all citizens possess equally. To have respect for the human dignity of a fellow citizen means to recognize that a fellow citizen belongs to the species *Homo sapiens* and thus to acknowledge that such a person must be treated according to a certain moral minimum that applies equally to all citizens. The equal moral standing of citizens often implies that they are to be treated in the same way, unless there are compelling reasons for treating them differently.

Throughout the history of democratic societies we have progressively learnt what differences we judge significant and which ones not. Although we will undoubtedly in future change our collective minds about these matters again, for now democrats have broad consensus that every citizen should have a set of rights similar to everyone else, be judged in terms of merit when applying for professional positions, be treated with medical care in order of need, be admitted to university in terms of previous academic achievements and so on.

Sometimes people miss the importance of solidarity as central value of modern constitutional democracies. Solidarity refers to agreement or unity between individuals in some or other respect, such as having common interests, shared values and similar sympathies to engage in social cooperation for mutual benefit. Brian Barry (2005: 183) defines solidarity simply as 'the sense that those who live together share a common fate and should work together'. We choose democracy as our political model for the simple reason that we judge it the best way for us to live together to enable meaningful cooperation for our survival and flourishing. We agree on core values, feel the same way about the diverse kinds of human lives we want to allow in our society and we have multiple shared interests in developing the well-being of our community.

Solidarity implies the following in a democratic context. Through institutionalizing a modern constitutional democracy we collectively define the nature of the relationships between ourselves and we set up a governmental system that will enable us as a society to make the best possible decisions. We implement our shared concern and care for every person (1) to have liberty rights that enable them to make their own choices, (2) to be treated as equal members of our species, (3) to

have access to the best possible education and training to develop their
potential and (4) to enjoy the riches of our natural and cultural heritage that we collectively protect and develop. We make joint decisions
on how to share the financial, administrative, managerial and other
burdens to run our society in ways that will enable us to engage in individual lives of our own choosing. We also decide our own procedures
for distributing, assigning and awarding the benefits that accrue from
our collectively organized lives. Thus, as citizens of modern constitutional democracies we show our solidarity with one another in the
way we cooperate to set up structures and spaces within which we
can safely and securely live lives that show our individuality within
the broader cultural confines of lives we collectively share, develop and
convey to future generations.

To what extent does poverty violate these core democratic values that
we all share, or make it impossible to implement the conditions these
values aspire to create for every citizen?

Poverty contradicts democratic values

Poverty violates equal respect for every citizen

One of the core values underlying democratic institutions is that all citizens
must be equally respected as human beings. Their dignity as members
of our species implies that they must be treated equally as persons with
liberties to design their own lives through similar opportunities to develop
their potential and participate in shared activities. Poverty implies a denial
of the equal dignity of every citizen. Let us review how I have defended
this strong statement in earlier chapters. The concept of poverty is almost
uniquely applied to humans. Poverty as a lack of economic capacities
causes its victims to live lives in which they cannot fully participate in
the range of activities expressive of their nature as human beings. Sometimes they may not even be able to maintain their physical health. To
describe someone as poor thus indicates when a person has fallen below
the standard of life thought appropriate for a human being in a specific
society.

The concept of poverty signifies two levels at which a person's standard
of living might have fallen below that of their peers. The concept of
extreme poverty implies that a person does not have sufficient economic
capacities to provide food, clothing, shelter, security and medical care to

maintain their physical health. The concept of intermediate poverty signifies that although people have adequate economic capacities to provide food, clothing, shelter, security and medical care to maintain their physical health, they cannot participate in any other activities regarded as indicative of being human in their society. They are deprived of full participation in activities such as the governance of a community's shared life to maintain social order, education to train and equip others to fulfil useful tasks, initiation ceremonies for welcoming new part-icipants in diverse social practices, thanksgiving events for expressing gratitude for services rendered in smaller or larger contexts, celebration of significant events on smaller (family) and larger (society) scale and entertainment that amuses and amazes others through expressing rare individual and team talents and skills.

Poverty as a condition that strips citizens of their human dignity is no natural disaster in which humans play no role. Rather, poverty results from the choices humans make about the values and organizational structures of their society and from the social forces they allow space to operate to produce unequal distributions of income, wealth and opportunities. The levels of poverty and riches in society are the collective product and responsibility of its citizens. Poverty and its negative con-sequences for the dignity of fellow citizens are thus the result either of what democrats do to their fellow citizens, or what they allow to happen to them.

An important part of having respect for one's fellow citizens is to acknowledge that public decisions are to be made collectively. If fellow citizens are treated with respect, they will both have opportunities to influence public decisions and such decisions will be justified to them on grounds they can accept (see Gutmann and Thompson, 1996). If powerful citizens manipulate or steamroller public decisions at the expense of poor citizens and on the basis of reasons poor citizens reject, they are showing them disrespect. The ethical norm for democratic deliberators is simply put by Iris Young: 'Deliberators should appeal to justice and frame the reasons for their proposals in terms they claim that others ought to accept' (2003: 103).

If the rich and powerful can dominate public dialogue through the use of their impressive resources to protect and advance their interests at the cost of poor people and thus silence the weak and vulnerable in the process, then core democratic values failed to protect the dignity and interests of those who need protection most (ibid.).

Poverty violates equal concern for every individual's interest

Democratic values require that governmental institutions show equal concern to protect the fundamental interests every citizen has in making something out of their own lives. Fundamental interests include things needed for basic human survival and health, as well as for self-reliant living in cooperation with others. Ian Shapiro articulates the basic interests of every citizen as follows: 'People have basic interests in developing and sustaining what is needed to survive as independent agents in the world as it is likely to exist for their lifetimes and to protect those interests by participating in decision-making that affects them' (2003: 132).

Poverty implies that citizens are not treated the same regarding their fundamental interest in securing their survival. Poverty thus violates the principle of the equal consideration of every citizen's interests. Poor people's fundamental interests in having enough food to sustain life and health, having shelter for protection against the elements and as shield against prying eyes, having proper clothes to wear to keep their bodies warm and to avoid public embarrassment and in being employed to be able to provide for such basic needs are ignored as if they do not qualify as fellow citizens who deserve concern.

People suffering from poverty have inadequate resources to provide for their basic needs of food, clothing, shelter and self-development. To ignore their interest in securing these things in their quest to enable their physical survival as human beings and to strive for flourishing lives, while others in society have an abundance of such means violates the principle of the equal consideration of each citizen's interests.

If fellow citizens have no concern for poor people and their basic interests, damaging consequences ensue. An example will demonstrate the point. To take note of poor people's interests and nevertheless dismiss the valid claims they have to all-purpose means necessary for the satisfaction of their basic needs (see Rawls, 1993) is to add insult to injury. To ignore their interests in having healthy bodies and developed capacities implies treating them as beings that do not possess human characteristics. For example, the failure to take seriously the link between poverty and illness is to show lack of concern for vulnerable people. This means that government and fellow citizens ignore both the fact that ill health is often judged to be a 'key characteristic of poverty' and that 'poor nutrition, inadequate sanitation and water and insufficient access to healthcare are identified in many studies as the underlying causal factors responsible for illness' (Kabir et al., 2000: 707).

The World Bank found that poor people generally suffer more from illness than the non-poor, while they have less access to healthcare (2001: 27). Note the dripping sarcasm in Tawney's remark when he articulates the impact of poverty on the health of people: 'The poor, it seems, are beloved by the gods, if not by their fellow-mortals. They are awarded exceptional opportunities of dying young' (1952: 70, 71). Non-poor citizens surely ought to show concern through interventions to eradicate such crippling effects of poverty?

Someone might argue that poor people are well enough treated in democratic societies, though their basic needs are unfulfilled. The argument is that they are accorded equal respect through political liberty rights and are protected from state intervention in their private lives. Although this statement is true, it is only a half-truth. Political rights and freedom from state intrusion are very important, but so are bodily health and educational opportunities. Therefore, to have equal political liberty rights is only part of what it means to be treated with the respect and equal concern due to a human being that qualifies as citizen of a constitutional democracy.

Isaiah Berlin rightly argues that to say the poor are treated well enough when they are only assigned equal political rights is to 'mock their condition', as these poor people need medical help, food or shelter before they can 'understand or make use of an increase in their freedom' (1969: 124). Berlin states that sophisticated forms of individual liberty, such as freedom of the press and freedom of contract, do not concern those people that live in squalor and oppression. How could they be concerned about the details of liberty rights, Berlin asks, if they do not have enough food, adequate shelter, sufficient warmth or a minimum degree of security?

There is no way that anyone can argue that a government has given concern to the fundamental interests of such poor people that is equal to the concern shown for the interests of other members of society. Clearly, for anyone to watch people suffer – and even die – as a result of poverty while they are able to ameliorate the situation without harming themselves in any morally significant way brings us to the 'end of all notions of human equality and respect for human life', as Singer (1981: 176) has put it so succinctly. Genuine concern for the fundamental interests of suffering poor people implies willingness to relieve their suffering through providing them with all purpose means to satisfy their basic needs.

Poverty leads to unequal political participation

Perhaps Berlin's correct focus on the urgent need of poor people for basic goods such as food, shelter and medical care made him overlook the important function liberty rights can fulfil for poor people. Through exercising liberty rights poor people can create awareness of their needs and publicize their sense of injustice at being ignored and sidelined. For these reasons the value of the equal political rights assigned to all citizens in modern constitutional democracies should not be underestimated.

In modern constitutional democracies all citizens have equal political liberties. These liberties are expressed in rights to freedom of association, expression, religion, conscience and movement. Poor people's lack of economic means and the burdens that result limit their capacity to advance their goals within the framework provided by a modern constitutional democracy (cf. Rawls, 1971: 202; Berlin, 1969). One cannot describe poor citizens as possessing adequately functioning political capacities, as they cannot effectively make their needs and interests heard, they cannot fully employ their collective political voice, nor can they adequately insist on the fulfilment of their rights (see Bohman, 1996: 124). Note how a recent commission in the UK describes the impact of such experiences of poor people as told to them: 'But the Commission was overwhelmed by the extent of the scepticism, mistrust and eventual disillusionment reported by people experiencing poverty who feel their voices are being ignored' (Report of the Commission on Poverty, Participation and Power, 2000: v).

The value (or worth) of liberties possessed by non-poor people is far greater as a result of their greater wealth, means, education and resulting capability available for achieving their aims (cf. Rawls, 1971: 204). The danger of this outcome is that liberty 'becomes the privilege of a class, not the possession of a nation' (Tawney, 1952: 185).

In contemporary discussions of democracy, supporters of the idea that deliberation between free and equal citizens forms the core of what democracy is about often point out how easily poor people's concerns are ignored and their voices silenced. These theorists point out socioeconomic inequalities can have strong impacts on democratic decision making. Poor people can be prevented from effective participation in public dialogue for reasons like not having enough time available, not having appropriately developed capacities and sufficient resources for engaging in democratic deliberation and not having clout enough to help set public agendas by offering possible alternatives (Bohman, 1996: 15, 18, 36, 65, 66, 108, 110; Dryzek, 2000: 86, 172; Young, 2003: 110, 113). The consequence is often that material inequality is turned into political inequality, thereby undermining equal participation through effective voice for poor people. This strongly diminishes the quality of public dialogue (Dryzek, 2000: 172; Bohman, 1996: 66).

Citizens bolstered by their wealth do not feel much need to shift their positions in public dialogue as their opponents are too weak to make them reconsider alternatives (Bohman, 1996: 65). As a result democratic decision making suffers, as significant sections of the political community do not have effective input to determine agendas, much less outcomes of public dialogue. They are virtually sidelined or even excluded from public dialogue, but made politically subject to the outcome of decisions they were too weak to influence (ibid.: 125, 126). In this way the democratic assumption is violated that people ought to participate as free and equal citizens with roughly equal voice and similar opportunities to influence the outcome of decisions that will influence their lives.

We have seen that when citizens are unable to make similar use of political liberties as a result of the unequal value those liberties have for them, there is a danger that economic inequalities can be translated into political inequalities. Drastically unequal distribution of economic capacities easily manifests itself in the political arena where poor people cannot compete on equal terms with non-poor people. Alcock refers to the 'debilitating consequences of poverty and deprivation for participation in political activity' (1993: 212). His description of the consequences is worth quoting in full: 'These include the direct costs of participation, such as membership fees, transport, socialising and keeping up to date and the indirect consequences of poor health, poor environment and lack of time, which inhibit involvement in any organised, active pursuits.'

The result of unequal political participation is that poor people's 'needs are often overlooked, neglected, or very insufficiently provided for' (Gewirth, 1984: 564). When some poor people lack economic capacities to use the print and electronic media, their organizational infrastructure and skills are also severely hampered. As a result such poor people lose their ability to speak for themselves so as to bring their needs and grievances to the attention of their governing bodies. They become unable to influence political decisions to favour their interests and views. Myrdal (1970: 63) captures best what happens when he describes the poor masses of the 1960s in India and Pakistan as follows: 'When it comes to public policy, the masses of poor people in the undeveloped world are the object of politics but hardly anywhere its subject.' Bluntly stated, things merely happen to poor people in these circumstances, they don't make things happen.

A result of the fact that poor people often have an inaudible and ineffective voice in local politics is reflected in what Ellis (1998) rightly refers to as an 'oft-stated finding of poverty research', that is, poor people are disadvantaged by governments in provision of services. These services tend to be 'biased towards the better off and more accessible locations, communities and social groups' (Ellis, 1998: 4, 5). Through this neglect governments contribute to the suffering and deprivation experienced by poor people.

This powerlessness to use political processes effectively to advance their interests – that often occurs amongst poor people – convinces them that politics offers them no hopeful solutions for their problems. This knowledge – gained from experience and passed on from one generation to the next – might lead poor people to 'passivity, deference and resentment' (Walzer, 1983: 311). Attitudes of fatalism and resignation can lead poor people to accept their situation as inevitable and to avoid or resist mobilization to protest and change their living conditions. They become powerless citizens.

Poverty can destabilize modern constitutional democracies

Dissatisfied citizens have various avenues to peacefully channel their protest and make their grievances heard without significant social disruption. Groups harbouring intensely felt grievances they believe are ignored by the rest of society can engage in angry protest action that might become disruptive and destabilize the democratic order.

Among the group of not so desperately poor people, feelings of relative deprivation might result from the lack of integration into society and the accompanying feelings of alienation. Whereas desperately poor people often resign themselves to their miserable situation of poverty and fail to see any possibility of improvement, moderately poor people often feel cheated of a more comfortable lifestyle. Sociologists describe these feelings in terms of relative deprivation.

Relative deprivation has both cognitive and affective aspects (cf. Uys, 1990: 57–70). The cognitive aspect refers to poor people's belief that they are being treated unfairly by society. The affective aspects of relative deprivation refer to poor people feeling dissatisfied and aggrieved because of their belief that injustices are perpetrated against them. They compare their personal situation with those of others in society and judge that the others have an unfair advantage or share privileges only available to a small elite group. These people become convinced that their unequal socio-economic position results from injustice. In societies with strong universal norms – such as modern constitutional democracies – these beliefs are intensified when poor people insist on sharing more equally in the benefits promised by the universal norms underlying democratic institutions.

A strong degree of relative deprivation amongst poor people does not necessarily translate into social unrest or political protest action, but the possibility is always there. Skilful politicians, trade unionists or community leaders can capitalize on feelings of deprivation and convert them into political campaigns that might become destabilizing. Resentment about unjust treatment by the social and political elite of society can easily spill over into a violent campaign in which destruction of property becomes commonplace, since large holdings of property are taken to be unjust. Moreover, such resentment can spill over into widespread acceptance, legitimizing, sanctioning and condoning of crime as unlawful means of redress and redistribution. Although many citizens will not necessarily commit crimes themselves, their passive acceptance of crime and unwillingness to cooperate with law enforcement agencies can create Robin Hood 'heroes' who steal from the rich to benefit the poor, or who steal from the rich simply to get back at those seemingly unfairly advantaged by the status quo.

Condoning crime or instigating political protest can easily generate more significant social conflict. The United Nations Development Programme (UNDP) holds the view that poverty can lead to conflict just as much as conflict can create poverty (1997: 66). Situations of low economic growth with minimal resources and few opportunities for sustainable livelihoods are thought to 'contribute to social conflicts of all kinds' (ibid.: 66, 67). Lewis (2004: 3) gives a global perspective of poverty's effects in international affairs, one often echoed by various political leaders and commentators over the past decade:

> The gap between rich and poor nations threatens global stability. Immigration pressures are becoming unsustainable; the poor sees moving to the rich countries as the only way to improve their way of life within their lifetime. The frustration, envy and wounded pride of the poor are causing rogue nations to seek power

and influence through the development of weapons of mass destruction and individual extremists to lash out against rich countries through terrorism.

A similar warning is sounded by Little when he says: 'If the world does not make progress in alleviating poverty, in improving the life circumstances of the world's disadvantaged people and in enhancing human equality, then it appears unavoidable that conflict and violence will continue' (2003: 247).

Despite the dangers of destabilization, poor people's resistance and their political mobilization to change their relative bad economic position must also be judged positively. To engage in such a struggle is a 'denial of powerlessness, an acting out of citizenly virtue' (Walzer, 1983: 311). Why does Walzer describe poor people's protest thus? Walzer interprets the parties and movements responsible for such protest action as 'breeding grounds of self-respecting citizens' (ibid.). For Walzer citizens are self-respecting when they resist the violation of their rights and challenge those who deny their humanity in any way. Citizens who deliberate with their fellow citizens, take responsibility for their views and protest the violation of their rights are exercising political power in defence of their rights. Such citizens respect themselves through using some of their rights to oppose actions and policies that violate their other rights. They respect themselves by not allowing others to violate any of their rights, or to deny them anything they have a legitimate moral claim to, through acts of commission or omission.

The UNDP highly values political mobilization of the poor as a significant factor in the eradication of poverty. They claim that 'poverty eradication and empowerment of the poor go hand in hand' (2000: 42). Without politically active poor citizens struggling for their own well-being, poverty eradication merely becomes, 'one form of social welfare or another' (ibid.). To eradicate poverty thus means that poor people must break the alienation between one another to transform themselves into activist democratic citizens 'with greater organizational capacity' so as to claim for themselves 'more power to influence their lives' (ibid.: 78).

Poverty demonstrates the fallibility and vulnerability of democracy

The discord between democracy and poverty demonstrates the fallibility and vulnerability of democratic political institutions. These institutions cannot by their mere institutionalization alone deliver fully on the promises implicit in the central, core democratic values. No democratic institution can succeed without a majority of citizens deeply infused with the spirit and tenor of fundamental democratic values. The institutions, procedures and rules of formal democracy may provide guidelines, but somehow the inner appropriation of these values expressed in outer care for every citizen is a major complementary factor that will determine the quality of a democratic society (see Shapiro, 2003: 135; Dowding, 2004: 35).

How must we understand the failure of democratic political institutions to address a disruptive and destructive condition like poverty? In the next section I will investigate possible reasons for this failure: the aspirational character of democratic values, the selectivity of our favoured interpretations of democratic values or the irreconcilability of the ultimate democratic values. Together these three reasons explain a large part of the failure of democracies to properly address poverty.

Do we have poverty because it is difficult to implement democratic values?

One possible reason inhibiting adequate equality of citizens to prevent debilitating poverty in modern constitutional democracies is the slow democratic process of consistently actualizing and implementing equal individual rights (cf. Habermas, 1994). Habermas points to the dialectic between *de jure* equality, that is, equality under law and as embodied in the constitution, and *de facto* equality, that is, equal treatment in practice and equality in life circumstances. What the law and the constitution promise do not necessarily exist in practice.

The actualization of equality must be driven by active democrats, organized in social movements that engage in political struggles, where those affected by inequalities articulate their dissatisfaction and justify alternatives though public debate (Habermas, 1994). Often such groups do not exist or are too weak. Another factor might be that a particular democracy does not have the financial resources to fund the proper, wide-ranging implementation of its core values. It might also be that not enough trained and educated people are available to serve as competent bureaucrats to implement well-meaning governmental policies. These explanations of the failure of democracies to deal appropriately with poverty aid our understanding. Combined with the next one we might have a workable explanation of the problem of the discordancy between poverty and democracy.

Is poverty justified by our interpretations of and dealings with core democratic values?

Whatever the exact formulation of the normative foundations of modern constitutional democracies – whether it be liberty, equality and solidarity or the deeper principle of equal concern and respect – conflict will occur between the different values embodied in these formulations. Such conflicts are often resolved by selectively focusing on some values only. A good example of how a selective focus on some fundamental values can be detrimental to poor people's interests comes from the strong emphasis on liberty as a fundamental value of democracy. Liberal political rights to enable political participation are combined with liberties to engage in free economic activity to create optimum conditions for economic growth. As a result many countries achieve economic growth without making any difference to the lives of poor people. The UNDP (1997: 71; 2000: 43) has found that economic growth without policies that embody at least some aspects of the values of equality and solidarity does not benefit poor people at all if the non-poor members of society have no concern to eradicate poverty. The UNDP suggests that poor people must mobilize themselves to 'overcome the handicap of too much income directed at the rich' (2000: 54). The choice of words in the UNDP report is significant.

The easy way of dealing with conflict between core democratic values is to be selective and choose only those values that suit your interests and those of your associates. The more difficult way of dealing with such conflicts is to find a compromise between core democratic values that protects the integrity of those values and the basic interests of all people involved. Let us look at how these two options promote or counter the incidence of poverty in a society.

The best explanation of the discordance between poverty and democracy is provided by the way poverty is justified by a selective focus on some core democratic values whilst ignoring and sidelining others. The above example of an almost exclusive focus on liberty at the cost of equality and solidarity illustrates the point. This selective focus on some values only amounts to an ideological distortion of the normative foundations of modern constitutional democracies. These justifications convince citizens that nothing is wrong with their society and that no action is thus needed to deal with poverty.

How does this kind of justification work? The existence and degree of poverty in violation of the normative foundations of modern constitutional democracies can be justified by various ideologies. These ideologies are perversions and distortions of the normative foundations, as they select aspects of those foundations that suit the interests of a specific group and ignore the rest. Economic inequalities are justified by using only some of the values generally accepted by citizens and embodied in the constitutions of modern constitutional democracies. Such justifications pretend to be in the interests of all citizens, but only serve to mask the interests of a privileged group. These ideological justifications of sectional interests present distorted versions of the normative foundations. They represent incomplete versions of these foundations, subtle disguises of the self-interest of a privileged group that masquerade as universal norms to benefit every citizen.

Thus, democratic countries where the poverty rate is high usually function on a selective interpretation of democratic values where some of the important ones are ignored or distorted. Not all the important values required for the full and effective treatment of every citizen as a free and equal person are simultaneously realized, but some are held back, sidelined or understated. As a result certain crucial values for the protection of poor and vulnerable people never become operative to play their important role.

Note the following illustration. Peter Singer (1993: 32) uses America as an example of a society where an ideology of individualism 'that simply encourages people to maximise personal advantage' reigns supreme. Individuals are in continual competition in pursuit of their self-interest. In such a society there is mutual hostility between individuals that undermines cooperation for collective goals. Singer fails to see how a society that has elevated 'acquisitive selfishness into its chief virtue' (37) can be classified as having an ethical lifestyle. His judgement suggests that this ideology of individualism is difficult to reconcile with the normative foundations embedded in the American constitution.

The ideological process of selective appropriation of moral values with the aim of promoting the interests of a particular group can be further illuminated by use of a modified version of a set of distinctions made by Ronald Dworkin (1986: 181–91). The normative foundations embodied in the constitutions of modern democracies can be called a coherent political programme that each generation interprets and actualizes. Such a coherent political programme consists of constitutive political positions, such as liberty, equality or solidarity, that are valued for their own sake. Constitutive political positions do not necessarily cohere and might have contrary implications. As a result difficult choices must be made that will involve compromises and sacrifices. Strategies used as means to achieve constitutive political positions are called derivative positions.

Ideological distortions of the normative foundations of modern constitutional democracies occur at the level of both constitutive political positions and derivative positions. People identify stronger with some constitutive political positions and then design derivative positions to implement their one-sided choice that excludes other fundamental values. Yet in a vibrant society with vigorous political debate and activity, one-sided choices made by one group can be debated, challenged or off-set by similar one-sided choices made by other groups.

However, in some societies the members of a dominant, powerful group are entrenched in influential positions which give them a strong and loud voice in society on public issues. As a result they can easily spread their ideas through the media to gain acceptance from those who are advantaged by their ideas and practices and even from some who are not. In the process they can easily marginalize other voices that articulate opposing views. When poor people are a powerless minority without access to, or without the means to use channels of communication effectively, they might be made inaudible by the loud voices and legitimizing functions of such ideologies. Lister argues that poor people's 'lack of voice' is simultaneously 'a symptom of the political powerlessness of people in poverty and a cause of their feelings of powerlessness' (2004: 172).

Isaiah Berlin (1969) believes that ultimate values are sometimes irreconcilable and equally ultimate ends often collide as they are in perpetual rivalry with one another. Therefore we must make difficult choices in which some values or ends are sacrificed for the sake of others. We cannot eliminate the possibility of such conflict, for such conflict is a permanent characteristic of human life. Conflict between ultimate values cannot be solved by clear-cut solutions, Berlin argues, but rather by different choices involving hard sacrifices. This is particularly true of the sometimes conflicting demands of liberty, equality and solidarity, as well as the often contrary claims based on equal respect or the equal consideration of interests. In many countries of the world we find strong regard for liberty that leads to its application in the economic and personal spheres as much as in the political sphere. The emphasis on freedom to do business and accumulate wealth without restrictions conflicts with the demand that governments tax citizens to redistribute income and wealth for the sake of providing all purpose means for poor and vulnerable people.

There is another way to look at this issue. One can interpret democratic institutions as the embodiment of core moral values such as liberty, equality, solidarity, justice and fairness. Taken together, democratic institutions provide us with a framework of safe spaces and fixed boundaries within which to live our lives. Within these spaces we create and construct our individual lives in conjunction and coordination with others. Together we also create shared public lives with other people, such as in the spheres of education, sport, business, entertainment and politics. The kind of lives we build within democratic spaces will not necessarily contain all moral values constitutive of modern democracies. Through exercising our liberties by making autonomous choices, we set constraints for our interpersonal interactions and determine aspirations we hope to achieve. Our chosen lifestyles and personal goals do again not necessarily reflect the full range of values democratic institutions require to function optimally.

What kind of shared human life emerges in and through countless individual and shared moral decisions in the spaces offered by democratic institutions depends on the moral qualities of the inhabitants and the ethical values they pursue. Again, selective use of democratic values to benefit selfish interests can significantly detract from the full and balanced realization of the comprehensive range of democratic values. This happens both in the lives of individuals and groups, such as political parties, socio-economic classes, or ethnic minorities or majorities. The closer citizens internalize and approximate the moral values undergirding democratic institutions, the better the moral quality of our shared lives will reflect democratic ideals.

Is destructive conflict between democratic values and selective appropriation of core values inevitable? Should attempted resolutions necessarily result in harm to poor people? My answer is no. Despite such possible conflicts, the core democratic values are each clearly enough articulated and well enough supported not to leave space for a sacrifice or abandonment of equality and solidarity in favour of (economic) liberty, for example. These two values especially require that no citizens must be left without the means to satisfy their basic needs or to take care of their fundamental interests. Unless values like equality and solidarity are mostly ignored, sidelined or distorted, poverty need not result from possible conflicts between core democratic values. Thus, this explanation adds another element to our explanation of the discordancy between poverty and democracy.

The best way to avoid conflicts between core values that can lead to poverty is to engage in dialogue to establish and revise compromises between core democratic values. To engage constantly in public dialogue about so-called 'constitutional essentials' is part of what life in modern constitutional democracies entail. Bohman (1996: 49) rejects any idea that we will ever have finality in our interpretation of the fundamental values of our society. To think such finality can be achieved is to ignore 'their constant dialogical respecification and renegotiation in all currently existing forms of democracy'. Shapiro (2003: 124) observes that not all people want consensus with others and might prefer to keep disagreements about fundamentals alive, as they 'may perceive consensus as oppressive and they may take pleasure in differentiating themselves from one another'.

Constant dialogue and continued conflict about fundamental values might be the best way to keep us conscious of the rich alternatives and complex applications suggested by our fundamental values. At best we can reach a kind of provisional, principled compromise through intense dialogue and protracted deliberation on the scope and application of our fundamental values. In such a compromise we agree on the outer boundaries that our fundamental values place on the depth, scope and reach of one another's implementation. No compromise can have intellectual integrity if the central thrust of any one of the core democratic values is not allowed to have full effect. An acceptable compromise is one that honours and acknowledges the central claims of each value according to the weight our considered judgement assigned them when we selected those values in the first place.

Poverty violates the integrity of modern constitutional democracies

Should citizens of modern constitutional democracies be worried about the harm that poverty does to the normative foundations of their societies? If so, why? I want to argue that citizens of modern constitutional democracies ought to be seriously concerned with the damage poverty does not only to their fellow citizens, but also to the moral values underlying their public institutions. They must even reconsider their own self-interest, as they themselves are violating the core values they profess to live by. The reason in support of my claim is as follows. Injustice harms not only its victims, but also those responsible for it. The harm to perpetrators of injustice that result from the injustice of poverty is the loss of integrity.

Plato (1993) has already argued in his book *Republic* that unjust people do not only injure their victims, but also their own 'souls'. Through doing injustice, people destroy parts of themselves constituted by moral values. Moral values form a defining element of any person's life, as morality forms an inescapable part of being human. A person's moral choices, concerned *inter alia* with what we ought to do or refrain from doing to other people and their interests, play a constitutive role in the definition of a person's identity. By acting against one's own moral values, a person erodes the legitimacy of those values and undermines one's own credibility. A similar argument applies to the way citizens of modern constitutional democracies deal with those of their moral values underlying the public institutions of their society.

Committing injustice causes loss of legitimacy to moral values and a lack of credibility for individuals and societies. Harm to legitimacy and credibility can further be explained by the concept of loss of moral integrity. Moral integrity has two meanings. The first refers to the sense of wholeness or integration of a set of moral values. Does a set of moral values cohere and combine into a reasonable, coherent whole? If a person or society acts according to values contrary to some of those publicly professed by the person's or society's set of values, then the integrity of the set of values is undermined or violated.

This kind of loss of moral integrity happens when democrats unjustifiably rearrange the weights and priorities of their value set so that one value trumps all other competing values in every circumstance. In such a case, for example, the value of liberty might be emphasized to exclude equality or solidarity from becoming properly operational. Free economic activity and strong economic growth are judged so important as to invalidate claims to equality and solidarity that would provide minimal standards of living to poor people. To sideline and repress some core values for the sake of the dominance of others leads to the loss of moral coherence of the total value set.

The second meaning of moral integrity refers to the degree of correspondence between the values a person or society professes and the values expressed in the actual lives lived by that person or society. A high degree of correspondence between values professed and values lived is indicative of strong moral integrity, which is an admirable quality. Lack of correspondence between values and life leads to loss of moral integrity, a condition generally frowned upon.

The most obvious example of a lack of correspondence between professed values and values expressed in lifestyle occurs in the ways democratic citizens consciously or unconsciously fail to act on those democratic values that make the eradication of poverty a moral imperative. This failure makes citizens, organizations, agencies and governments of modern constitutional democracies lose moral integrity which de-legitimizes their moral values and makes them lose credibility as trustworthy associates. They lose credibility because they selectively obey only those moral values that protect their own interests, whereas they ignore those contrary to their own immediate selfish interests that would have functioned to eradicate poverty for many people.

The way we selfishly obey only those moral values that secure our interests shows best when we take into account that we refuse, or are unwilling, to collectively help poor citizens escape a condition that can seriously harm their lives. It is not the case that we can plead ignorance of the true causes and mechanisms of poverty, nor can we defend our in-action by pointing to the exorbitant cost or the lack of knowledge how to deal with a perplexing human condition. Note how Gordon (2002: 73, 74) articulates clearly that we have no excuse that offsets our collective unwillingness to aid the poor:

> Ending poverty is largely a matter of lack of political will. It is not a problem of lack of money or scientific knowledge on how to eradicate poverty . . . Yet the costs of meeting the basic needs of every person in the world are relatively small compared with the vast wealth available. The practical policies and instit-utional mechanisms needed to end world poverty are well known and widely understood.

Conclusion

In this chapter I have argued that poverty threatens the well-being of democratic societies. My focus was on the harm poverty does to the moral values underlying contemporary democratic societies. These harms are serious enough to threaten the short and long term interests of citizens. Poverty harms a society through the negative conditions that arise as a result of dissatisfaction leading to political conflict or civil unrest, the loss of the power of core moral values through a lack of legitimacy and the loss of personal moral integrity by a large group of citizens who act selfishly through justifying their interests ideologically at the expense of the most vulnerable in society.

A high incidence of poverty threatens the moral foundations of democratic societies, as the fundamental values embodied in democratic societies seemingly commit members of those societies to address issues of poverty. My claim is that failure to do something about poverty means neglecting, ignoring or deliberately violating some fundamental values of democratic societies. This failure has negative consequences for all involved, not only the victims of this failure. The harm the phenomenon of poverty does to democratic values gives good reason why democrats should take poverty a lot more seriously, as this kind of harm to a society threatens the interests and well-being of all members of contemporary democracies.

What is the significance of my analysis of the discordance between poverty and democracy? What is the rationale for my defence of core democratic values against any acts of commission or omission that result in weakening the impact of those values? The significance of my defence of core democratic values is to safeguard some of the strongest instruments we have for protecting our fundamental interests that can also assist us best in the struggle to eradicate poverty that diminish and destroy people's lives. These core democratic values fulfil important functions in both contemporary democratic countries and in those undemocratic ones where citizens are struggling to get democracy accepted and instituted. How can these functions now be explained best in terms of their value for every citizen, especially those afflicted by poverty?

The first function of these values is to provide mirrors within which citizens can look to determine whether they are being appropriately treated as human beings with dignity by fellow citizens and government officials in their countries. Do they see the values of liberty, equality and solidarity reflected in the way they are treated by the individual and collective actions of their fellow citizens?

A second role for these democratic values is to act as guarantees of opportunities for citizens to engage in fitting self-enhancing actions. When citizens generally adhere to democratic values, every person is guaranteed reasonable opportunities, like everyone else, to engage in activities judged worthwhile in the quest for creating and maintaining a decent life. Do poor people feel instead that they only experience powerlessness and frustration through being unable and disempowered to utilize available opportunities?

To allow fellow citizens to live their lives according to their conscience within the boundaries of shared values lets the third role of democratic values become manifest. Democratic values function as beacons of hope that either individually or collectively we can develop lifestyles that fittingly express our humanity. These values become our guide to the promised land, a place where we can live according to our promises to ourselves and one another. They enable us to create a world in which we all can live our lives to the full both in accordance with our own judgement and in respect of other people's right to do similarly. Do poor people merely observe a world that excludes them, where others blessed by fate, nature, family privilege or social co-incidence can realize their dreams?

The fourth role of democratic values flows from the third: they create expectations that the best life we judge possible for ourselves might become a reality through the empowering role of our shared lives appropriately organized. These expectations make democrats restlessly search for better ways to organize society to enable fulfilled individual lives, as democracy offers the promise of giving everyone opportunities to improve their lives as much as they themselves want and are capable to do. Do poor people know more of a denial of hope, the squashing of possibilities and ignorance of co-operative ventures, where their lives are constricted, not empowered and their potential are withering away and not developed?

Perhaps the fifth function of democratic values will now come as no surprise: they function as instigators of protest whenever citizens feel they get too little of the freedoms and opportunities rightfully owed them. Do poor people feel a smouldering resistance to their lot in society, that they let out through small acts of active or passive resistance? Do they sometimes show no adherence to social values, as abiding by those values has never brought them any benefit? Do they sometimes not care for others, as no one seems to care about their continued inhuman existence?

Thus far I have argued that poverty has harmful consequences for the lives of individuals with their various environments as well as for the political system in which they function. How must we make sense of this human condition that has such devastating effects? In the next chapter I present a framework of ideas to help us understand this phenomenon that so often shatters human lives.

7 • Why Poverty is Such a Complex Affair

Most people know how to apply the concepts 'poor' and 'poverty' and have a reasonable understanding of the condition that they refer to. Many people believe they know what the causes of poverty are. The explanations of the causes of poverty prevalent in a society fulfil a strong guiding role for non-poor people's actions and attitudes towards poor people. They guide people to what is going on in their society and how they should react to it. These explanations of the causes of poverty are socially shared amongst many and thus influential in determining if and how social policy and collective action should alleviate or eradicate poverty. Everyday explanations of poverty are the result of people's lived experience of their own or others' poverty over a period of time, their moral values, their prejudice and a possible trickle down of the results of social scientific studies. There is no guarantee that such common explanations provide appropriate understandings of poverty or give us adequate guides for addressing and alleviating poverty. The main reason why many of these explanations of poverty fail is their simplicity in dealing with complex problems.[1]

In this chapter I propose a set of propositions as a limited theoretical framework within which the phenomenon of poverty can best be explained. The theory consists of ideas that are not controversial and thus need no complicated defence. In developing the theory, I use results of social science research for information about poverty to provide the data set in need of explanation. The results of good social science research are based on well-developed theory and carefully planned empirical investigation, are more detailed and sophisticated, logically more coherent and probably have higher truth content than everyday explanations of poverty.

What is poverty and why is it such a complex affair? I have defined poverty in earlier chapters as a lack of adequate economic capacities to maintain physical health and engage in social activities distinctive of human beings in a particular society (cf. Dieterlen, 2005: 163). Economic capacities refer both to resources as well the ability to utilize resources effectively. If I include capacities in the definition I do not assume that ordinary people automatically possess the requisite knowledge or skill to deal with resources fittingly. Note how a range of metaphors used in the chapter illuminate poverty as a phenomenon that is both clearly observable and yet has an elusive nature.

What is the broader context of the characteristic activities of human beings in our world within which the condition and elusive nature of poverty becomes visible and explicable? I offer the following set of propositions to provide a theory for understanding poverty.

1. Humans share with all other living beings the imperative to ensure their survival or face death. As all other living beings, humans require adequate food, water and shelter to sustain life. All living beings must find appropriate resources to satisfy these survival needs. In so far as poverty is a lack of means for survival, or an inadequate supply of resources to satisfy basic needs, poverty is a condition humans share with other living beings. From this basic perspective poverty means that human beings are without resources needed for survival or have too little thereof. They are short of economic resources and thus stand in need of basic requirements for a minimally acceptable human life.

2. Most living beings are adapted to particular habitats, require specific diets and possess specialized bodily equipment to acquire and consume needed resources. Living organisms use specialized bodily functions to utilize resources they locate in their habitats to ensure their fittingness for survival. Inappropriate disturbance of the interlinkage between habitat, diet and species capabilities, coupled with inability to adapt timeously to changing circumstances, often result in a population crash or even extinction. In so far as poverty is a lack of knowledge and technology to find and use resources humans share this fate with other living beings, that is, being unable to adapt successfully to their environment.

    If a lack of developed capacities result from the absence of appropriate knowledge and technology, then human beings will not be able to do the proper things to match the offerings of their environment suitably to the requirements set by their basic human needs for survival or flourishing. Thus, they cannot find a proper fit between their needs, their knowledge and skills and the natural and human resources available in their environment.

3. In contrast to most living beings, humans have highly specialized functions that do not require a specific habitat or diet for survival, but are

open to adapt to a wide variety of conditions on our planet. Whilst most living beings are equipped with specialized bodily functions that ensure survival by means of focused activities, humans have bodies that can be developed and trained to execute an almost infinite array of immensely detailed functions in the quest for survival.

Michael Landmann, building on the theories of Gehlen, Portmann, Uexküll and Lorenz, compares the specialized bodily equipment of non-human beings with the unspecialized non-focused nature of human bodily equipment. He describes the human lack of overriding instincts and the unspecialized nature of our organs that have not developed to fulfil specific functions as positive characteristics. Not adapted to fulfil specific functions implies adaptability to fulfil a variety of functions that provides an immeasurable evolutionary advantage for our species (1966: 152).

The creative, innovative human mind compensates for this lack of specialization through its ability to adapt the human organism to almost all planetary conditions. Even our helplessness at birth and our long road to adulthood demonstrate the importance of educating our minds in state-of-the-art knowledge and technology available in our cultural sphere. Through applying these insights and adapting to new circumstances, we create new innovations to sustain and improve our quality of life. If people cannot succeed in doing so, they become poor in the sense of underdevelopment. They cannot grow their minds and train their bodies to gain insight and learn skills to locate resources and convert them into life-sustaining products.

Our non-specialized nature forces us to create culture, Landmann argues, as a means to survive as individuals and species. Humans are creators of culture through which we design worlds for ourselves, that is, we transform the earth and its natural resources into habitable places where humans can find food, shelter, clothing and company with humans and other living beings (see also Rossouw, 1972). These worlds and the knowledge they are built on are transferred to people elsewhere in time and space, thus providing them with advanced starting points that they can further explore and adapt (Landmann, 1966: 191). In this way humans are part of historical processes of learning to cope with our world in our quest for survival and flourishing (ibid.: 193). Many cases of poverty result from the inability to transfer what experienced, skilled people have learnt to a younger generation.

Even our best innovations to ensure survival and our most intricate creations to express our nature in flourishing can never be final answers to the question how beings like us humans ought to live (ibid.: 198). The amazing array of possible lifestyles human beings have explored throughout history testifies to the multiplicity of options available to us and the flexibility of our minds in adapting to an endless changing set of natural and cultural circumstances. Failure to adapt timeously can mean failure to find the all-purpose means necessary to avoid poverty.

Human intellectual powers to design tools combine with educable bodily potentials to create and operate tools that mimic and enhance our finest characteristics to enable survival in almost any of our planet's climatic conditions. Various aspects of our bodies, such as muscular strength and agility, limbs, jaws and senses are far surpassed by the specialized functions of many living beings. Nevertheless, our non-specialist nature combines with our enormous brain power to enable us to create technologies, develop behaviours and to discipline our bodies in extraordinary ways. These abilities have enabled us to become the dominant species, even though we are by far the latest arrival of life on earth. Sachs (2005: 31) acknowledges the fundamental importance of technology in our recent history by saying it has been 'the main force behind the long-term increases in income in the rich world'. Little (2003: 42) spells out the role of technology in economic improvement by saying that new technologies are 'one of the central elements' to better economic performance by contributing to an 'overall increase in productivity or efficiency'.

Van Peursen claims technological innovation is a core characteristic of our species by pointing to similarities between various technologies and different aspects of the human body. Through technological innovations we improve our bodily capacities for labour spectacularly by deliberate design, manufacture and improved functionality of tools (Van Peursen, 1972: 103–4). Humans can do this, Van Peursen says, because of what he calls the organ of all organs, or the tools of all tools: the human central nervous system (ibid.: 105). The brilliance of our brain capacity shows in its amazing ability to project human bodily functions into machine, energy and information technologies. Through development of these innovations technology becomes an extension and manifestation of human bodily existence (ibid.: 107) and an increasing exteriorization of the functions or abilities of human beings (ibid.: 108). The prime example of complex, integrated innovations that mimic our intricate brain functions is today's information technology (ibid.: 109).

Through our plastic nature we not only collectively adapt to the environment, but also shape it according to our needs more powerfully than any other species can dream of doing. We convert our knowledge about the world into strategies to survive and flourish. If humans cannot use their minds properly to design and inculcate capacities that facilitate technological innovations for finding and processing natural resources necessary for human living, poverty will result. In this case poverty becomes like disease, where certain human functions do not work properly and as a result the normal state of health is negatively affected.

4. Humans have communicative and social skills to define for ourselves what it means to be flourishing humans and our innovative technologies put these definitions into practice. Implementing such definitions is facilitated by the development of the complex social organization that produces flourishing human communities through their mastery of the art of learning from others. The successful acquisition and transfer of knowledge and skills relevant to the demands of everyday living is a hallmark of societies that have accomplished acceptable states of well-being for its citizens.

Plato long ago described why humans find it practical to live in groups to ensure survival. For Plato the rationale behind the formation of human communities is partially an economic one. This rationale lies in the awareness that individual human beings have 'needs' or 'requirements' that they cannot fulfil on their own (1993: 369b, c). He uses the lack of self-sufficiency in providing for one's individual needs as an explanation for the origin of human society. Individuals who experience that they are not self-sufficient in providing for their own needs and requirements form a community where they gather other human beings as their 'associates and assistants' to help them 'fulfil various needs' (ibid.).

People thus form communities because they need one another's assistance. Plato refers to three needs as being 'the most basic and most important' (ibid.: 369d). They are 'food for existence and for life', 'our need for somewhere to live' and our need for clothing (ibid.). Later on in the *Republic* Plato defines 'necessary desires', which seem to be something similar to these needs. Necessary desires are those 'which we're incapable of stopping', 'whose satisfaction is beneficial to us' and which can be regarded as 'essential to human nature' (ibid.: 558e). These needs, or necessary desires, are fulfilled through mutually beneficial trade: 'people trade goods with one another, because they think they will be better off if each gives or receives something in exchange' (ibid.: 369c).

When human beings live in a community where they cannot satisfy their 'necessary desires' despite living in interdependent relationships with others, they are not self-reliant. They cannot acquire adequate economic capacities that they require for their needs, that are suitable and fully answer the minimum purpose of staving off deteriorating health and a life judged unworthy of humans. What they can acquire is insufficient and thus not fitting for a minimally decent human life.

To best provide for the needs of humans, labour specialization is needed. Plato presents several reasons why one person should do only one specific job. Differences between people point to a 'wide variety of natures' which makes individuals 'inherently suitable for different activities' (1993: 370a, b). Accommodating individual talents with specialized jobs has good consequences, which include better productivity, improved quality of products, simplified labour processes and greater chances of success (ibid.: 370b, c). To neglect the need for specialization, or to be unsuccessful in attempts at sharing the work that needs to be done to keep life and limb together can be another source of poverty.

5. A basic challenge for our species is the need to identify, locate, extract, convert and consume resources for survival. These resources can be (i) edible products found or cultivated by means of natural resources like soil, water or organic material; (ii) materials for designing, manufacturing and constructing new composite materials, tools, buildings and infrastructure, (iii) living beings to provide or produce things we need as food, clothes or tools, (iv) ideas and innovations that improve or enhance any aspect of our lives and (v) skills, talents, knowledge or insight that can provide services to others. In this context more of Plato's ideas still make sense today. To deal with resources appropriately now, modern societies have developed labour specialization in accordance with Plato's ideas, although one might surmise that the degree of labour specialization today might perhaps be unimaginable for someone from Plato's age.

Some poor societies or individuals struggle to successfully do the things that could provide them with the requisite economic capacities to escape poverty. In such cases poverty resembles disability, as a condition that limits a person's activities or expresses a want of the abilities that would have enabled them to fulfil functions sufficiently rewarded to stave off poverty.

6. We use resources in different ways that require variable degrees of human intervention. Words that refer to the location and conversion of food resources, like 'collect', 'harvest', 'produce', 'slaughter' and 'prepare' reflect these degrees. We consume or use some resources directly, like fruits and flowers. Others need simple preparation, like meat and seeds that we process and cook, fry or bake. In some cases we use complex processes to produce food, for example, followed by even more detailed processes of design and manufacture to deliver highly intricate products such as beverages or fancy sweets.

Locke had keen insight into the intricacy of the processes involved in locating and converting resources into products that enable human survival. His example of the human labour needed to locate and convert resources to bake bread in seventeenth-century England provides fascinating reading (Locke, 1966 [1690]: 23–4). He analyses the labour and materials necessary for baking bread as follows:

> For 'tis not barely the ploughman's pains, the reaper's and thresher's toil and the baker's sweat, is to be counted into the bread we eat; the labour of those who broke the oxen, who digged and wrought the iron and stones, who felled and framed the timber employed about the plough, mill, oven, or any other utensils, which are a vast number, requisite to this corn, from its being seed to be sown to its being made bread, must all be charged on the account of labour and received as an effect of that. (23)

Let's briefly look at a contemporary example. Imagine the complexity of an analysis of all dimensions related to the labour, materials, energy, science and technology embodied in the processes of manufacturing supercomputers. Sophisticated computer programming for complex calculations, intelligent use of materials for storing information and a deep understanding of electromagnetism are just some of the things required. The amount of knowledge involved, the sophisticated labour skills and the technological know-how required to design, manufacture and run supercomputers are simply amazingly complex.

Again, some poor people might be part of those who fail to find a useful role in such labour processes. They do not find a role as they might not be adequately qualified for participation because their capacities were not developed, they might not have the ability to discharge the functions, or they might have been prevented from accessing employment through prejudice. Some societies fail to properly imagine, plan, develop or maintain such processes that have become inadequate, wasteful or inefficient. Such failures often result in poverty as well. Little (2003: 42) says that inefficiency matters because it is 'equivalent to a waste of resources – resources that could otherwise be used to satisfy human needs'.

7. Humans have the intellectual and bodily characteristics that allow them to locate and convert resources in ways almost infinitely more complex than animals. Many living beings do amazing things in their quest to locate and convert resources for survival and flourishing. Beavers construct dams and underground chambers, squirrels store food for winter, birds navigate intercontinental flights to migrate thousands of kilometres to escape cold winters, sea turtles navigate their way across oceans, ants cultivate mushrooms, lions hunt as teams and plants effortlessly convert sunlight into energy, a feat that we struggle to accomplish despite our huge collective scientific effort. However magnificent and beyond our capacities, none of these activities rival our combined set of doings in terms of complexity, range, use of knowledge and deliberate, conscious planning.

   Many millennia ago humans lived mainly as hunter-gatherers. We then relied more on finding natural resources, as do other species, when our numbers were small and plant and animal resources abundant in relation to our population size. However, in the last couple of millennia some areas of the world had increasing human populations who had to rely on diminishing resources. These growing populations placed huge demands on the collective ability of societies to locate and convert resources to ensure the survival of all members.

   John Locke lived during a time when the opposing hunter-gatherer lifestyle of the First Nation Americans and the intensive agricultural-urban technological lifestyles of the British colonists seemed like competitors for being the best or most rational overall. Locke provides a fascinating insight into the mind of a progressive intellectual of the newly modernizing and technologically innovating Western culture on the location, conversion, exchange and distribution of resources. He is scathing in his judgement of the use Native Americans made of their land compared with the productive cultivation of land in Devonshire. In his view the lack of labour by the Native Americans to improve the land is the cause that 'a thousand acres yield the needy and wretched inhabitants as many conveniences of life as ten acres of equally fertile land do in Devonshire, where they are well cultivated' (Locke, 1966 [1690]: 20).

Locke's judgement is underpinned by two assumptions. One is that human labour, as he broadly defines it, magically transforms the earth's resources into something much more valuable than before. Locke praises human labour and looks down on natural resources. In his discussion of bread as an example of what human labour can produce, he remarks that nature and the earth 'furnished only the almost worthless materials as in themselves' (23). Locke thus seems to have a prejudice against natural resources in favour of products manufactured and cultivated by humans that add value to natural resources. His prejudice shows most clearly in his remark that 'land that is left wholly to nature, that hath no improvement of pasturage, tillage, or planting, is called, as indeed it is, waste and we shall find the benefit of it amount to little more than nothing' (22, 23). Locke's low opinion of living off the fruits of the wilderness is too extreme, although he had good insight into the value human cultivation creates. More than three centuries later Sachs (2005: 28) affirms Locke's appraisal of human labour by making this judgement on human cultivation of the earth over the past five centuries: 'Vastly improved farm yields were achieved on the basis of technological advances.'

Nevertheless, Locke totally misses the labour involved in the hunter-gatherer lifestyle practised by our ancestors for millennia. Considerable knowledge and skill – characteristic aspects of Locke's broad definition of labour – is necessary for survival through hunting, for example (see Liebenberg, 1990). Hunters need knowledge of plants to know which branches are best for bows and arrows. They make poison from plant material which again requires considerable knowledge of plant properties. Similarly, knowledge of animal behaviour and characteristics proves essential to select the right kind of animal to kill without being harmed themselves. The detailed knowledge and skill involved in tracking animals need thought processes that Liebenberg convincingly argues are similar to the thought processes involved in twentieth-century natural science.

Locke's misinterpretation of the value of the hunter-gatherer lifestyle shows how easily one can miss the skills relevant to successfully acquire economic resources from a particular environment. Clearly hunter-gatherer communities had a wide range of skills suited to their circumstances, skills that had a bearing on their specific context and were pertinent to the challenges they faced. For these reasons they survived adequately through their lifestyle for many centuries.

In an overpopulated world with intense stress on the productive capacities of the global biosphere, Locke's views on the transformative power of human labour are also pertinent for us to understand that poverty is sometimes the result of our deficiencies. We often have a shortage of knowledge and skills for proper cultivation of the earth's resources and we lack smart innovation to productively transform whatever we have available into useful products for survival. This shortage of knowledge and skills means that large parts of the world's population are consistently in situations where they cannot obtain sufficient economic resources as required for decent human living. Little (2003: 40) describes how the output, efficiency and productivity of an economy can be improved through the discovery and application of new technologies. Furthermore he thinks more efficient systems of management can be designed; the labour force can be expanded; workers can be better educated (and therefore more productive); more land and other natural resources can be brought into production; and economic institutions can be enhanced for greater efficiency, incentive, or equity (ibid.).

8. Once a particular community successfully locates and converts resources for survival and builds a flourishing social life, several new demands arise. New needs and wants for more sophisticated products and services develop, which in turn put increased pressure on the community's abilities to locate new kinds of resources and find novel ways of converting them to suit and fulfil new demands.

    Plato gave a good, although biased, description of how other needs and wants arise in a society once survival has been secured. He realizes that the 'true community', one that is in a 'healthy condition', could easily develop into an 'indulgent' or 'inflamed' community (Plato, 1993: 372e). Dissatisfactions with 'the provisions and the lifestyle' of the community based on the mutual provision for one another's necessary desires would lead to a multiplication of what Plato defines as 'unnecessary desires'. These desires are ones that 'can be dispensed with', provided people have been trained to do so (ibid.: 559a). The presence of these desires 'certainly does no good and may even do harm' (ibid.).

The harm of the unnecessary desires to the healthy community is an increase in size for the community until it becomes 'bloated and distended with occupations' (ibid.: 373a). A negative consequence of the increase in size of the community and number of occupations is that the community's land becomes too small. The need for land leads to the possibility of conquering other people's land – thus war against neighbours becomes a distinct possibility (ibid.: 373d). As Plato indicates, conflict about resources has often led to war in the past. Many observers predict intensified conflict over resources like oil and water might in future again lead to war.

In contemporary societies the amount and value of products and services that cater for what Plato terms 'unnecessary desires' have multiplied exponentially. One reason is the sheer volume of people who have enough money to indulge such desires. Another reason is the human ability to symbolize economic value in money and thus hoard it limitlessly. Many well-to-do people claim their high incomes as fully and completely their own deserved rewards that they can use for their own purposes as they wish. Therefore, many rich people spend their large share of their society's financial resources on a variety of luxury items as their hearts desire. The claim by the rich that they are entitled to the satisfaction of insatiable demands for luxury goods and services is an important factor that keeps in place the deep inequalities that characterize many societies.

9. To deal with new demands for consumer goods and services successfully, three things must happen. New sources of materials and products must be located, current conversion processes must be improved and new recruits must be inducted into conversion processes.

Throughout history the need to find new sources of materials and products has led to explorations of anything from continents to atoms, from familiar living beings and materials to unknown spaces and complex cellular mechanisms. In this context science and technology appear as typically human activities of exploration and construction that play 'pivotal roles' in human development (Sachs, 2005: 18). If population growth exceeds the carrying capacity of the available environment based on current economic activities, explorative activities to find new resources or identify new needs for services are imperative to avoid slipping into poverty. Failure to do so will lead to the gradual growth of an underclass with no employment. Note the importance of employment. A recent study in the UK indicates that 'loss of employment is the single most significant cause of entry into poverty' and therefore poverty can best be eradicated through employment as the 'surest factor in triggering exits from poverty' (Smith and Middleton, 2007: 13).

Discovery, invention, cultivation and production of new materials and products have made better location of valued resources and more complex conversions possible. These increasingly complex conversions allow humans to construct artificial worlds, like modern cities, in which lifestyles with food and accessories undreamt of earlier have now become commonplace. These new human worlds have significantly altered the basic prerequisites and thus increased the resources required, that enable us to live lives worthy of our species membership.

The processes of locating and converting resources need new recruits to learn existing processes and develop new ones. Traditions of learning and apprenticeship develop that enable new recruits to master the current state of the art in location and conversion and infuse the recruits with problem-solving skills to deal with new challenges. Young people receive education and training to familiarize them with their world and current ways of exploiting its possibilities.

Failure to properly educate and fittingly train a new generation for continuous growth and development of their knowledge, insight and skill can mean competent workers are not available and innovative renewal of existing practices will not occur. Such stagnation in a world where markets encourage global competition can easily lead to poverty.

10. Some people are better able to locate and convert resources than others. In the slowly diversifying populations of larger growing human communities with ever more complex needs, some have expert knowledge about the location of resources, others have versatile skills in conversion processes, many are involved in exchanges and some determine appropriate distributions of resources. Such people are more highly valued by their society for their greater contribution to the central processes that sustain collective survival and develop communal flourishing.

In this context entrepreneurship emerges as a basic human characteristic that some people have displayed throughout history. Entrepreneurs typically see opportunities to locate new resources and develop new materials, products and services. They can also find ways and means to bring such new benefits to clients or customers through establishing viable, sustainable businesses (Barringer and Ireland, 2006: 5–10;

Baron and Shane, 2005: 4–13). Absence of entrepreneurs or an entrepreneurial spirit often stunts the development and growth of activities that contribute to the production of economic resources that create opportunities that others can take up to escape poverty.

11. The products of locating resources and converting them are exchanged and traded in different ways. Markets have evolved over thousands of years as appropriate forums and mechanisms for exchanging consumer products and determining their value, although they have diversified, become endlessly more complex and are often regulated to a greater or lesser degree. The concept market refers to an endless variety of human constructions within which humans can negotiate deals and trade relatively freely.

Michael Walzer (1983: 95–128) interestingly explains how fundamental the exchange and distribution of goods are in human communities, of which markets provide an example. He states that humans conceive and create goods which we then exchange and distribute among ourselves. These processes of exchange and distribution are not only strictly economic matters. Walzer says that 'the market is a zone of the city, not the whole city' (109). We attach and ascribe meanings and value to all goods, regardless whether they are sold in economic markets or not. Our exchange and distribution of goods depend on such meanings. Our patterns of exchange and distribution change when the meanings and values we assign to goods change. Injustice, Walzer (1983: 100–8) argues, occurs when these meanings are not respected by some and goods are distributed for wrong reasons in violation of generally accepted meanings.

Markets are thus not necessarily magical spheres of perfect freedom where everyone automatically gets their just desert. They are human constructions, deeply influenced by factors such as population size, power relations, geography, laws and regulations, available resources and so on. A fresh produce market in a small town will differ vastly in the dynamics of supply and demand from a similar market in a mega-city. Markets for fresh produce in Europe are deeply influenced by governmental subsidies for farmers and by European Union policies that only allow selected countries to sell products complying with strict regulations. Giving outsiders selective access to markets is different from a common twentieth-century practice to close markets to outsiders. Closed markets often have negative consequences. For Sachs (2005: 48) closing markets to

outsiders means 'countries also closed them off from global economic progress and the advance of technology', which in turn led to
'high-cost local industries which couldn't compete internally' and
'a great deal of corruption'.

Ideally markets are places where everyone can offer products or
services that will get their due reward. However, markets can be distorted in various ways that benefit some and destroy others. Some
competitors in markets create their own advantage by using their
strengths to go ahead of others or to get the better of them, sometimes
through unethical means or supported by biased or unjust governmental policies. There is no guarantee that smaller, vulnerable, less
well-off competitors will necessarily be in favourable positions compared
to others, as they are often without the strength or ability to compete
on an equal footing. Thus, brave attempts by poor people to make
livelihoods through market activity might not succeed if equal access
and fair trading are not enforced.

Various other economic factors can lead to poverty. Macro-economic
trends can impoverish many people unable to adapt or without
adequate reserves to see them through. Poor people do not have any
control over events such as economic depression, a lack of employment opportunities, a downturn in the economy, or the ways in which
an economic system limits their options. Similar macro-economic
trends with major impacts on poverty are recession and inflation.
Recession can cause massive unemployment resulting in poverty,
whereas strongly rising prices of consumer goods can be devastating
for poor households and those close to it (May, 1998a: 54). They
have little savings or other reserves for lessening the impact of price
hikes on essential goods (Wilson and Ramphele, 1989: 251–3).

A rapid macro-economic change, such as from an agrarian to an
industrial economy, can quickly and unexpectedly cause widespread
unemployment and poverty amongst people unable or unwilling to
adapt to new circumstances (Grosskopf, 1932: viii, 48–53). If the
new economy demands a foreign (international) language, such as
English, for participation, many newcomers could be sidelined from
a potential remedy for their poverty (Malherbe, 1932: 364).

Modernization of sectors of the economy can also cause poverty.
For example, technological and scientific developments in agriculture
has led to the mechanization of ploughing, harvesting and weeding
of maize. As a consequence the need for manual labour vastly diminished, causing major unemployment for workers dependent on the

agricultural sector (Wilson and Ramphele, 1989: 242–3). Whereas technological and scientific developments benefited farmers, while disadvantaging the labourers no longer needed, inadequate or wrong farming practices often led to the impoverishment of farmers themselves. Wasteful exploitation of land and outdated farming practices often led to poverty. Furthermore, many farmers failed to adapt from one style of farming to another. For white farmers in South Africa at the end of the nineteenth century the transition from living as conquering pioneers and settlers off the richness of the African land to becoming farmers on small patches of land was difficult. Many farmers showed an inability to adapt. This was compounded by the practice of fairly dividing a farm between sons (and sometimes daughters) which led to farms becoming smaller and thus non-viable economic units (Grosskopf, 1932: 115–16; Willcocks, 1932: 170).

Besides macro-economic trends, lack of economic know-how and business practices can significantly harm poor people and those at risk of becoming poor. Some people become poor as a result of their own lack of knowledge, sophistication and experience of consumer matters. They waste money on non-essential goods and spend money in ill-considered ways (Terreblanche, 1977: 105). They literally impoverish themselves. Some businesses exploit these consumer weaknesses through shrewd marketing, offering easy credit to people who do not have adequate financial means and who cannot foresee all the implications of easy credit schemes (ibid.: 106–9). In default of monthly payments, these people often lose the purchased item and lots of urgently needed money. Similar patterns manifest themselves in the way poor people borrow money from relatives, friends, acquaintances, shop owners and micro-lenders (May, 1998b: 63). Micro-lenders who lend small amounts of money to poor people exploit their vulnerable position of being unable to loan money from commercial banks. Some of these lenders charge exorbitant interest rates of up to 100 per cent and more. Shrewd exploitation of consumer weaknesses thus impoverishes many people.

12. Almost since time immemorial human social organization, through politics, played a role to facilitate, direct, stabilize, stimulate or stifle resource dealing processes, that is, processes of location, conversion, exchange and distribution of resources. Collective human action, through anything from smaller groups to larger institutions, constantly intervenes in more or less beneficial or harmful ways. A good example

is the role of governments in markets. Sometimes governments restrict markets, sometimes they allow unrestricted freedom. Governments impose standards for some marketable items in the interest of consumer safety and make it more or less difficult to set up new businesses through licensing, etc.

The extent of collective action through politics to enable individuals to become involved and competent in the resource dealing processes is not the same everywhere. All governments decide on their role in facilitating and enhancing resource dealing. These decisions are reflected in the degree of intervention in markets and the kind and level of taxation on different income groups. Adequate enablement is of critical importance to ensure continued success in the quest for survival and flourishing. Tax income can be redistributed to ensure that all members of society get opportunities to develop their talents and have support during life's mishaps.

The percentage of tax income invested in enabling education and the construction of necessary preconditions for resource dealing processes are further aspects of government interference that impact positively or negatively on resource dealing processes. The importance of these preconditions is stressed by Sachs (2005: 3) who says that 'without the preconditions of basic infrastructure (roads, power and ports) and human capital (health and education) markets can cruelly bypass large parts of the world, leaving them impoverished and suffering without respite'.

When a government deprives a section of the population of opportunities to develop and display their human capacities and talents, those people are being oppressed. Sometimes a government refuses to provide people support when they are in need and the absence of such support can cause or perpetuate poverty. To take such decisions without allowing the people most affected input to state their case, thus ignoring their views, amounts to domination. Those in serious need of governmental aid are thus excluded from appropriate consideration. The government fails to act to their advantage by improving their unfavourable position due to lack of economic capacities which places them at a distinct disadvantage compared with the opportunities their fellow citizens can access.

13. If some groups dominate their particular communities through accumulation of excessive rewards for their role in resource dealing processes, other groups may be significantly disadvantaged through

their meagre share of resources so that it weakens the central social project of location, conversion, exchange and distribution of resources in a particular community. In this way poverty disables the capacities of segments of society to contribute their share to the joint societal project of ensuring survival and enhancing flourishing. Eventually the existence of such disabled segments harms society as a whole. Similarly, powerful political groups can employ political processes and mechanisms to determine and enforce distributions of resources that deliberately advantage some citizens and exclude or neglect others. They deny citizens voice and vote to struggle for their fair share in resource dealing processes.

Amartya Sen shows the vital impact of social organization in facilitating or thwarting resource dealing processes that create or eradicate poverty. He sets up an argument for the importance of freedom for human development. Sen states his claim in strong terms: 'freedoms are not only the primary ends of development, they are also among its principal means' (1999: 10). Freedom is thus not only important as one of the measures to gauge the outcome of development initiatives in a society, but is crucial for the success of processes of development themselves. Sen is talking not only about political, social and economic freedoms, but also about opportunities and security. He correctly points out that these different kinds of freedom reinforce one another. Favourable development outcomes, Sen argues, is 'thoroughly dependent on the free agency of people' (4). Individuals can only develop their capabilities and determine their own lives if they have adequate freedoms to make their own decisions, associate with whomever they wish, choose to participate in the labour market where they think best, publicize their queries and concerns, protest their maltreatment or neglect, target unjust policies and distributions and develop their resource dealing capacities. Sen is not alone in arguing for the vital importance of social and political freedoms for the socio-economic development of human beings to liberate them from poverty. Sachs (2005: 33–4) confirms Sen's argument in his discussion of the reasons why the Industrial Revolution occurred first in Britain by pointing out the crucial role played by British socio-political freedom.

Quality of life is significantly influenced by events in the present or the recent past, especially events of a political or economic nature (Wilson and Ramphele, 1989: 152–66). For this reason such events figure prominently as explanations of causes of poverty. In countries where sections of the population are excluded from participation in the political processes at national, regional and local levels, one can expect politics to have a major impact on the incidence and degree of poverty.

One obvious reason for the impact of politics on poverty is that politicians at different levels of government make decisions about the use of public resources. Systematic and prolonged bias in public expenditure in favour of a section of the population can substantially impoverish those who are excluded. Local, regional and national governments decide on priorities for public spending, thus determining the allocation of public resources to what they think worthwhile causes. Their priorities determine the amount and placement of public facilities and the people who benefit from them. Areas inhabited by poor people often do not have infrastructure accepted as normal by other sections of the population. Services such as street lighting, telephones, decent public roads and public transport are often unavailable. The absence of such services further detracts from poor people's quality of life and makes crime prevention more difficult.

In contrast to an unjust society where one group dominates political institutions to benefit its own members, a constitutional democracy opens up opportunities for every citizen to participate in political processes. Citizens elect their own representatives to speak on their behalf during the formulation and implementation of policy. In addition, citizens can mobilize themselves to form pressure groups advocating policies to benefit the poor, or use opportunities for public comment on draft policies offered by a democratic government.

The issues and interests of poor people are often not heard or noticed by politicians, even in constitutional democracies. Due to their lack of income, poor people mostly do not have sufficient resources to influence public opinion through costly ways, such as advertisements, lobby groups or paid officials. Their public action is often constrained by the shame of poverty and others often champion their cause. The lack of power of poor individuals and their resultant weak bargaining position often make them vulnerable to be politically ignored (cf. Alcock, 1987: 207; Terreblanche, 1977: 115–16).

Racism can play an important role in causing poverty. In a political system based on race some races get benefits and privileges, while the others – victims of racism – are disadvantaged to the point of being severely impoverished. The view of the ruling racists on the place that the subordinate races ought to have in society can lead to various measures with the function to keep them there. The view that ruling racists have of subordinate races are often based on vague impressions, single cases and prejudice. Such a view combines with rationalizations of their privileged position to distance themselves from any responsibility for the conditions of poverty or their improvement. In this way poverty is both caused and maintained by racist attitudes.

But racism can also impoverish racist people – the perpetrators of racism – who look down on other races. Poor racist people have often refused to do work that are done by members of the supposedly inferior race. It is not whether the nature of work is hard, difficult, gruelling or degrading that counts, but whether it is work only done by members of the disadvantaged race (cf. Grosskopf, 1932: 166–72). This attitude led to many missed job opportunities; thus, also to continued unemployment and poverty.

Politics can influence the extent of poverty in various other ways. Banning or restricting special interest groups aiming to mobilize people already poor or at risk of becoming poor can substantially weaken their bargaining position (Wilson and Ramphele, 1989: 161). For example, banning trade unions leaves many workers in low paying jobs without effective bargaining power against exploitative employers. Similarly, if people are not allowed to mobilize themselves they cannot effectively resist government policies aiming to relocate them elsewhere without their consent. Such relocations often caused poverty in apartheid South Africa, because people were dumped at places where making a living was impossible because of overcrowding or adverse climatic conditions (Wilson and Ramphele, 1989: 161). Relocations also destroyed communal and family ties which functioned as buffers against the worst effects of poverty, thus further weakening people's resistance against poverty.

Relocations were part of the comprehensive apartheid policy to relocate people belonging to certain groups in specified areas, rather than ad hoc measures to remove people from large dam sites or proposed industrial areas. If a government tries to contain members of a group to a specific area, it can severely impoverish such people. Laws restricting people's movement from rural to urban areas, as well as constraints on housing construction in urban areas, can lead to the overpopulation of rural areas, pressing their carrying capacity far beyond its limitations. It leads to an overwhelming pressure on the land, which cannot carry the burden being placed on it (Wilson and Ramphele, 1989: 39, 43). Under these circumstances normal production quotas are significantly lowered, leading to further impoverishment.

The political actions referred to above are examples of acts of commission that governments at various levels can do to impoverish people. There are numerous acts of omission that can do the same, or simply perpetuate existing conditions of poverty. No provision for unemployment insurance, inadequate old age pensions or no proper schooling can all contribute to poverty. Though there are limitations on government spending, acts of omission will only be acceptable if government actions and policies are judged to be equitable. The result of pursuing unjust policies often is the impoverishment of sections of the population.

Related to acts of omission is the lack of knowledge, expertise and skills of government officials to formulate or implement appropriate policies for addressing poverty. Lack of management skills to co-ordinate governmental programmes across different government departments or bureaucratic attitudes unsympathetic to poor people can also slow down the delivery of services to poor households and communities.

Most people are not aware how events in the past function as causes for people's poverty in the present. However, the assumption that the past has shaped and formed the present leads to significant perspectives for understanding poverty. If we do not understand how the present has grown from the past, we will not be able to transform the present into a different future. Many examples exist of how events – even from the distant past – still influence poverty today (cf. Wilson and Ramphele, 1989: 5, 7, 190–204).

Some South Africans are descended from slaves. Slavery as practice existed from the seventeenth century up to the early nineteenth century in South Africa. The slavery experience of many generations made them dependent on and subordinate to people who owned them as property. Slaves were also subject to the racist attitudes of their owners which had to keep them down and in their place, being that of lowly servants with meagre incomes. These experiences were internalized as negative self-images and transmitted from generation to generation. The interaction between bad working conditions, few opportunities for development, racist attitudes and practices, and low self-esteem created an interlocking set of circumstances forming one of the main factors leading to chronic poverty amongst their descendants. This shows how events in the distant past can still have effects on the quality of people's lives in the present (Terreblanche, 1977: 80–8).

Take as example how the apartheid policies from before 1994, based on privileging white people at the expense of black people, will reverberate through the South African society for many years to come. Many social science studies done in South Africa show convincingly that the inequalities resulting from apartheid might become self-perpetuating. The contemporary high levels of inequalities were established over decades by a government manipulating public funds to enrich a racially defined minority whilst impoverishing the majority of black people. The history of mining and capitalist development over the past century is deeply intertwined with the growth of inequalities and governmental exploitation of the black labour class. To undo the impoverishing effects of more than a century's exploitation, domination and oppression will take time, resources, expertise and an attitude of self-reliance.

14. Many forces independent of human influence can also thwart, distort or short-circuit the complex human activities involved in resource dealing processes. Natural disasters such as hurricanes, volcanic eruptions, floods, droughts and tsunamis can devastate resource dealing processes. Climates can enhance or destroy the cultivation and production of food and clothing. Geology can determine which mineral resources are available. For example, Sachs (2005: 35) shows that Britain's coal resources freed the society during the Industrial Revolution 'from energy constraints that had limited the scale of economic production throughout human history'.

Geography can make access to markets and interaction with other cultures easy or difficult. Sachs points out how Britain's favourable geography contributed to its industrial innovations and economic growth during the nineteenth century. Some of these favourable conditions are Britain's 'low-cost sea-based trade' with continental Europe close by, 'extensive navigable river ways for internal trade', 'highly favourable environment for agriculture' and the close proximity of America to provide raw materials and a 'safety valve' for 'the exodus of impoverished people from the British countryside' (Sachs, 2005: 34). Epidemics can devastate the economies of continents or exacerbate existing poverty by dealing fatal blows to key actors in resource dealing processes. Note the upshot of Sachs's discussion of the role of malaria in African poverty: 'malaria sets the perfect trap: it impoverishes a country, making it too expensive to prevent and treat the disease. Thus malaria continues and poverty deepens in a truly vicious circle' (199).

15. Let me review the discussion so far by pointing out how normal human activities can be derailed by myriad human actions to produce poverty. Human resource dealing processes, that is, the complex series of human activities consisting of the location, conversion, exchange and distribution of resources, can be short-circuited and thwarted in a diversity of ways, some of natural and others of human origin. Humans can directly or indirectly influence these activities as follows.

A particular community might be without sufficient resources or run out of resources and fail to find replaceable ones. Population growth might outstrip available resources and conversion skills. Societies might neglect the transfer of knowledge and development of skills for the location and conversion of resources. Fewer recruits, or recruits with lesser knowledge and skill might fail their particular community in locating, converting or exchanging resources in the quest for survival and flourishing. A skewed or restricted allocation of opportunities to members of society for participation in location and conversion of resources might diminish the society's capacity to ensure survival. A disproportionate distribution of rewards to some participants at the expense of others on grounds such as the supposed extraordinary value of their work or their group membership can create poverty as well as resentment and conflict.

Some forces of human origin that thwart or short-circuit resource-dealing processes operate at continental or global levels. Such forces, for instance, macro-economic trends and environmental degradation, are presumably under human control, but difficult for one decision-making body to manage or control. These forces result from countless actions by individuals and institutions and combine to form almost impersonal forces that humans struggle to deal with appropriately.

In summary, poverty is the result of any of thousands of possible kinds of failure or obstruction somewhere in the highly complex series of processes involved in the location, conversion, exchange and distribution of resources. Whole human societies become poor when the highly complex processes of location, conversion, exchange and distribution of resources are short-circuited or fouled up on such a large scale that significant parts of the population are classified as poor. Individuals are, or become, poor when they do not have, or cannot find, any rewarded role within these processes, or are excluded from them, for whatever reason.

An enriched definition of poverty

I want to propose an enriched definition of poverty in the light of the foregoing theoretical explanation of poverty. According to this definition, people are poor if they cannot obtain adequate economic resources, or do not have the requisite economic capacities to deal with resources fittingly to maintain physical health and engage in social activities distinctive of human beings in their respective societies.

Their poverty is due to the fact that they do not have roles or functions rewarded in their society's quest for the location, conversion, exchange or distribution of resources, nor are they compensated for this lack. They cannot realize the appropriate social activities characteristic of humans in their society. They also do not participate in the fundamental collective human quest for ensuring the survival and enabling the flourishing of human communities. In a double sense they are thus excluded from fully realizing their unique human characteristics.

Can this theory work? A case study

With this theory I hope to explain most kinds of poverty. Due to the complex interplay of various factors in the genesis and maintenance of specific people's poverty, each case of poverty must be analysed and judged on its own merits. I claim that my theory provides a comprehensive perspective that enables fine-grained attention to the detailed particulars involved in any case of poverty.

Let us test this claim with a brief example: imagine Paradise as a 10,000 km² area in rural Ciskei in the South Africa of the middle 1980s. Paradise has lost almost all its lush vegetation and wildlife. The area is overpopulated and overgrazed. Soil erosion degrades the small plots used for subsistence agriculture. Most people survive through remittances from men working elsewhere in urban areas. The people are desperately poor with almost no hope of ever recovering from their miserable existence. Why did Paradise die? Was it soil erosion or overpopulation of humans and animals? Was it an inability to transfer knowledge and skill of farming to new generations? Did communal land ownership cause a collapse of profitable farming practices through the so-called tragedy of the commons, where individuals who ignored the collective impact of their choices to increase their use of shared land by thinking that their small incremental increases of land use will have no big impact when added up with those of others?

Perhaps some of these factors played a role. Overgrazing that might have resulted from communal ownership, an inability to acquire and transmit knowledge about state-of-the-art farming methods and soil erosion might all have played a part in the impoverishment of the affected community. However, before even considering these factors the role of devastating wars, conquest by foreign powers and subsequent decades of political oppression must first be accounted for. Political oppression included inferior or absent enablement of inhabitants to become competent participants exploiting their full personal powers somewhere in the processes of resource dealing.

Although overpopulation is a major factor in this specific case of poverty, overpopulation itself was caused by conquest of land and subsequent restrictions of migration to urban areas. Large-scale political events were the primary factors that set impoverishment in motion. These events kept poverty going into modes of desperation from which escape became virtually impossible until political liberation occurred. Political liberation on its own that merely entrenches democratic rule will not eradicate poverty by itself. Only liberation that entails individual and communal enablement, as well as empowerment in resource dealing processes, can effectively eradicate this particular community's poverty. This view will be argued for in more detail in a later chapter. It is enough to note all the factors and prerequisites that must be in place to enable and ensure successful, sustainable resource location and conversion, as this gives us a glimpse of what the eradication of poverty presupposes.

Why do I refer to poverty as a complex affair?

In conclusion I argue that poverty is a multidimensional complex human phenomenon that in each case consists of a complex interweaving of contingent circumstances and factors. Something is described as complex when it consists of a number of parts that vary in kind and importance. Language is a common example of something described as complex. It consists of many kinds of words and sentences that combine in endless ways according to some basic rules.

In complex phenomena the relationships between parts differ, are intricate and complicated. Human beings are often described as complex, in part because of the intricate and complicated relationships between differing parts, such as mind, hormones, emotions and body. Nevertheless, in complex phenomena these parts combine into a complicated whole with characteristics of its own. A skyscraper requires the complex construction of many different materials in varying relationships, but nevertheless the skyscraper forms a complicated whole with describable characteristics.

The combination of parts into a whole can be described in various ways. The parts can be interwoven, connected together, involved in various degrees, intimately mixed, intricately intertwined, entangled, or united. The ways different parts are combined in human beings differ from the combinations of parts found in skyscrapers or language. When phenomena, events or behaviour are called complex in ordinary language, this indicates that people judge such events, phenomena or behaviour not to be easily analysed or understood. Rather, it is difficult to determine the factors involved and disentangle them. Not even the best minds in medical science can easily analyse the functions of the parts of the human brain as a complex phenomenon, nor explain their complicated interactions.

What does it mean to call poverty a complex human phenomenon? Myriad things occur daily in the endless processes of locating, converting, exchanging and distributing resources to ensure survival and enable flourishing. When one or more of the significant things in resource dealing processes go wrong in ways not easily fixed, poverty may result at individual, household, group or societal level. Thus, what poverty consists of, the effects it has on persons and the causes thereof, have many different parts related in many ways (cf. Wilson and Ramphele, 1989: 14). Importantly, these parts combine to form a unique configuration in each individual case. Nevertheless, the configuration exhibits characteristics easily recognized as belonging to the complex, multidimensional phenomenon of poverty. The complexity of poverty can be seen in social science research by noting both its multiple indicators and causes.

In order to understand each individual case of poverty, we must draw a profile that would do justice to the complex configuration of indicators and causes operative in a particular individual's case. Factors involved can be personal, communal, national, continental or natural. To profile individual or group cases, profilers must be conversant with current poverty research that provides checklists of possible intervening factors. Profilers must also be deeply attentive to all circumstances and conditions actually impacting on a specific case. A detailed quantitative and qualitative description of the scope and extent of a specific case of poverty is needed. Added to that a detailed analysis of all possible factors involved in causing or reinforcing poverty must be given. Sachs (2005: 73) states 'there are myriad possibilities for the persistence of poverty even in the midst of economic growth. Only a close diagnosis of particular circumstances will allow an accurate understanding.' Sachs calls this 'the art of differential diagnosis' (ibid.: 79). Differential diagnosis implies understanding 'which of these many variables is posing particular obstacles in specific circumstances' (ibid.).

In profiling cases of poverty, broader contexts must be accounted for. Often individuals, communities or countries find themselves in spaces where several complex societal systems, such as local, regional or national governments or economies, intersect with regional, continental and global trends. The manner of such intersections could amplify the effects of some factors and strengthen their causal role. Furthermore, it has to be determined why a specific individual, community or country was susceptible or vulnerable to the set of circumstances and factors that led to poverty. The combined results of such a detailed investigation, constructed to present a personal, communal, regional, national or continental profile, are the necessary prologue to any appropriate and effective aid. Such profiles are also prerequisites for any detailed moral evaluation of the manifestation of poverty in a given context.

In this chapter I suggested a theory to explain the complexity of poverty. Whether this theory turns out to have explanatory value depends on its capacity to guide human development in such a way that poverty can be eradicated permanently.

At the end of Part 1 of this book, I hope to have presented arguments, ideas and evidence to establish the following: poverty has a wide range of dimensions complexly assembled in every case. To properly understand poverty, we need a comprehensive grip of the multidimensional nature of poverty that highlights the diverse range of harmful impacts poverty might have on individual humans. Only such an understanding provides an appropriate illumination of the salient issues for moral evaluation as a prelude for aid and action. Such a moral evaluation shows how the many dimensions of poverty violate a wide range of generally accepted moral values.

In Part 2 I argue that the eradication of such a complex phenomenon as poverty in its myriad configurations, with the potential to inflict such a wide range of harmful effects on people, their relationships and institutions, needs a counter of aid and collective action consisting of a similarly comprehensive set of strategies and interventions based on appropriate moral values. In the next chapters I thus argue in defence of an ethically justified style of aid, I show how a decent theory of justice can, at least in principle, counteract or prevent all manifestations of poverty, I indicate why poverty needs to be tackled through collective efforts, indicating eventually that only collective action through core governance functions can completely eradicate poverty and prevent its recurrence. Once these governance functions have been effectively established, it becomes possible in principle to uproot all forms of poverty remaining from events that occurred even in the distant past.

Part 2

**The Complexity of Moral Ways
to Eradicate Poverty**

8 • Ethics for Eradicating Poverty

The eradication of poverty has recently become a priority on the agendas of governments and international organizations. Lots of articles, books and reports have been written on how to rescue one billion people who suffer from extreme poverty worldwide.

Is it possible that any kind of aid is good enough when people are suffering severely from poverty? Note the stringent criticism that Cullity (2004: 35) articulates that many people express against the work of many poverty relief organizations. They refer to a way of thinking about aid to the poor,

> that infantilizes the poor, treating them as victims to be acted upon. It treats poverty-related need and suffering as an act of god, rather than a political problem which needs to be met by political action. It creates patterns of short-term interference and manipulation without long-term commitment . . . perpetuates the problem it is supposed to be addressing. It acts as an alibi for the failure to support genuine political reform and it simply feeds resources into the structures of manipulation and injustice that enforce the subjugation and disempowerment of the poor. (ibid.)

I will not assess the validity of these harsh criticisms here. They do, however, indicate that ways of aiding poor people can be deeply controversial and must be thought through clearly.

Two of the important things that can go wrong when people give aid to poor people are as follows. The aid giver's assessment of either the causes or effects of specific poor people's poverty can be wrong. As a result the aid giver gives the wrong means to address the causes or effects and thus the aid is ineffectual. Furthermore, aid based on a wrong diagnosis can humiliate people. For example, to give caviar to someone dying of thirst is a waste of resources. However, to misinterpret the person's urgent need for water through a lack of caring attention also constitutes a humiliation of the sufferer. Alternatively, the aid giver can have wrong ideas of the goal aid is given for. For example, some aid givers think emergency relief will simultaneously liberate poor people from so-called long-term poverty traps. Although aid as emergency relief is an admirable humanitarian activity, it will not necessarily help people caught up in long-term poverty traps to effectively escape their misfortune.

In this chapter I want to argue in defence of the following general normative ideal as guidance for dealing with poverty, that is, eradicate poverty (1) by first identifying the particular manifestation of poverty in each case (2) and then further through enabling agents to exercise their freedom in a rights-based community (3) so as to optimize their well-being and self-fulfilment (4) by using their human capacities optimally (5) through interdependent cooperation with others.

My defence of this normative ideal will proceed through arguments for the following claims:

1. poverty is an inhuman condition and must therefore be eradicated and not merely alleviated;
2. aid givers must correctly identify the causes and effects of poverty by using the best possible scientific know-how and engaging in dialogue with poor people;
3. possible restoration and definitive development of human agency are crucial steps in the effective eradication of poverty;
4. exercising individual freedom within a rights-based community that enables autonomous decision making in the light of the best available knowledge plays an important role in the eradication of poverty;
5. poor people's well-being can be improved by enhancing their ability (i) to enjoy the essential preconditions for competent human action; and (ii) to access conditions and utilize opportunities needed to acquire and use capacities and resources to improve the quality of their lives;
6. the use of reason to determine the best course of action, (i) in the light of available resources and (ii) through consideration of other people's interests, will contribute significantly to the eradication of poverty;
7. the deep intertwinement and complex complementarity between individual agency and societal arrangements imply that aid must be based on an integrated and multi-faceted approach to transform both individuals and human communities.

My arguments for these claims will have both normative and pragmatic aspects. Note how these two aspects are interwoven. There are normative requirements how poor people ought to be treated when aided and pragmatic requirements for efficient use of limited resources. The pragmatic requirement for the efficient use of limited resources acquires normative significance in the following cases. (1) Precious resources must be used in the interest of as many people as possible from the overwhelming numbers of poor people worldwide. To relieve as much human suffering as is feasible is always morally good. (2) Poor people must be helped as effectively as possible. They must not be given the impression that they are being experimented on, nor should they be given false hope or groundless expectations. There can be no moral justification to raise the hopes and lift the expectations of suffering people that help has finally arrived only to dash those hopes and expectations through inept or corrupt behaviour. To do so is simply cruel.

I

The first claim I want to defend is that poverty is an inhuman condition and therefore must be eradicated and not merely alleviated. This claim rests on the assumption that 'to alleviate poverty' means to make this human condition less severe, whereas 'to eradicate poverty' means to remove or destroy poverty completely. An even stronger meaning of eradicate goes back to the original meaning of the Latin word 'eradicate' which means 'to tear up by the roots'. I want to use the word eradicate with this strong meaning in mind, that is, the idea of getting rid of poverty completely through rooting it out.

Does a moral obligation exist to eradicate poverty? I claim we have a moral obligation to completely root out poverty. If I assume that humans have a general moral responsibility to intervene when fellow human beings suffer inhuman treatment or conditions, then we have to intervene if it can be proven that poverty is an inhuman condition. When is a condition or act inhuman? We call something inhuman when a condition or an act implies that human beings are treated in some or other way as beings of significantly lesser value or worth than their fellows, or live in conditions that devalue their status as human beings in meaningful ways. How can I prove that poverty is an inhuman condition? My definition of poverty provides a clue.

I claimed in Chapter 2 that poverty is a distinctively human condition that denies human beings opportunities to live lives that express their humanity and thus forces them into lifestyles not worthy of their species. I defined poverty first as intermediate poverty, which means that although people have sufficient economic capacities to provide adequate food, clothing, shelter, security and medical care to maintain their physical health, they cannot participate in any other activities regarded as indicative of being human in their society. In this case people are unable to afford participation in characteristic aspects of human life, that is, they are people without sufficient money, wealth or material possessions to afford anything more than the barest necessities to keep themselves physically alive and well. People who are intermediately poor are excluded from living lives expressing their humanity in socially defined ways.

I then defined poverty further as extreme poverty, which means that its victims suffer additional harmful effects than those suffered by people subject to intermediate poverty only. People living in extreme poverty do not have sufficient economic capacities to provide sufficient food, clothing, shelter, security and medical care to maintain their physical health. In everyday language this means people do not have enough means to procure even the necessaries of life. Such people cannot secure their survival and are dependent on others for help. Gifts, community assistance, allowances, governmental aid or charitable relief stand between their bare subsistence and ill health or even death.

Poverty as a lack of economic capacities makes it impossible for its victims to develop and deploy their capacities to engage in social life, disables people from giving their full input in employment, diminishes their range of activities as full members of society and restrains them from utilizing opportunities they would otherwise qualify for. For poor people a lack of economic capacities implies some things cannot be acquired, some activities cannot be engaged in, because the prerequisites are not there, the enabling circumstances to make something of their lives are absent. The things, support, circumstances and resources to acquire what is necessary to engage in a normal human life are not accessible to support their life's project. They are disabled in their quest to live a life worthy of humans as defined by their society. They cannot empower themselves sufficiently to exploit the opportunities available to them as human beings seeking to live lives comparable to those of their fellow citizens.

My definition shows that in all cases of poverty the people concerned live lives judged – in important respects, but not all – to be below the minimum standard of what is considered to be a life worthy of human beings as set out by their society. If this definition succeeds in depicting poverty as an inhuman condition, then non-poor people have a moral obligation to use all available means to eradicate poverty.

Does each one of us really have a moral obligation to assist human beings who suffer from inhuman conditions? If so, why? This matter has been intensely debated by philosophers in the last decade and I will briefly summarize some of the main arguments.

Despite the wealth of recent literature on how to eradicate poverty, most philosophers and ethicists have steered clear from many of the ethical issues involved with the concrete phenomenon of poverty and its harmful consequences. Much work has been done on the issues of distributive justice and inequality, but less on the actual ethics that ought to guide and shape aid to poor people.

All attempts to justify a binding moral obligation to aid victims suffering from poverty depend on convincing people to accept a specific set of moral values. Thus, suppose a person selfishly agrees to the protection and opportunities provided by graciously interpreted and benevolently specified sets of democratic values, norms of justice, conceptions of human rights or universal moral principles respectful of human dignity, then that person must accept that a consistent application of these sets of moral values implies that poor people can claim similar protection and opportunities from them. Thus, protection claimed for yourself must be granted to poor people as well, if you want to apply such values consistently with integrity.

Why challenge a selfish person intent on demanding selective application of moral values with the importance of consistent application of ethical values to all persons? The reason is that for those moral values to protect any specific individual, they must be applied consistently and equally to everyone. If not, any individual – including the selfish person – will be at risk of not being considered as worthy of those values in their hour of need as the values are only applied irregularly and inconsistently. If individuals rely on things like their religious or cultural affiliation, or their social of economic status to ensure moral values are applied in their favour, then the moral basis of their claims on society are undermined.

II

My second claim is that aid givers have a responsibility to correctly and reliably identify the cause and effects of poverty through the use of the best possible scientific know-how and by engaging in dialogue with poor people. I will first present an argument that defends the claim that despite poverty's similar appearance everywhere, its origins and contributory factors can come from a diversity of sources. If this claim is true, then I can argue for the thesis that aid givers have a moral responsibility to accurately identify the origins and causes of poverty in every case before they give aid to poor people. I further discuss whether the latter can be done in any way without engaging poor people in dialogue.

The claim that a selection of factors from a diverse series of origins and contributory factors cause each individual case of poverty in its familiar universal manifestations has been defended like this in a previous chapter. I have indicated that poverty can only meaningfully be understood in the context of human resource dealing processes, that is, the complex series of human activities consisting of the location, conversion, exchange, distribution and consumption of resources. A basic challenge for our species is to identify, locate, extract, convert, exchange and consume resources for survival and flourishing. These resources can be (1) edible products found or cultivated by means of natural resources like soil, water or organic material; (2) materials for designing, manufacturing and constructing new composite materials, tools, buildings and infrastructure, (3) living beings to provide or produce things we need as food, clothes or tools, (4) ideas and innovations that improve or enhance any aspect of our lives and (5) skills, talents, knowledge or insight that we can apply to provide appropriate goods or services to ourselves or others.

Within this context poverty can be understood as follows. People are poor if they cannot obtain adequate resources or do not have the requisite capacities to deal with resources fittingly to maintain physical health and engage in social activities distinctive of human beings in their respective societies. Their poverty is due to the fact that they do not have roles or functions rewarded in their society's quest for the location, conversion, exchange, distribution or consumption of resources, nor are they compensated for this lack.

Myriad things occur daily in the endless processes of locating, converting, exchanging, distributing and consuming resources to ensure people's survival and enable human flourishing. When one or more of the significant things in resource dealing processes go wrong in ways not easily fixed, poverty may result at individual, household, group or societal level. Poverty is thus a consequence of any of thousands of possible kinds of failure or obstruction somewhere in the highly complex series of processes involved in the location, conversion, exchange, distribution and consumption of resources. Poverty thus occurs when human resource dealing processes are short-circuited and thwarted in a diversity of ways by forces of either natural or human origin.

If the claim is convincing that despite poverty's similar appearance everywhere, its origins and contributory factors can come from a diversity of sources, then aid givers must draw individual profiles to do justice to the complex configuration of indicators and causes operative in each specific case. Factors involved can be personal, communal, national, continental or natural. To profile individual or group cases, profilers must be conversant with current poverty research that provides checklists of possible intervening factors. Profilers must also be deeply attentive to all circumstances and conditions actually impacting on a specific case. A detailed quantitative and qualitative description of the scope and extent of a specific case of poverty is needed. Added to that a detailed analysis of all possible factors involved in causing or reinforcing poverty must be given.

In profiling cases of poverty, broader contexts must be accounted for. Often individuals, communities or countries find themselves in spaces where several complex societal systems, such as local, regional or national governments or economies intersect with regional, continental and global trends. The manner of such intersections could amplify the effects of some factors and strengthen their causal role. Furthermore, it has to be determined why a specific individual, community or country was susceptible or vulnerable to the set of circumstances and factors that led to poverty. The combined results of such a detailed investigation, constructed to present a personal, communal, regional, national or continental profile, are the necessary prologue to any appropriate and effective aid.

Without such detailed profiles, aid givers would only be able to provide emergency aid to prevent poor people from dying or to avoid that poor people suffer serious harm. Aid givers without an in-depth understanding of individual cases of poverty will not know which causal factors of a specific case of poverty to address so as to effectively eradicate poverty. Aid givers without appropriate knowledge will be wasting donors' resources, misdirecting aid workers and frustrating poor people's expectations. Aid givers will be responsible for these negative consequences if they engage in poverty eradication without the guidance of individual profiles of poverty in each case. For these reasons one could claim that aid givers have a moral responsibility to accurately identify the origins and causes of poverty in every case before they give aid. They thus have obligations both to people donating and those receiving aid.

Should people receive aid without any questions being asked? In the case of emergency aid to prevent loss of life and serious illness the answer is yes, as serious harm to people in desperate circumstances will be avoided through timeous, appropriate responses. In other cases of aid the answer is not that simple. Aid will have to be conditional, if ideas on the interdependence of humans and the restoration and development of agency are taken seriously. Anyone receiving a form of aid other than for emergency purposes will have to be willing to become self-reliant and live in inter-dependence within their communities. This is mandated by an ethical obligation to make proper use of aid to become adult human beings that take full responsibility for their own lives as far as they are capable of. If there are any people or circumstances that prevent aid accomplish-ing such goals, these obstructions must be removed as well, as far as is possible. The functions and effective working of aid cannot be abandoned, sacrificed or wasted as a result of exploitative relationships or dominating political regimes. Somehow ways must be found to simultaneously address individual factors, as well as social, political and economic reasons for poverty.

But can one responsibly profile the poverty of an individual or group without explicitly engaging poor people themselves in dialogue at every phase of the process of profiling? There are several reasons that count against such exclusion. One reason is that poor people possess an inside, felt experience of their condition and its history that represents know-ledge and insight unavailable from other sources. If poor people's experi-ences are ignored by aid givers who treat them as if they have nothing meaningfully to contribute to their own improvement, it would be difficult to get poor people's cooperation and identification with any interventions designed by benevolent outsiders. Moreover, to ignore the contributions poor people can make to their own restoration as fully participating members of society would be to treat people already dehumanized by the condition they suffer from as mere objects without their own voice or will.

In contrast, if poor people who possess privileged, exclusive infor-mation about the human problem to be resolved are engaged in dialogue as equal participants, the process of profiling their case of poverty can become the imaginative first step in resolving the poverty problem. The personal involvement of poor people in this process will empower them to restore their human functioning to optimum levels. Treating poor people as valuable individuals in possession of information indispensable for the accomplishment of the shared social goal of eradicating poverty will initiate the transformation and healing of poor people. They will experi-ence themselves as worthwhile partners with valuable contributions in the reconstruction of human communities, as human beings with dignity.

If poor people are listened to and taken seriously in these ways, two consequences might follow. One possible consequence of fellow citizens recognising the humanity of poor people and their desperate plight is that poor people's self-respect and sense of dignity can be positively affirmed. The other possible consequence of listening to poor people and taking them seriously can be on the non-poor people who will become aware of the human desperation poor people suffer.

Human face-to-face contact with the intent of listening and understanding can significantly challenge people's perceptions and beliefs. Meaningful interpersonal communication between humans who regard themselves as of equal dignity can transform people's grasp of their moral obligations towards their conversational partners who are in great need. For these reasons dialogue between free and equal citizens intent on finding solutions to intractable problems of poverty can transform parties from both sides in ways necessary to effectively eradicate poverty.

III

The third claim in this chapter is that possible restoration and definitive development of human agency are crucial steps in the effective eradication of poverty.

The concepts 'agent' and 'agency' are often used in philosophy without being adequately defined or discussed. Nevertheless sufficient work has been done to present a simplified model of human agents appropriate for illuminating the dynamics of human poverty so that its effects on persons can be countered (see Donald Davidson, 1980; Charles Taylor, 1985c; Amartya Sen, 1984, 1992, 1999; Onora O'Neill, 1986; Michael J. Sandel, 1982; Barry Barnes, 2000; Michael E. Bratman, 2001; Lawrence H. Davis, 1979; Brian Fay, 1996; Vinit Haksar, 1998).

An understanding of human agency illuminates the challenges humans face to ensure survival and to accomplish flourishing. To survive and flourish humans must locate, extract, convert, exchange and consume appropriate resources. To be successful in dealing with resources, humans must be the kind of agents one can describe as competent performers. They must perform daily a wide range of functions more or less effectively to secure their survival and enhance their flourishing. To be poor means that a host of things can go wrong that disable aspects of a person's daily functioning enough so as to cause people to become flawed performers unable to adequately secure survival. The notions of agent and agency can usefully explain some of the intricacies involved in the struggle to eradicate poverty by illuminating the ideas of competent and flawed performers.

Our universe is full of agents, but only our planet has human agents. The concept agent at its basic level refers to something with the potential to exert power, produce an effect, cause an outcome or influence its environment. This 'something' is a locus of one or more forces that can be activated under the right conditions to start a chain of events. A chemical agent such as acid, for example, has characteristics that interact with other agents to facilitate particular outcomes, produce specified effects or induce repeatable reactions.

Lifeless chemical agents, such as acid, form one end of a continuous spectrum of agents of increasing complexity with higher degrees of agency. At the other end of the spectrum we find human beings with a plastic nature that calls for agency operations to design appropriate habitats with our superior minds through the use of resources found in our world. These habitats serve as sites for making a living that ensure physical survival and enable flourishing lifestyles.

Human beings are notably characterized by their agency, that is, their ability to act in a multiplicity of styles, exert power through a wide range of means and to intervene constantly in a variety of events. Obviously human agency has limits, as we cannot act to alter the movements of the stars, cannot effectively intervene in the course of terminal disease nor bring to bear appropriate force on two individuals to make them fall in love. Nevertheless, our collective agency as humans on earth seems powerful enough to alter the climates on our planet.

Through our agency humans can loosen the grip of environmental constraints on our lifestyle, for example by finding a new source of energy. Through our agency we can also change the impact and restraint that cultural conventions and societal structures have on us. What are the basic characteristics of human agents through which we accomplish so much?

Human agency manifests itself primarily in what we are and what we do, that is, in our being and doing. What we have chosen to do and eventually carried out, as well as the kind of person we have chosen to be through our everyday behaviour, reveal our agency in operation. Our agency can thus be seen in our ability to be sources of activity through which we act intentionally, author events, produce effects, make things happen, bring about change and cause consequences. Agency also manifests itself by our nature as centres of experience through which we process information about our world to become aware of its possibilities and make decisions about appropriate courses of action in the light of values and goals we have set and appropriated for ourselves.

To be sources of activity and centres of experience we as agents need cognitive capacities and powers of action as prerequisites. Our cognitive capacities give us an awareness of our environment that enables us to perceive our situation within it. We make working assumptions about the ways the world works, the nature of living beings we interact with and opportunities available within our cultural settings. Our cognitive capacities enable us to recognize and define problems and empower us to judge problems to determine an effective response. Through gathering knowledge of our position within our world, we can reflect on alternative courses of action to eventually arrive at motivated, reasoned decisions about our choice for intervention in our state of affairs. Our ability to reflect on our action means that we can explain and justify the chosen course of action that we have executed. We can also evaluate those actions with reference to our perspective determined by our own goals and values and try to alter them, or their consequences, if necessary. However, through imaginative powers of sympathetic identification we can also judge our action from the different perspective of others affected by our doings and thus note and accommodate their point of view.

Our powers of action can be observed in the ways we exercise our free will, that is, how we activate our ability to 'summon our will', to act out of our own volition to determine our course of action. We need to be enduring selves capable of longer term planning and decision making to give full manifestation to the scope and extent of the exercise of our free will. The depth of our exercise of agency only becomes apparent by means of setting goals and purposes for our lives through which we implement our chosen lifestyles and demonstrate the value we attach to various activities, things and persons. Thus, our exercise of agency shows in the ways we shape our destiny within the scope available for human decision making and appropriate action.

Individual human agents can never be viewed apart from their social context. For this reason we can justifiably refer to ourselves as interdependent social agents, as individual humans acquire much of their agency from their immediate social environment. Fay (1996: 192) argues that the 'capacity to act is an achievement that requires a great deal of learning'. Individual human agents are always embedded within looser or tighter knit communities where they are taught social roles and rules that enable and mould their range of possible action. Through processes of enculturation and appropriation individual agents are capacitated to become more or less competent performers within their socio-cultural world, while the possibility always stays open that they can modify and alter the roles and rules to better suit their overarching goals of physical survival and human flourishing.

Not only should we speak of individual humans as interdependent social agents who are empowered to act on their own within a social context, but we must also speak of groups of interdependent social agents who act collectively to achieve shared goals. We can refer to such collective units as agencies. These groups can be more loosely organized, such as a mob that arises almost spontaneously in reaction to some or other event, to tightly knit groups produced by institutions rigidly organized according to authoritarian chains of command, such as an army or even a country properly ordered by laws and managed by governments.

Note how powerful some collective agents such as a developed country or a multinational company can be. Compare the capacities available in a developed country to do things through manufacturing, cultivation and production processes, make events happen through highly qualified citizens such as a trained and equipped military or through capable advertising or events agencies, to improve citizens' lives through health services and government bureaucracies and to perceive different worlds through media empires and scientific fields of research. Look in comparison to some of the world's poorest societies that are weak in so many respects compared to a strongly developed country. No infrastructure, insufficient human resources, lack of technological skills, corrupt government officials depleting limited tax income and inadequate cultivation of agricultural land significantly lowers the collective agency of such often desperately poor countries.

Perhaps the most important fact about human agency in the context of poverty is that the level of agency in individuals and societies is not a constant value, but rather a wide ranging variable. Individual agents exercise more or less agency, to the extent that one can easily talk of a spectrum of agency levels ranging from passive patients to active agents. The level of agency activity in individuals can be influenced by various factors. Obviously the arbitrary fortunes of talents and characteristics that come from one's genetic make-up have significant effects on the agency levels an individual can reach. We can ignore this factor, as our collective human agency can thus far not affect our genetic make-up.

Far more important is the influence some human beings can have on the agency levels achieved by others. If it is true that our socialization and enculturation within a specific community equip us to act as agents, then the contents, quality and availability of agency empowerment in our communities will determine the kind and level of agency activity we can achieve.

The effects of poverty on some poor people's agency are often similar to what happens to people under political oppression. In the context of political oppression the oppressors not only deny the oppressed people opportunities to develop and nurture their agency, but often also dominate, humiliate and degrade the oppressed people to such an extent that they sometimes even lose their awareness of themselves as agents. In such cases the oppressed people tend to regard themselves rather as patients, that is, as people who cannot act independently and autonomously. Even in their own eyes they become people who are acted upon, people who are passive recipients of whatever others dish out rather than active agents who respond to life's challenges as equals to all others in their world.

In the case of some poor people the lack of proper education and training to develop several agency functions and the powerlessness that results from lack of economic capacities often cause serious harm to the quality of agency operations expressed. The kinds of things they cannot observe or appreciate, the decisions they cannot take or implement, the useful labour functions they cannot imagine or fulfil, the celebrations they cannot organize or attend, the long-term planning that they cannot visualize or entertain – the list of scarred, tainted or injured agency functions almost does not stop. For this reason the restoration of agency functions must get serious attention.

IV

The next claim I want to argue for is that exercising individual freedom within a rights-based community that enables autonomous decision making in the light of the best available knowledge plays an important role in the eradication of poverty. Amartya Sen (1999) has strongly argued this point. To accomplish this implies that poor individuals either had their agency restored to at least partial functionality or they had found space and resources to activate their agency functions in their own defence and on their own behalf. To take responsibility to fight politically for the eradication of one's own poverty is simultaneously a significant affirmation of one's self-worth and dignity as an equal citizen (see Walzer, 1983: 310–11). Such affirmation is important to poor people who often struggle with unfair accusations blaming them for their poverty. They also sometimes lose sight of their own value as human beings.

Within a rights-based community citizens have guaranteed opportunities to participate in political processes that can influence their lives (see Walzer, 1983: 281–311). If a state has assigned its citizens rights to basic subsistence, poor individuals can actively campaign for the alleviation or even eradication of their own poverty through insisting on the enforcement of their rights (see Shue, 1980). If basic socio-economic rights are not available in a democratic state, citizens can nevertheless use several other political rights as leverage to urge their government to be more responsive to the lack of fulfilment of their basic needs. Citizens can organize protest meetings in terms of their right to freedom of association to express their dismay and opposition to being invisible to the authorities. In terms of their right to freedom of information citizens can get access to governmental documents on budgets, policies and records of service delivery. This information creates chances to expose failure of government services, preferential treatment of some citizens and corrupt government officials who squander limited public resources for their own benefit and to the detriment of vulnerable citizens.

Exercising individual rights according to one's available wisdom can thus contribute to highlight one's poverty and make government officials and non-poor fellow citizens aware of unfulfilled basic needs and fundamental rights being denied.

V

The next claim states the following: poor people's well-being can be improved by enhancing their ability (1) to enjoy the essential preconditions for competent human action (see Rawls, 1971; Shue, 1980; Gewirth, 1978, 1982); and (2) to access conditions and utilize opportunities needed to acquire and use capacities and resources to improve the quality of their lives.

Why is it important that every person enjoy the essential preconditions for competent human action? Many poor people's daily functioning to secure survival or to enhance flourishing is hampered or hamstrung by their lack of the all-purpose means (Rawls, 1993) or primary goods (Rawls, 1971) needed for competent, effective action in support of these goals. People without enough food, without adequate clothing, without shelter that provides a good night's rest, without the means to get transported to a place of work or without appropriate education, training or equipment to do a job within their capabilities cannot play any meaningful role to cooperate in the process of eradicating their own poverty.

If this is true, then aid givers must focus at least part of their aid on enabling poor people to get access to the means they require to become effectively functioning human beings who can collaborate fully in their own escape from poverty. For example, emergency aid to provide adequate food to victims of poverty is thus an imperative, but so is aid to empower poor people with capacities and competencies to become self-reliant through interdependent cooperation with others in society.

Why should poor people be assisted to access conditions and utilize opportunities needed to acquire and use capacities and resources to improve the quality of their lives? No one can assume that any person automatically possesses knowledge, skills and capacities to earn a living. Human beings are raised within cultural settings where they learn established social roles. The quality of whatever education is available within the context, and in response to the needs, of a particular society determines the employability and career-readiness of young people.

Many poor people did not get any appropriate education to enable them to do socially valuable jobs, or have no access to opportunities for continuous learning or further education and training to hone their skills or develop their capacities in order to contribute in socially rewarded ways. For this reason the eradication of poverty requires considerable investment in the growth and development of people's capacities to equip them with knowledge, insight, skills and attitudes that will empower them to contribute their part to society and be rewarded sufficiently to survive comfortably. In this way they can taste the satisfaction of being independent citizens that take care of their own subsistence and share the value of meaningful work with their peers.

VI

The sixth claim I want to defend is as follows: the use of reason to determine the best course of action, (1) in the light of available resources and (2) through consideration of other people's interests, will contribute significantly to the eradication of poverty. Both aid givers and aid receivers will have to apply their minds to determine the best course of action in every situation. Aid givers will have to use reason to determine which state-of-the-art knowledge and research findings apply in cases where they are involved. Aid givers will have to reason about the best options for investing limited funds to make the biggest impact in the eradication of poverty. There is no self-evident set of priorities for investing limited funds to eradicate poverty, other than perhaps that emergency relief has a prima facie claim to be considered first.

Other than emergency relief, should the provision of food, shelter and clothing be attended to first, or should money go to projects that will enhance the capacities of individuals and communities to help themselves, or should aid givers invest in infrastructure such as roads, water and energy provision to enable job creation projects to proceed more effectively? These choices can have a fundamental impact on the long-term sustainable eradication of poverty.

Careful consideration of available ecosystem services and possibilities for their sustainable utilization must be combined with a critical scrutiny of the levels of human resource development that could be mobilized to effectively and sustainably utilize these ecosystem services. Through rational reflection that takes into account past experience, state-of-the-art knowledge, best practice and the considered opinion of everyone involved we can make wise decisions that we must be willing to revisit, re-evaluate and overturn, if necessary. Only by constantly applying rational thinking can aid givers and poor people as equals together determine through dialogue how strong a focus on which priorities will make the most significant difference in the lives of people who need small miracles to ensure survival and well-being.

Aid receivers will also need to apply their minds to the same issues as aid givers, as they can never fully realize their status as citizens of equal worth and dignity who are active, competent agents if they allow others to make decisions on their behalf. Aid receivers with privileged knowledge of their own recent history, needs and preferences will have to engage aid givers as equals in dialogue to determine priorities and set preferences for the processes tailored to enable the eradication of their own poverty. Taking responsibility for the reconstruction of their lives in collaboration with respectful people who have more resources and power than they do will restore poor people's sense of being equal members of a community of interdependent social agents who cooperate to ensure a society that mutually benefits everyone. They also have to take responsibility for the ways they use aid, as aid comes from well-meaning people who give some of their resources for the betterment of people suffering poverty. The express willingness to account for aid is another way to activate and exercise agency functions crucial for a successful, sustainable escape from poverty's traps. Obviously the traps of aid must also be avoided, such as aid givers creating dependency or exacting favours that might lead to corruption.

Through reasoned dialogue and reciprocal interaction with poor people as equals, aid givers (including rich and powerful people) can perceive suffering and inhumanity through observing directly poor people's bodies, faces and homes, listening to their voices and hearing what they think and feel. If such unmediated experiences of poverty occur, important developments can follow. To experience suffering individuals encountered in the flesh will challenge non-poor people to justify their public policy choices to such citizens who are not able to have lives that qualify as human by their society's standards. The non-poor will have to reflect on economic and tax policies that disadvantage the poor, as well as wage policies that channel excessive rewards to certain classes of skilled employees and risk-taking entrepreneurs. They will have to make up their minds whether they can defend policies and practices that impoverish other people to the face of those people directly affected by the suffering such policies and practices cause.

As democrats they will have to give reasons face to face to fellow citizens why some non-poor citizens can command massive shares of societal resources and consequently deplete available means that could have enabled suffering people in inhuman circumstances to have minimally decent lives. Above all, they will have to account why poor people's issues are not properly listened to, why poor people's plight is not genuinely seen, or why nothing is done to improve their lot. Through honest, reasonable exchange of perceptions, experiences and ideas, poor people cannot be ignored at will anymore, nor can the non-poor blissfully continue to pursue their interests whilst knowing how others pay part of the cost of their privileged lifestyles. Stuart Hampshire says that poverty will be 'immediately felt' as an evil by 'any normally responsive person, unless she has perhaps been distracted from natural feeling by some theory that explains them away: for example, as necessary parts of God's design' (2000: xii). Such a face-to-face discussion gives a good chance to rip away such theories and expose the harmful effects poverty has on fellow human beings.

VII

The last claim I argue for is the following: the deep intertwinement and complex complementarity between individual agency and societal arrangements imply that aid must be based on an integrated and multi-faceted approach to transform both individuals and human communities. Lister argues that of 'particular significance for the study of poverty is the extent to which, on the one hand, structure enables or constrains the agency of different groups and, on the other, the agency of different groups is able to impact on structure' (2004: 126).

If both individuals and societies can be depicted as agents with varying agency levels, then restoration of agency levels and empowerment of agency functions must take place for both. In the preceding sections I have already shown that individuals' agency can be influenced deeply by their society, be it through the quality and availability of education and other resources or the restrictions or spaces set up by socio-political arrangements, cultural values or economic policies and practices. Societies can thus empower and enhance individuals in their struggle for survival and their quest for flourishing or not. Similarly, enthusiastic competent individuals can strengthen and develop the human potential available in their society, thus positively changing the agency functions of their society.

In his book *Republic* Plato presents a brief example that beautifully illustrates the point above (1993: 329e–30a). Themistocles, an Athenian, is rudely accused by someone from Seriphus that 'his fame was not due to his own merits but to his city'. In his counterattack Themistocles acknowledges the influence of Athens on his success, but denies that he himself is devoid of individual merit: 'It's true that I wouldn't have become famous if I were a Seriphian, but it's also true that you wouldn't if you were an Athenian' (330a). Seriphus did not have the empowering effect on individuals that the social space, cultural climate or education of Athens had on its citizens. Nevertheless, only citizens with the appropriate talents that could flourish in the Athenian world, like Themistocles and unlike his accuser, were the ones who became famous in Athens.

If both the above truisms are accepted, that is, (1) that individual and society are deeply intertwined, in the sense that their fates are linked and have a reciprocal influence on each other and (2) that individual and society have a complex complementarity, that is, that strong individuals with properly focused outputs can, though not necessarily will, benefit their society and weak societies often, though not always, fail to equip their members for successful survival, then interventions to eradicate poverty must never focus on either individuals or society alone. Any interventions to eradicate poverty must ensure that a multitude of factors are in place in society that will enhance the ability of poor individuals to acquire capacities and learn responsibilities that will ensure their escape from poverty. Not only individual transformation to equip people for survival and flourishing, but especially social transformation is necessary to create and establish conditions favourable for the effective eradication of poverty. Issues such as governmental budget priorities, a state's macro-economic policies and entrepreneur-encouraging practices need as much attention to transform a society as individual empowerment through education and training, or feeding and housing schemes. Little points out that in giving aid we should 'pay close attention to the factors and institutions that most directly influence human well-being throughout society' (2003: 39).

If the deep intertwinement and complex complementarity between individual and society are accepted, then aid needs to be redefined in several ways so as to capacitate both individual and society in various ways as is necessary. Aid must aim to restore and enhance agency functions so that individuals and societies can become self-reliant, interdependent human agents. The contents of 'aid' can be various, such as money, clothing, food, temporary shelter, education and training, equipment, infrastructure, advice, ideas and services (electricity, water, transport, etc.). The style of giving aid can also not be only of one kind. In some cases aid could take the form of sounding board discussions, or consultative dialogue. In other cases aid can be money, accompanied by dialogue ending in binding consensus about its expenditure. What is clear is that any form of aid must respond in detail to what Sachs calls a differential diagnosis of poverty (see Sachs, 2005) and must be offered and given in dialogue with recipients treated as people of equal worth every step of the way. This style of giving aid is required, because poor people are equals in dignity and worth, though they are not equal in economic performance, nor adequate in the survival stakes or best in the flourishing business.

Conclusion

In this chapter I have defended the view that poverty is an inhuman condition that we have a moral obligation to root out completely. The most humane way of doing so is to accurately define the cause and effects of each case of poverty and to address them fittingly. We must involve poor people fully in the process of eradicating poverty so as to restore their humanity by empowering their agency so that they can effectively claim and exercise their rights to live lives worthy of human beings.

These ideas cover only certain aspects concerning the eradication of poverty, that is, the normative ideal of aid that would eradicate poverty. But that is not enough said yet. Poverty occurs within broader social environments ultimately determined by the values of justice that are accepted, implemented and enforced in a society. How can these values of justice contribute to the eradication of poverty? In the next chapter I argue that an adequate theory of justice can address – and prevent – the principal manifestations of poverty.

9 · Justice as Poverty Prevention

One of the oldest answers to the question: 'What is justice?' is as follows. 'Justice', so many philosophers throughout history have replied, 'is to give everyone their due'. This answer had considerable staying power, as it has been approvingly quoted for more than two millennia.[1] Many theories of justice, so their authors claim, were attempts to work out its meaning in detail.[2]

One could argue that Rawls (1971, 1993, 2001) worked out everyone's due in terms of the distribution of benefits and burdens and the assignment of rights and duties as determined by his two principles of justice applicable to the basic structure of society. Or that Robert Nozick (1974) worked out what everyone is due in the light of strong liberty rights that function as side constraints on human action. Perhaps we could say that Michael Walzer (1983) determined everyone's due in the light of the principles of justice that apply in specified spheres of justice and guided by the meanings shared by citizens of a political community. Or we could agree that David Schmidtz (2006) made an ever better attempt to show what everyone is due in his pluralistic theory that looked at desert, reciprocity, need and equal shares as elements of justice. Yet no theory explicitly interrogated this adage and examined its presuppositions.

Despite the approval and a few detailed expositions seemingly interpreting this adage, very few, if any, detailed analyses of it exists. In this section I am presenting an analysis of this adage as prelude to a theory of justice with the power to prevent poverty. I will proceed as follows. I will interrogate the adage that 'Justice is to give everyone their due' by looking at the meaning of the concepts and the assumptions embedded in this sentence. The results of this analysis will be presented in a series of propositions that will gradually build up to a theory of justice.

In this theory I argue that justice is a cluster concept with a core meaning that unfolds into a kaleidoscope of dimensions like the facets of a finely cut diamond.[3] The upshot of this discussion is that justice turns out to be analogous to a diamond: the beauty of justice is seen in its ability to be fair to everyone involved and thus to protect the fundamental interests of each person. The strength and power of justice is found in its ability to cut through the most complicated, tangled mess to sort out intractable conflicts of interest equitably. This diamond amongst our moral values can prevent any future forms of poverty and eradicate all existing versions, except those cases based on voluntary choice for lifestyle reasons.

In what follows I set out my analysis of the centuries-old depiction of justice mentioned in the first paragraph according to a set of propositions that build on each other.

1. The adage 'Justice is to give everyone their due' has a clear normative dimension. If something is *due* to a person, it means that something is *owed* to that person or is *payable* to him or her. Thus, something belongs to a person by right. The person can thus claim this 'thing' from one or more other persons who have a moral obligation to give this something to the person who has a right to it.[4]

    Thus, something is a matter of justice if persons can legitimately claim that 'something' from us as a moral obligation we owe them, justified through shared public moral values. Let me explain. The moral imperative in some ethical theories that requires adherents to show charity towards people does not imply that any person can legitimately claim that I must be charitable towards them. I have considerable leeway how I show charity and towards whom. The moral imperative not to kill anyone is different. Most societies have a strong moral obligation that its members do not in any way kill another human being. This duty is something we owe to every other human being.

    Matters of justice are like this: it concerns moral obligations we owe every human being who qualify appropriately in terms of specified principles of justice. Others can claim those things from us as a right that can be enforced. Similarly, the reasons supporting such moral obligations are judged to be reasons that typically 'imply general moral rules applicable to all relevantly similar cases' (Kane, 1996: 377).

2. In the adage 'Justice is to give everyone their due' it is clearly assumed that some human being has *something that can be given* to another. One person has control over some object, action, feeling or whatever that can thus be transferred to another person. This implies that no person can justly promise their lover the moon and the stars, as they cannot be given in any normal sense to a beloved. Human beings do not have control over certain things and events and thus cannot give things like a rainy day or freedom from terminal disease to one another. Similarly, justice requires that no one should give anything to someone else that does not legitimately fall within their purview.

Debates on justice do not focus on issues that cannot be changed by collective or individual human action. People are often mistaken about what circumstances or conditions in society humans have the power to change or not. For example, people sometimes accept their poverty as 'natural,' as if human intervention is powerless to change some or other force of nature that operates on humans. In such cases a negative human condition is seen as something 'natural' rather than the result of human doings that can be called 'unjust'.

Why do people sometimes judge social conditions as if they are unalterable natural occurrences? Stuart Hampshire explains blindness to injustice with reference to the fallacy of false fixity (1989: 59). What this fallacy does is to represent particular social arrangements in a specific society as being unalterable or unavoidable features of human life, as they are part of a natural, divine or societal order that cannot be changed or made otherwise through deliberate, conscious human action (ibid.). The continued existence of poverty and persistent inaction by those capable of eradicating poverty are often justified in this way as matters that do not fall under the purview of justice.

Rejecting the fallacy of false fixity means that justice becomes possible when people realize that they must take charge of, and responsibility for, the social forces which they produce, sometimes as by-products of private, individual decisions and sometimes as the result of inadequate or wrong collective decisions (Pitkin, 1981: 344). If these forces are left unattended, we can become subject to them and they can 'dominate our lives and limit our options' (ibid.: 345).

3. Perhaps the most obvious question to ask about the adage 'Justice is to give everyone their due' is the simple issue of who is 'everyone'. Do we owe a moral obligation to give their due to everyone in our family? Or perhaps to everyone in our town? To everyone in our province? Perhaps we have this obligation towards everyone in our country? Or maybe to every person in the world?

The simple question 'Who is everyone?' raises the fundamental matter of how we determine towards whom we have obligations of justice. Can we justly decide for ourselves which people we include amongst those we are prepared to treat justly? And do we unilaterally decide whom we exclude? If we do decide this way, what are we going to do if the ones excluded start pressing their claims of justice against us? One obvious choice that humans have made so often throughout history is to ignore such claims. If the claimants become persistent, one could employ all manner of methods to shut them up, from deliberate ignorance through domination by means of oppression, up to cruel repression through violent conquest. However, the human cost over the longer term to everyone involved, such as death, serious injury, hatred and bitterness, makes this option unattractive, as human history is replete with examples of suffering caused this way that any straight thinking human being would want to avoid.

Thus, the moral injunction to treat all people with equal respect and thus to allow all persons input to set up arguments why they ought to be included in our definition of 'everyone' might be the most practical option after all. Even better if we allow them equal access to decision making about such matters so that consensus can be found on who deserves treatment in terms of justice. In the process of shared decision making we will transform the 'we' and 'them' into an 'us' that includes every human being as a legitimate claimant of justice. Dialogue in the vein of moral solidarity can develop a new kind of relationship based on 'a knowing that transforms the self who knows, a knowing that brings into being new sympathies, new affects as well as new cognitions and new forms of intersubjectivity' (Harvey, 2007: 27).

4. Note that 'every human being' has thus far only become 'everyone' who must receive their due. What exactly it is that is due to everyone has not yet been determined. In the recent past many philosophers would easily have answered the question about who 'everyone' is and what everyone is due. A general assumption was that 'everyone' is our fellow citizen and thus is owed full citizenship rights, however they might be defined. This assumption has been challenged in fundamental ways by the emergence of the so-called global village and the focus on gender and family relations. The upshot of these challenges enables us to determine the nature, scope and strength of our obligations of justice towards 'everyone' in a much more satisfying way.

I want to argue that the interplay between three factors is decisive for our understanding of obligations of justice towards other human beings.[5] All three factors link with the assumption discussed above, that is, justice concerns moral obligations concerning matters and events that humans have control over. The first factor is that people are owed some kind of obligation of justice if our actions and the consequences thereof have an impact on their lives. If what we do affects someone else's life, we owe that person at least something, depending on the nature and degree of the impact. If our cutting down trees in the equatorial rain forests detrimentally affects the climate in a country thousands of kilometres away, a relationship of justice arises as a result of this impact.

A second factor that establishes a relationship of justice is when humans interact in some or other way or participate in the same events. Explorers and local inhabitants that meet deep in a desert owe one another at least some basic duties of justice, such as respecting lives, limbs and property. Similarly, participation in international sports events generate obligations of justice that competitors owe one another, like following rules and competing fairly in terms of the rules, not to mention to have respect for the life and limb of their opponents.

Obligations of justice are created by a third factor as well. Wherever humans form part of a sphere of decision making, they develop obligations of justice towards one another. A sphere of decision making is any part of human life subject to the decisions of some or other authority. For example, within a family certain decisions made by one or more members of the family may be binding for family members only. In contrast decisions by a country's government bind all citizens (and in some cases all non-citizens) within its territory.

The nature, strength and scope of obligations of justice vary according to the degree to which each of these factors is present and the interplay and overlap between them. Note two examples. Within the nation-state citizens have a major impact on one another's lives, participate in all kinds of shared activities and interact in myriad spaces, whilst they are subject to their government's sphere of decision making as expressed in laws and policies. In the relation between two faraway countries on different continents there might be minimal impact of one on the other, although there might be some kind of trade or other interaction between citizens at some global sporting event. These countries on different continents would not even share in any form of regional decision making, but still be subject to the spheres of decision making exercised by global institutions such as the United Nations Organization or international sport governing bodies. Clearly the nature, strength and scope of the obligations of justice between citizens sharing a country will be more than those between the citizens of these different countries continents apart.

The advantage of this view that obligations of justice are determined by the interplay between interaction and participation, impact and spheres of decision making is that every individual person will have *a shifting site* of obligations of justice dependent on the person's positioning in terms of these three factors. Such obligations will most possibly vary throughout the person's life, if the person's relationship to these three factors changes as well.

5. Perhaps the most difficult question to answer is the following. How do we determine what is someone's due? Humans have been fighting one another about the answer for centuries, sometimes in the most violent, cruel fashion and at other times by means of the most sophisticated, abstract philosophical arguments. For this reason we are not clueless as to how to go about to determine someone's due. We know how destructive violent conflict about such matters can be and how such clashes can harm and destroy people's lives. We also know that often seemingly endless dialogue and deliberation do resolve conflict in peaceful ways about what everyone is due. Such peaceful successes open up vistas of respectful cooperation in perpetuity.

We know that in deciding someone's due, we must be guided by two other well-established maxims. We must treat similar cases similarly and thus we owe it to claimants of justice to accurately determine similarity and difference between cases. We must also tailor our actions and decisions about justice in proportion to the facts and reasons given in a specific case, as Aristotle (1925: 1129^b13–134^a14) has so precisely pointed out long ago. Although helpful, these two maxims do not assist us in determining the exact contents of what a person is due.

We have already determined that the most practicable as well as the most reasonable way to determine who is 'everyone' is to allow everyone input and an equal say in working out an answer. If, for the same reasons, we do the same in this case, we must ensure that co-operative processes are in place to enable such decision making. In the way most human societies have thus far dealt with this issue, two important things stand out. One is that the wide range of 'things' that can be owed to a person forces us to think in refined, nuanced ways about the reasons why a particular person could claim any specific thing. The other important thing that stands out is that we have many decentralized spheres of decision making where we determine what we owe one another. Some brief comments about each might be apt.

6. If justice is a matter of what is due to a person, then we must be aware of the wide range of 'goods' and 'behaviour' someone might claim from us. A person might claim anything from us that ranges between

rights to political participation, a decent wage, to keep agreements, a prize, a lighter tax burden or financial provision for a legitimate need when unemployed. It seems obvious that decisions about the legitimacy of such claims will have to be based on different considerations that are appropriate to the matter at hand and fair to everyone involved. Some examples will be provided below when I defend the claim that a proper functioning theory of justice is the best way to prevent or eradicate poverty.

7. Within the context of the normative associations entailed in the adage that 'Justice is to give everyone their due', there is little doubt that in order to establish what exactly it is that we owe someone and the reasons why we owe it, we would need an attitude of equal concern and respect for every 'someone' with whom we deal. To show respect to someone means to have regard for the person, to give due attention to who and what the person is and what the person has to say, to esteem the person for what they are, to show due appreciation for the person's characteristics and to treat the person in a manner worthy of the person's fundamental nature. Only by treating a person in this way can we begin to properly understand the reasons why a specific person claims something from us. Similarly, when more than one person claims the same thing from us, like a prize or a prestigious job, we must in addition give each claimant equal consideration, by taking into account every characteristic relevant to the matter at hand. Thus, respectful treatment of every claimant to allow them to portray their relevant characteristics in full is as important in working out what justice requires, as is the requirement to give equal consideration to everyone's case. To dismiss anyone's case out of hand or to deprive anyone of an equal hearing implies that justice has not been served. The persons involved did not have a chance to state their case so that those obligated could determine accurately what the person is due.

8. If we have determined loosely who everyone is and have decided vaguely how we are going to decide what someone is due and why, can we get some inkling of general things that everyone is due? I want to set up an argument that there are at least two basic things that every human being is due in terms of justice, regardless of whatever else we might define as requirements of justice. I claim that no human being can ever be owed to be destroyed or seriously harmed without very strong reasons that are generally accepted. Similarly, it can never

be due to any human being to deprive them of opportunities to develop a minimally decent life for themselves, unless very strong, generally accepted reasons exist to the contrary. The argument goes as follows.

Requirements of justice in any human society can be classified into two major groups, that is, those requirements that prevent harm to human beings and those that establish the conditions for humans to live individual and shared lives worthy of being human. Thus claims for justice are for matters that will both avoid the great evils of human conflict as well as put in place prerequisites for living one's best possible life.

In a general sense everyone is due those values that would enable them to pursue the good life as they choose it within legitimate boundaries for that pursuit to protect both their interests and those of others. The values of justice must thus be able to protect everyone's fundamental interests through recognizing them as human beings, ensure they have a minimal set of means required for living a decent human life and protect them from negative and harmful acts. Citizens must be enabled to gain access to conditions under which they can live the best lives they want and are capable of, within the constraints of what is owed to other people. Thus, certain things must be avoided and others must be provided for justice to be done. Only in this way can justice serve one of its primary functions acknowledged so often by political philosophers, that is, to enable social cooperation that benefits everyone.

Stuart Hampshire (1989: 90) argues that all moral judgements and arguments presuppose that the great evils experienced by human beings must be avoided. Although background to all moral theorizing, Hampshire says the concept of justice in particular can only be fully understood when the 'forces of destruction' that justice intends to avert, are taken into account (68). Justice is thus necessary to human associations for preventing the great evils – such as murder, indiscriminate killing, physical assault, rape, hunger, starvation, oppression and domination – from being inflicted on people and for stopping minor conflicts escalating into major disasters.

What could justify us doing things like these to another human being? What reasons must we have to kill someone, to injure their bodies, to enslave them, to take away their liberty, to cause them suffering or to humiliate them? What circumstances must prevail to make such actions seem 'due' to another human being? Throughout human history we have seen these kinds of actions are rarely, if ever, justified. If we claim self-defence as reason enough, it only points to the fact that our mechanisms of conflict resolution or our procedures for holding people to account for violations of precepts of justice have not been properly developed.

Although Hampshire may be right that the impetus for a conception of justice is the goal of avoiding the great evils of human experience through resolving conflict timeously, that is by far not its only function. The sustaining power of the quest for justice is the endeavour for a society where each claimant of justice can enjoy the fullest life possible for, and worthy of, human beings (Frankena, 1962: 26). As Schmidtz (2006: 11) argues, justice is 'a framework for decreasing the cost of living together', whose main point is 'to free us to focus less on self-defence and more on mutual advantage and on opportunities to make the world a better place'.

Therefore issues such as the safety and security of body and mind, the recognition of one's human dignity, freedom to live one's life according to one's own judgement, access to income, wealth and property and participation in public decision making are the proper stuff to be addressed in a theory of justice. Again, it is not clear that we can ever have strong enough reasons to convince another human being standing in front of us that we can legitimately deny any reasonable request for opportunities to attempt to develop a minimally decent human life. For us to be regarded as reasonable by those with whom we interact, we must be willing to take 'serious note of critical scrutiny from the perspectives of others', as Sen (2009: 197) argues. So can we deny fellow human beings such basic opportunities on grounds that they cannot reasonably reject (see Scanlon 1998)?

Claimants for justice thus can legitimately try (1) to secure for themselves treatment that recognizes them as human beings and to avert treatment that does not and (2) to gain access to conditions under which they can live the best lives they want to and are capable of (Frankena, 1962: 21; Rossouw, 1995: 7).

A conception of justice with these constant elements aims to protect the fundamental interests of all members of society and therefore serves as a pact of reconciliation between persons from diverse groups, such as ethnic, religious, cultural, racial or income groups (Rawls, 1971: 221; Rawls, 1985: 207). Through protection of everyone's interests, reconciling opposing groups and creating expectations of stable behaviour and actions, a public conception of justice creates a well-ordered and peaceful society where members are generally inclined to act justly.

9. An interesting assumption underlying the adage that 'Justice is to give everyone their due' is that whatever a person is owed is *given* to that person. Justice therefore always seems to be justice that is *seen* to be done. Not only must we fairly determine what we owe one another, but we must effectively carry out our decisions of justice. A theory of justice means nothing for citizens if it is not fully implemented and properly enforced. John Rawls argued that not only does a well-ordered society advance the good of its members by protecting their interests, but it is also effectively regulated by that conception of justice (Rawls, 1971: 5). To be an effectively regulated society means that everyone accepts the principles of justice and knows that the other members of society do the same. Furthermore, institutions generally satisfy the principles of justice (Rawls, 1971: 5). As a result, members of the society develop a strong desire to act justly and the conception of justice is generally adhered to.

In what follows, I will present fragments of a liberal egalitarian conception of justice to give examples of how a properly defined, understood and realized concept of justice is capable of preventing great evils, containing and resolving minor conflicts and creating conditions in which human beings can flourish, in short, how justice functioning this way can prevent and eradicate poverty. This exposition will demonstrate how justice has the ability to prevent all forms of poverty and could effectively be employed to guide the complete eradication of existing poverty. I choose a liberal-democratic conception of justice as being approximately representative of modern constitutional democracies that have to some degree embraced the ideal of a welfare state, that is, the ideal that free and equal citizens must have some kind of collective protection against the ravages and vicissitudes endemic to human life on earth.

Issues and categories of justice

To ask questions about justice is to ask what everyone is due. If justice is a cluster concept with a core meaning that unfolds into a kaleidoscope of dimensions such as the facets of a finely cut diamond, how do we get to see this brilliantly shining gem? We have to apply the above analysis of the adage that justice is what everyone is due to six major issues that raise questions in our society about our due. I will thus first briefly review the results of the analysis above, then mention the issues thought to be matters of justice and finally present examples of how the justice of such matters can eradicate and prevent poverty.

The adage to give everyone their due means the following. Some things or behaviours under individual or collective human control can be claimed from us by right. To determine who we judge as legitimate claimants of justice, what they can claim and for which reasons must be determined fairly by giving equal respect and consideration to every person. In the process similar cases must be treated similarly and justice must be dispensed proportionally to the matter at hand. Not only must we make a proper assessment of what is due to whom and for what reasons, but such decisions must be properly implemented so that justice really can be given, or be seen to be done. In general there seems to be no prima facie reasons to harm or humiliate others for reasons of justice, as there are no reasons evident for deliberately depriving anyone of reasonable opportunities to make a decent living.

These ideas must now be applied to the core questions to be answered if one wants to know what someone is due in contemporary society so that the brilliance of justice can shine to illuminate our world so that the darkness of poverty can be eliminated. We must first determine to whom justice is owed and what it means to recognize human beings as claimants of justice. Then we must explore what preconditions enable fair cooperation among human beings. A further issue deals with the nature of prerequisites that will enable every claimant of justice to get access to opportunities to make worthwhile lives for themselves. In the process of making worthwhile lives, human beings first gather means to ensure survival and enable flourishing. Thereafter they accumulate material possessions, claim honours and work to achieve sought after positions in society. How to distribute these things raises important issues of justice.

Although having an appropriate conception of justice that is fair to every person is important, such a conception means nothing if not effectively implemented. Therefore any worthwhile conception of justice must ask questions how to justly ensure compliance with its own dictates. Furthermore, questions must be answered about the ways to change unjust laws, policies and practices so that a society can become more just in its treatment of every person.

The moral issues raised by the concept of justice can thus be sorted into a framework of justice consisting of six distinct categories that feature prominently in the current philosophical literature on justice.[6]

These categories form the facets of the diamond: they are justice as recognition, justice as reciprocity, justice as enablement, justice as distribution, justice as accountability and justice as transformation. They have emerged in recent debates on justice as constitutive of many current conceptions of justice. In what follows, I present the normative requirements of a framework of justice with these six categories present in many theories of justice and operative in many contemporary constitutional democracies.

Through this skeletal presentation of a comprehensive view on justice I hope to show that such a conception of justice can protect fellow citizens from the evils caused by the phenomenon of poverty. Similarly, the dictates of justice will enable us to treat poor people fairly by securing optimum conditions for the development of each one's potential to build a worthwhile human life.

Poverty and the Justice of Recognition

The first issue deals with identifying members of our species as human beings who are owed justice of the kind under discussion. The main matter involved in justice as recognition is to find ways of appropriately recognizing the humanity of fellow beings, thus to acknowledge their dignity or worth. This issue cuts to the heart of the moral harm poverty causes its sufferers, that is, the loss of their human dignity and worth. In the case of poverty this loss results from poor people not being able to engage in activities that express their human nature, a disability caused by their lack of economic capacities. Note how poor people conveyed their views on this matter to a UK commission recently when the commission concludes that 'The lack of respect for people living in poverty was one of the clearest and most heartfelt messages which came across to us as a Commission' (Report of the Commission on Poverty, Participation and Power, 2000: 3).

In contemporary constitutional democracies, the humanity of fellow beings is recognized when justice requires treating all citizens with equal respect. Equal respect implies that citizens must be viewed as fellow human beings with similar worth and be awarded equal political rights for meaningful participation in the democratic political system. It can be explained as follows.

Equal respect is part of the normative foundations of contemporary constitutional democracies. It is universally applicable to all citizens of a country. This is recognition respect, which means that kind of respect we owe all persons simply because they are human beings, regardless whether they are rich or poor (Darwall, 1977: 38, 39, 45). To have equal recognition respect for every human being means that some things are due them because they are human, regardless of wealth, poverty, desert, merit, race, moral or religious views and lifestyle.

The basic thing due to citizens accorded equal respect is to be recognized as human beings of equal moral worth, that in contemporary constitutional democracies implies being holders of equal political rights. This is accepted as standard practice in most contemporary constitutional democracies. The first principle of John Rawls's theory of justice spells out what basic liberties for each individual mean. Equal basic liberties include the right to vote and to be eligible for public office, together with freedom of speech and assembly, 'liberty of conscience and freedom of thought; freedom of the person along with the right to hold personal property; and freedom from arbitrary arrest and seizure as defined by the concept of the rule of law' (1971: 61).

To be a holder of equal political liberties does not automatically resolve all forms of injustice. For example, despite having been assigned equal basic liberties, black people and women have had major political struggles in contemporary constitutional democracies to secure their equal treatment as citizens. Racism and sexism, that often flourish despite the existence of equal political liberties for everyone, are sometimes causes of poverty or reinforce and exacerbate the harmful effects of poverty.

Although equal political rights do not by themselves necessarily eradicate poverty, they can directly contribute to such efforts through enabling equal participation in societal decision making processes. Note how Rawls demonstrates this point. When he applies his first principle of justice to the political procedures defined by the constitution, he argues that it leads to the idea of equal representation of every citizen in the decision making process. According to Rawls, this implies that each vote of a citizen should have 'approximately the same weight in determining the outcome of elections' (1971: 221–3). This means that political representatives should each represent the same amount of voters in at least one of the chambers of a national assembly (good reasons might exist for suggesting a different form of representation in the other).

Equal political representation can have great significance for poor people as it will enable them to 'express their interests and experience in public, on an equal basis with other groups', thus avoiding group domination (Young, 1990: 95). According to Young (185), democratic institutions should facilitate such public expression of needs and interests of people who are socially marginalized or silenced, as such expression is a major instrument for countering social oppression. However, effective representation in the major political institutions of society is not enough. Young encourages the involvement of all persons in collective discussion and decision making in all the 'settings that depend on their commitment, action and obedience to rules', such as schools and workplaces (191).

Young's call thus represents a moral claim that poor people must be represented and thus empowered to participate in decision making in any setting of society where their interests are at stake and where citizens govern themselves in one way or another. If poor people have effective representation and are assured that their voices are heard by those in power, they might not feel, as they often do, that they are being deprived, that their interests are neglected, their protests ignored and their claims to equal citizenship insufficiently fulfilled. A recent UK commission on poverty concludes that 'genuine participation in decision making by people experiencing poverty has great rewards', in part because it is a 'means of empowering individuals and communities' (Report of the Commission on Poverty, Participation and Power, 2000: 6).

The requirement of equal respect as a duty of justice protects poor people from negative behaviour from non-poor citizens. For example, looking down on poor people with contempt because of their poverty is not acceptable. Blaming poor people for their own poverty through one-sided explanations attributing poverty to their biological, genetic or moral inferiority, or lack of favour with the gods seems also like actions intended to humiliate poor people as human beings of far lesser worth. Stereotyping poor people as though they all are the same and their poverty has the same explanation similarly amounts to behaviour violating their shared humanity.

Equal respect further implies that simply because another human being exists, we are wrong to treat that person in some ways and right to treat the person in other ways. For example, no person may inflict bodily injury on any person without having sufficient reasons, acceptable in a court of law, for doing so. Note how such a requirement of justice can protect poor people.

Most poor people's bodies are at greater risk of dangers than those of other citizens. Women collecting firewood or water are at risk of sexual harassment and assault. Many poor women are at particular risk of domestic violence. Most poor people are at risk of interpersonal violence and crime – phenomena that are far more prevalent in poor areas than elsewhere. Having to rely on cheap energy resources such as wood and paraffin exposes some poor people's bodies to pollution and high risks of fires. Fires easily burn down some of their houses, often made of highly flammable material like wood or plastic. Fires also spread rapidly in their densely, often overpopulated areas. The risk of premature, preventable death increases with the choice of energy, such as wood and paraffin and the lack of adequate food to ensure a healthy body resistant to disease.

Equal respect furthermore requires that people must be respected in their own terms. Adults must be treated as adults, children as children. Poor children sometimes suffer massive injustices. Some frustrated, tired and highly stressed poor parents inflict cruel punishment on their children's bodies. Some parents or supervising adults push or sell children into prostitution to earn extra income, leaving major psychological scars. The need for extra income often forces some poor children to work when they should still have played. The adult responsibility of full-time or part-time labour, inside or outside the household, robs many poor children of their special childhood opportunities for psychological growth and intellectual development.

Thus, to give all citizens their due by fully recognizing their human dignity and worth will significantly impact on the lives of poor people. Nickel (2005: 394) argues simply in this matter, that is, that we respect a person's dignity 'when we protect his life and agency and when we prevent others from imposing treatment that is severely degrading or unfair'.

Poverty and the Justice of Reciprocity

The second issue of justice is to determine on what basis humans who are owed justice ought to cooperate. What do we owe one another in terms of cooperation required for individual or group purposes? In this category, called *justice as reciprocity*, issues arise that deal with the nature, scope and contents of fair terms of cooperation between citizens at inter-personal, social and institutional levels.

It is not without reason that the idea of a contract has been – and still is – so influential in modern political philosophy. Many aspects of the public lives of citizens, of their social lives as members of communities and associations and of their personal lives as individuals in interpersonal relationships can be characterized in terms of quasi-contractual agreements where two or more parties make an implicit or explicit agreement that defines their relationship, specify duties and responsibilities and outline benefits and advantages. Hampshire (2000: 4) argues that 'fairness in procedures for resolving conflicts is the fundamental kind of fairness . . . acknowledged as a value in most cultures, places and times'.

How to determine fair terms of cooperation at different levels in society and what qualifies as being fair cooperation between different people are important issues of justice. Rawls explicitly asks under what conditions rich and talented people can expect the willing cooperation of the poor and disadvantaged members of their society. If we accept that both rich and poor people are needed to make the effective functioning of society possible, can the well-to-do citizens both respect their fellow but disadvantaged citizens and have an attitude that those citizens must merely accept the terms of cooperation as dished out and dictated by the powerful elite? What would be just ways of cooperation that give every citizen the respect they are due?

The procedure for determining fair terms of cooperation must itself be evaluated in terms of justice, as an unfair procedure generally does not lead to a just outcome. Thus, all procedures for determining outcomes that affect any aspect of justice need moral evaluation to determine whether they allow justice to prevail. For example, the procedures of criminal courts need evaluation to determine whether they are fair toward the victims, the accused, the prosecutors, the defenders and the judge so that retributive justice will be satisfied. Similarly, the procedures for selecting national sports teams must be judged whether they are just toward all serious contenders for such coveted positions.

The terms of cooperation mutually agreed upon can be presupposed in social conventions, embodied in promises, agreements and contracts, or specified in responsibilities and obligations (see Mill, 1939: 931). In modern constitutional democracies many strong agreements are written in the constitution or laws of a state. The terms of cooperation can be found in many other places as well. They can be raised knowingly and voluntarily as expectations by us through our own conduct, as when charitable donations over time raise expectations of continued or improved aid. Promises by aid agencies or agreements with local governments or businesses can also lead to informal assumptions of terms of cooperation between aid-givers and the needy.

Government policies outlining strategies and plans for eradicating poverty are promises to poor members of the electorate that a vote for the party will change their lives. Similarly, when rights accorded to poor people to have their basic needs fulfilled are included as part of a bill of rights in a state's constitution they raise expectations. Poor people can legitimately expect that government and non-poor citizens will fulfil their correlative duties and take up their responsibilities. The rights of poor people do indeed make government and non-poor people respondents of those rights, which imply the latter have duties to fulfil those rights and responsibilities to provide poor people with the goods the rights assign them.

Michael Walzer (1983: 65, 79, 82–3) illustrates justice as reciprocity through his focus on the importance of a moral bond between citizens – recognized as humans of equal moral dignity – which allows all to participate in determining the extent to which a society must provide for its members' needs. Such a moral bond that expresses the requirements of justice as reciprocity can protect poor people, not in the least by also having a positive impact on their self-respect.

Walzer's awareness of the conditions of poverty provides the background for his view of a moral bond between citizens, expressed in his interpretation of the idea of a social contract. For Walzer a social contract is an agreement between citizens to make collective decisions about the goods necessary to the common life of people in a society and to implement those decisions (1983: 65). All citizens must be able to participate in debates about the meaning and implications of the social contract, otherwise their interests would be neglected and excluded. For this reason Walzer describes the social contract as a moral bond between weak and strong citizens, which commits them to continually re-negotiate the terms of the contract to accord with their shared understandings of needs.

Walzer's version of the social contract as an expression of solidarity between citizens has enormous positive value for poor people. It offers a view of citizens having moral ties with one another, committed to engage in dialogue about the nature and extent of communal provision for needs they regard as important. Poor people are thus equally respected, as they have a voice to promote their interests, the opportunity to present their distress and a chance to negotiate the terms of any relief or aid provided to them. Walzer's idea of a social contract furthermore implies that the contents thereof will depend on the values, convictions and beliefs of citizens in a sovereign state, which can change over time. It also affirms his strong emphasis on the value of political community, which in this case implies that citizens have stronger obligations to poor people within their own community than to those outside.

Some poor people can be vulnerable to injustice when unfair procedures are used to determine fair terms of cooperation. Often their powerless political position might have excluded them from participation in designing the procedures. As a result such procedures might be discriminatory to their interests. More likely, perhaps, is the possibility that the procedures are applied to their detriment, as they are sometimes too powerless to resist the pressure and manipulation exerted by powerful members of their society on weak or immoral implementers of procedures, like corrupt judges in courts of law.

Poor people are also very vulnerable when other groups in society refuse to implement mutual agreements or to deliver on promises made earlier. Poor people often do not have the authority to demand that others in society keep their side of agreements, or they sometimes do not have the power or self-confidence to resist unilaterally broken promises.

Poverty and the Justice of Enablement

The third issue of justice has to do with the opportunities human beings need to fulfil their potential to live worthwhile human lives. What kind of opportunities are due to us so that we can develop worthwhile lives of our own choosing? Therefore justice as enablement concerns the extent to which institutions, laws, policies and human behaviour enable or constrain the self-development and self-determination of people in society.

When people are constrained to develop and use their capacities, they are being oppressed. When people are hindered to participate in determining the course of their lives, they are being dominated (Young, 1990: 22, 37). Oppression and domination are thus the modes of the injustice of disablement. Oppression and domination need not necessarily be the result of individual actions or the consequence of identifiable social actors, such as governments or businesses. As Young argues, they could result from many actions by individuals and institutional actors that combine into conditions, circumstances and institutions that constrain the lives, opportunities, skills and talents of groups of people.

Justice as enablement has as goal to empower persons to become inter-dependent citizens competent to contribute appropriately to the effective functioning of society through fitting social cooperation. Individual citizens can be enabled through various means such as education and training, provision of information, consumer protection, safe spaces created by political rights and laws and so on. Little argues that individuals 'can only take advantage of social opportunities when they have had a chance to develop their human capacities to a reasonable degree and this requires fair access to social goods as education, health care and nutrition' (2003: 104).

Poverty is an example of a condition consisting of many possible elements that can constrain people's lives significantly and disable them into lives far below their capacity. Lack of economic capacities to engage in empowering education or meaningful self-improvement immediately springs to mind. Greater susceptibility to disease and less economic capacities to care for one's personal health are other disabling factors. The lack of opportunities for participation in generally accepted social activities and sharing in the richness of social interaction with fellow citizens is another factor that disables poor people.

In a sense, poor people are economically disabled people. More accurate would be to refer to poor people as people disabled in various ways and to different degrees through lack of resources that they can convert through education, training and experience into skills and competencies. The independence of people can suffer in different ways as a result of poverty. Poor people's independence is restricted by the way that poverty curtails their ability to make decisions about their own lives for lack of resources they command and opportunities they are able to utilize.

Why is interdependence so important to human beings as a measure and facilitator of enabling growth? What is the link between justice as enablement and healthy relations of interdependence between citizens? In what follows, I want to spell out the significance of interdependence as part of justice as enablement, an issue that matters a lot to individual citizens. I argue that independence depicts the degree to which citizens have been enabled to be self-reliant within their network of interdependent relationships.

Interdependence characterizes healthy relationships where adult people experience both dependence on and independence from other people. All humans are mutually interdependent – they are dependent on others for certain things, others depend on them for other things and all of them are independent with respect to part of their own range of needs and interests. The dependence relevant here has to do with the basic components of daily living. Most adults are not entirely dependent on others for moving around their own bodies, for washing and dressing themselves, for supplying their own basic means of life and so on. This means that there are certain things that human beings normally do for themselves and mostly want to do for themselves, without always needing others or being dependent on the assistance of someone else.

Let's have a look at some of the disempowering disabilities caused by poverty that an effective conception of justice as enablement can prevent from occurring. Some very poor people can be dependent on others for food, clothes, income, housing, transport and for raising their children.

These are things most people want to do or provide for themselves, or pay others to do or provide them. To be dependent on others for those things means one has to rely on the goodwill of generous benefactors, which can be degrading. If a very poor person does not want to be dependent on others for these things, the only alternatives available might be to go without them or to steal to have them. Both alternatives can add further harm to very poor people. Furthermore, dependent people can not easily engage in mutually interdependent relationships, as their ability to give something of themselves to others is often severely restricted.

Dependency and feelings of resignation on a personal level easily turn into political powerlessness. On the other hand, political powerlessness and inequality suffered by some poor people can reinforce personal dependency and resignation. Poverty leads to inequalities in the democratic process as some poor people do not have the means available to compete with the more affluent groups. Poor people often experience that their democratic rights are of lesser worth as a result of their meagre means to utilize such rights. If some poor people's further lack of command of resources is added to their lack of political influence, their experience of being socially disabled is strengthened. Adding political powerlessness to some poor people's lack of social and economic power increases their dependence on the decisions of others to determine the course of their lives.

One important result of social and political powerlessness is that many poor people's bargaining power with political authorities is limited. Consequently their ability to secure adequate public services is limited. Often poor areas are neglected in the provision of public services such as education, electricity, roads, water provision, recreation facilities and health services. This often contributes to environmental degradation, adding to the pressure placed on the environment by aspects of poor lifestyles, such as desperate needs for firewood, inadequate space for animal grazing, overcrowded housing conditions, lack of public amenities and services aiming to beautify urban surroundings. An environment without adequate services and amenities that lacks opportunities for self-development, recreation and aesthetic enjoyment further constrains poor people's self-development.

It is striking to note to what extent personal aspects associated with the phenomenon of poverty disable many poor people to develop themselves and constrain their scope to determine their own lives. Many poor people's bodies suffer from an inadequate diet, leading to stunted growth, more diseases and less resistance to them than other people. Furthermore, their bodies have pain and scars that result from interpersonal violence and the damage and dependence caused by substance abuse, like alcohol, for example. These effects on the bodies of poor people constrain children's physical development and diminish the health and fitness of adults needed for motivated work. Hungry and painful bodies have diminished abilities for concentration on work that needs to be done, thus decreasing poor people's performance in their daily work.

Meaningful interpersonal interaction is an enabling factor that can draw forth our best qualities. The nurture provided by family life can strongly enable people to develop their talents to become their best. The social bond of family life is at great risk for many poor people. Fractured family relations can severely constrain healthy psychological development and consume vast amounts of whatever precious little energy poor people have left after other struggles to survive. Domestic violence over the distribution of household resources and the division of household duties place further constraints on family members, usually women and children, who suffer from male violence. Their freedom of speech and personal autonomy are restricted through violent domination. In many cases, poor parents are too tired or stressed to take proper care of their children. In other cases, children grow up apart from their parents with other family members, thus deprived of the valuable resource of parental guidance and nurturing love that parents can give. Poor children's psychological and emotional development can thus often be constrained through these factors.

Poor people are often disabled to fully participate in the richness of meaningful interpersonal relationships outside their family. Poor people are sometimes not capable of maintaining social relationships through lack of funds to invite people over, or because they cannot afford to participate in the lifestyles dominant in their communities. They might not have enough money available for the food, clothes and proper interior decorations needed to sustain certain kinds of social relationships. Money for membership, the right clothing or gear and lack of time might disqualify many poor people from social activities such as participation in cultural organizations, clubs or sporting events. They do not have the money to develop those aspects of their lives.

As a result of the social isolation many poor people often find themselves in, they are stereotyped or stigmatized by non-poor people. This behaviour means that non-poor people look down on poor people, refuse to associate with them and treat them with disrespect in social interactions. These actions become another constraining factor in the lives of poor people, making it difficult to present themselves with self-confidence in social situations other than those with their closest family or friends.

Poor people in some conditions more often use interpersonal violence for resolving conflict. This more excessive use of violence becomes another constraining factor in their lives, as violence leaves not only physical signs of abuse, but mental scars as well. Fear and distrust become part of life, with destructive effects on interpersonal relationships and the social fabric of poor communities. Sometimes moral decay follows when people become desperately poor and struggle to survive. Crime often follows as consequence of moral decay, creating further pressure on vulnerable people who sometimes have fragile social networks of support. Crime and violence disable individuals through creating fear and increasing anxiety by destroying the trust that cements social bonds.

In the light of the explanations above poverty can be described as a disabling condition that places many restrictions on people's ability to determine their own lives and develop themselves. Lack of self-respect, reinforced by public stereotyping, undermines many poor people's confidence to change their situation. Lack of basic skills as a result of inadequate access to educational and self-improvement opportunities make it difficult to design creative solutions to the problems of poverty. Lack of time and money places further constraints on people's ability to change their lives, as does the inability to tap into social and political resources that can help to address problems of poverty collectively. On the whole, then, poverty is a major disabling condition.

We generally assume that aid enables most poor people to improve their lives. However, some poor people's dependence on aid disables them. Let me explain. Some desperately poor people experience themselves as powerless to change their situation. They often have a negative self-image and feelings of inferiority. As a result they resign themselves to their desperate condition. Experiencing poverty over a long period can strengthen these feelings and create a so-called 'culture of poverty' in a community. Even aid can deepen these feelings through making people dependent and thus disable poor people to develop their own initiative and take care of themselves. Poverty can thus constrain people's ability to function as mutually interdependent and relatively self-sufficient citizens.

Full and effective implementation of a view on justice as enablement can comprehensively prevent this disabling condition from wreaking its havoc on human beings.

Poverty and the Justice of Distribution

The fourth issue of justice concerns the goods every person can or should have. What 'goods' and 'services' do we owe one another and for what reasons? Thus in the oft-discussed category of *justice as distribution* the equitable distribution of goods that can be distributed like and analogously to, material possessions is at issue. These goods are means for living the best way that you choose and are able to. So the major issue revolves around the 'fair assignment of benefits that result from joint efforts' (Little, 2003: 97). How can a liberal egalitarian conception of justice illuminate some of the issues of distributive justice?

Most participants in the debates on justice assume that a major part of the concept of justice refers to the distribution of goods. Working on this assumption, John Rawls defines the concept of justice as referring to the principles used to guide the adjudication of conflicting claims to more of the benefits and less of the burdens that result from the life that a group of individuals share together in a specific society (1971: 9–10).

From this skeleton Rawlsian definition of distributive justice we see that justice as distribution has at its centre the notion of an allotment of things (goods) to (specific) persons – whether the allotment of benefits such as income, wealth, goods, offices and privileges, or the allotment of burdens such as hard work and lack of adequate income (Frankena, 1962: 9). To secure distributive justice in a specific society the adjudication of conflicting claims should be done according to principles of justice that lead to a division of benefits and burdens that create a proper balance between such claims. The application of such principles of justice must prohibit the making of arbitrary distinctions between persons in the process of the adjudication of conflicting claims to society's distributable goods (Rawls, 1985: 165).

Obviously we often employ different criteria in this context, depending on the nature of goods, services or whatever else is at stake. In some cases we award prizes for excellent achievement or a financial bonus for work performance beyond the call of duty. In other cases we pay wages for work well done or we choose team members based on recent performance. We appoint employees based on merit and potential and we provide assistance based on demonstrated need. Let us look at one or two examples of justice as distribution that will show the power of justice to prevent or eradicate poverty.

A good indicator whether distributive justice prevails in a society is to note what different people have in terms of income and wealth. What people have depends on how the resources and opportunities available in a society have been divided. For example, wealth is one of the benefits of a society. Who are the wealthy people in a society and how did they acquire their wealth? Distributive injustice exists when the benefits and burdens available in a society are unfairly divided between different individuals and groups in a society. Benefits are wealth, income, property, opportunities to education and good employment. Burdens are hard or dirty work and taxes, for example.

But what is a fair distribution? For a liberal egalitarian conception of justice it means at the very least that no citizen is without the basic goods and services to acquire the minimal living standard appropriate to their society. No wealthy citizen can give any acceptable reason to a poor citizen for possessing excessive income and wealth while the poor citizen suffers from deprivation of all kinds. If these two imaginary citizens stand face to face as free and equal citizens endowed with a set of equal human rights, what morally acceptable reasons could the rich citizens have to justify their opulence at the expense of the poor people's decrepitude? If the rich recognize poor people as their equals, they should want to 'seek terms of social and political organization that could not reasonably be rejected' (Krause, 2001: 319) by any of them. Thus, what are the terms that the rich then impose on the poor? Why are the rich not willing to offer their poor fellow citizens the chance to veto those terms as unreasonable?

Investigating suspected distributive injustice requires answers to several questions, as originally formulated by Robert Nozick in his historical, unpatterned theory of justice (1974). Let's say there is a pattern of one group of people being far more wealthy than another. Two questions must be asked. One question deals with the origin and history of the wealth or poverty of these people. We must establish how the rich people acquired their wealth. They might have had a better education. If this is true, then the reasons for them having better educational opportunities must be investigated. Rich people may have acquired their wealth from their ancestors. If this is so, then the way their ancestors acquired their wealth needs to be looked at. Did they perhaps illegitimately acquire their wealth?

Next, the investigation must focus on how wealth was transferred through generations to determine whether these transfers were fair. If rich people legitimately acquired and transferred their wealth to current generations, then their riches might be justly possessed (see Nozick, 1974: 150–3). However, if their wealth was based on unfair access to better opportunities for self-development or economic advantage than those available to other people, then their wealth is based on injustice that needs to be rectified.

Their wealth might also be based on unjust acquisition of resources through conquest or political domination. In such cases of unjust distributions, compensation is called for.

However, a moderately unequal division of benefits and burdens is not necessarily unjust. There may be good reasons why the president of a country gets a bigger salary than a teacher. What should be looked for is whether there are patterns in the division of benefits and burdens that could be judged skew and unfair. For example, do women teachers generally get lower salaries than their male colleagues? If the answer to the question is yes, there is good reason to investigate whether some kind of injustice is responsible for these patterns of some people being worse off than others.

John Rawls provides an interesting defence of an unequal division of the benefits of society that nevertheless is in the interests of the poor. He justifies an unequal distribution of income and wealth in his second principle of justice as necessary incentives to elicit the full cooperation and optimum productivity of the more talented persons. The principle goes as follows: 'Social and economic inequalities are to be arranged so that they are both (a) to the greatest benefit of the least advantaged and (b) attached to offices and positions open to all under conditions of fair equality of opportunity' (1971: 83). In terms of this principle, inequalities in a society should (1) provide incentives to the innovative and productive members of society and (2) benefit the least advantaged persons, otherwise such inequalities are unjust. Thus, high incomes for professionals such as doctors and engineers can only be justified if they lead to an improvement in the lot of the least advantaged people.

This aspect of Rawls's difference principle expresses care for poor people, as their interests must dominate when deciding which unequal divisions of income and wealth can be justifiably allowed. Rawls (1993 and 2001) stresses the importance of each citizen having a social minimum of all-purpose means with which to make a decent life. His difference principle provides an articulation of the democratic ideal of solidarity (fraternity) which could significantly improve at least the relative income and wealth of poor people.

An appropriate conception of distributive justice can protect poor people significantly, as they in general suffer many distributive injustices. Classifying people as 'poor' means by definition that they have very little income and practically no wealth compared with the abundance others in society have. The degree of inequality in some societies is staggering. If the gap between rich and poor becomes so pronounced that the rich live in luxury with holiday homes and luxury cars, while the poor can hardly afford enough food, live in houses that fail to protect them against the elements, have to make do with dangerous fuels that endanger their health and life and have to walk long distances to collect water of questionable quality, then their position relative to others in society seems radically unjust.

In the area of the household, gender relations have a profound influence on distributive issues of justice. Male domination is currently strongly contested, as it is believed to be unjust. Nevertheless, men continue to dominate and negatively influence the lives of many women. Enforced stereotypes about the role of women within the household make their lives particularly difficult in situations of poverty. The distribution of resources and responsibilities within a household can become matters of intense conflict, often resolved through violence or the threat thereof. As a result of male dominance, many poor women have most of the responsibility for household management and duties. Some poor women take hours to fetch water, collect firewood or to do washing and cleaning. These domestic services are mostly unpaid labour that deprives women of free time for self-improvement or productive activities. The unequal division of household duties on gender lines often severely disadvantages women to the benefit of men.

Justice as distribution deals not only with the distribution of benefits, but also burdens. Doing hard work, such as cleaning up dirt, is one of the burdens of a society. Who does this work and did they have other choices? The distribution of work opportunities – especially the more negative ones that have inadequate pay – is a difficult problem. How should these jobs be distributed? They must be done, are difficult and hard to do, but nevertheless leave those doing them poor as a result of low pay. Michael Walzer presents specific proposals which can help to alleviate the plight of these poor people in his discussion of hard work (1983: 165–83).

Walzer defines hard work as harsh, unpleasant and difficult to endure. People usually do not choose such work if they have any alternative, as it has a negative status in society and often leads to poverty, ill health, dishonour and degradation. Whereas the risks and dangers of military service can be equally divided amongst citizens, the risks and dangers of coal mining do not come from a public enemy. This difference, as well as the strong bond between miners and the fact that their work is best done with experience, does not necessitate an equal sharing of this work amongst citizens.

Nevertheless, the work of miners does serve the interests of the political community and for this reason the political community should ease their burden in various ways, such as supporting research into mine safety, making health care available for their specific needs, enabling early retirement and ensuring decent salaries and pensions (Walzer, 1983: 170). Thus, instead of exposing mine workers to hard, gruelling work, degrading poverty and many risks to their health and well-being, they are regarded as fellow citizens of equal moral standing, who are treated as such in their dangerous work. Through trade union membership they gain a voice in determining the contents of the communal social contract.

To ensure the eradication of existing poverty and the prevention of any future poverty will thus require the effective enforcement of a conception of distributive justice that treats every citizen fairly as an equal.

Poverty and the Justice of Accountability

What do we owe one another when we do actions that do not fall within the requirements of justice, or when we refrain from actions that are required by justice? The fifth issue of justice deals with different ways to ensure humans comply with a shared conception of justice. In the category *justice as accountability* the focus is on how to assign responsibilities and to find appropriate sanctions, penalties or punishment for those persons who violate society's accepted principles of justice. Justice as accountability also has its focus on rewards for just behaviour. Accountability presupposes a clear vision of what injustice is and clarity on the concept of responsibility, so as to be able to accurately determine who must be held responsible for doing justice and who must be called to account for specific injustices and to what degree. The well-known idea of justice as retribution is part of this category and implies appropriate punishment in whatever sense and through whichever legitimate institution or person if violations of precepts of justice have been fairly determined. John Stuart Mill regards 'the desire to punish a person who has done harm' as one of the two 'essential ingredients in the sentiment of justice' (1939: 936).

What does responsibility mean? Responsibility has different meanings, but the one relevant here is the following. Responsibility means that a person has an obligation to do something since they have to attend to matters they have control over and because something or someone is within their care or their sphere of influence. Thus, responsibility means that a person is answerable for the manner in which they execute such duties. Some persons or groups could thus hold persons or other groups to account for their actions in respect of such duties over which they have control or ought to have control. To hold people responsible for their actions is an integral part of a democratic society. People must demand that politicians, bureaucrats and ordinary citizens explain or justify any kind of conduct that they regard as violating precepts, principles and norms of justice. Citizens can demand accountability, that is, government officials justifiably give publicly acceptable reasons why certain laws were made, why they chose policies and why they set specific priorities.

Justice as accountability presupposes that we have reliable ways of identifying injustice. Injustice has to do with actions or events that harm, injure or constrain people. Injustice might occur when people are denied their rights or refused their valid claims to society's benefits. Injustices are brought about by individual or collective human agents and thus socially controllable or politically avoidable. To accurately identify injustice and hold people responsible, a distinction between injustice and misfortune is necessary (see Shklar, 1990). Misfortune is unavoidable and cannot be altered through human intervention. Injustice, by contrast, is brought about by human beings and can thus be socially controlled or avoided.

The distinction between misfortune and injustice can become blurred in some cases. Nevertheless, this distinction matters. Misfortune must be accepted, while injustice can be rectified and compensated. If poverty, for example, is the result of inevitable and unalterable events, it has to be accepted. If poverty results from events that are alterable and avoidable, it becomes an injustice to be rectified and compensated. Poverty caused by natural forces, such as drought or floods, could be considered a misfortune, though only if there are no people who have the responsibility to prepare for such disasters, issue warnings of imminent disasters, repair the damage done and prevent similar catastrophes from recurring.

The difficulties of distinguishing between misfortune and injustice can be explained as follows (see Shklar, 1990). Earthquakes and famines are usually explained as misfortune. This might not be true. Although they are natural and unavoidable, people today expect that governments will warn and protect them from natural disasters. Furthermore, people can make the impact of natural disasters worse. For example, buildings collapse during earthquakes because 'contractors have violated construction codes and bribed inspectors', people die because they were not warned of the dangers or public authorities fail to make 'serious preparations for the eventuality' (Shklar, 1990: 2). The impact of floods, for example, can be exacerbated where forests are plundered and destroyed or where agricultural practices and urban developments strip land of natural barriers and sponges that reduce the impact of raging torrents of water.

Once we have determined injustice and the people responsible, we must still decide on the degree of responsibility people have for injustice. The degree of responsibility for injustice is strongly affected by the distinction between active and passive injustice (Shklar, 1990). Active injustice occurs when perpetrators of injustice deprive people of possessions or opportunities, harm other people's bodies or lives and violate their dignity. Passive injustice results from persons who are indifferent to injustice happening. Passively unjust persons are people who tolerate injustice and ignore the claims of victims of injustice. Shklar depicts citizens who are passively unjust as any of us: 'when we do not report crimes, when we look the other way when we see cheating and minor thefts, when we tolerate political corruption and when we silently accept laws that we regard as unjust, unwise or cruel' (1990: 6).

Passive injustice can also be found at governmental level where a lack of motivation and caring, or a shortage of competence, efficient skills and lively agency exist among officials. One often finds so-called 'weak states' that cannot effectively administer their own conception of justice (see O'Neill, 2001). These states do not have the economic resources, the educated labour power or the political will to implement and enforce the conception of justice accepted and professed by members of their society. They thus cannot 'do very much to secure or improve justice within their boundaries' (O'Neill, 2001: 190). Justice, argues O'Neill, must be 'built by a diversity of agents and agencies that possess . . . varying ranges of capabilities' (ibid.: 194).

Passive injustice is important when discussing the link between poverty and justice as accountability. The idea of passive injustice helps us point out the responsibility of non-poor people for allowing people to continue living in conditions of poverty. In many societies non-poor people often allow poor people to die from ill health, fail to protect them from injustice and exploitation, do nothing to alleviate their lack of food, clothing and shelter and fail to enhance their opportunities for self-development and growth. Although non-poor people do nothing to visibly exacerbate the lot of poor people, they also do nothing to change or improve their situation, while the non-poor presumably have the ability and means to do so. Standing by while some people suffer from so much difficulties inflicted by a social disease like poverty makes non-poor people guilty of acting unjustly through violation of the positive intent of principles and norms of justice.

Poverty and the Justice of Transformation

What do we owe one another when our ideas and practices of justice are in need of meaningful change? The sixth issue of justice rests on an acknowledgement that conceptions of justice change over time and therefore just ways and means must be found to comply with a new, improved conception of justice. Thus, in *justice as transformation* problems of changing existing institutions, practices and behaviour are explored. Matters such as rectifying past injustices, compensating victims of serious injustices and dealing with the legacy of physical, social and emotional harm inflicted by past injustice are discussed.

In the case of poverty the issues would be how to transform the condition of poor people to one of self-sufficient, mutually interdependent citizens with self-respect. If this is the end goal, the question must be how poor people can take the initiative to drive this transformation for themselves while enlisting the needed help from others. Despite the importance of allowing poor people to take the initiative in their own transformation, listening to victims of poverty and speaking on their behalf might be appropriate in cases of desperate poverty where people may have been so affected by poverty as to need others to help them to help themselves.

How should citizens of contemporary constitutional democracies deal with victims of poverty? Judith Shklar judges a modern constitutional democracy to be the best available response to the sense of injustice, for the reason that it does not 'simply silence every expression of the sense of injustice' (1990: 117). Furthermore, people committed to a constitutional democracy accept 'expressions of felt injustice as a mandate for change', instead of resorting to repression as most other regimes would do (ibid.: 85). Listening to poor people would be important to determine their needs and their sense of society's injustice against them.

The awareness of victims in Western democracies in recent times has been politically significant, as the sense of injustice created thereby has 'not merely festered, but has led to new institutions' (Shklar, 1990: 37). The openness to accusations of injustice made by citizens functions as a 'protection against oppression' for them (ibid.: 55) and as an invaluable asset for all citizens who have an interest in 'maintaining high standards of public service and rectitude' (ibid.: 5). Openness to demands that injustice be rectified thus fulfils a vital function in protecting the moral and social health of a constitutional democracy.

Knowing that fellow citizens take them seriously as fellow-citizens-who-are-victims, poor people might explore opportunities for political protest against the injustice of their specific cases of poverty. Transforming any social condition through public means will require political mobilization that is dependent on adequate public space for political protest. For this reason one must note the extent of civil liberties available in society and the degree to which dissatisfied citizens are tolerated to act on them.

Protest enabled by the spaces provided by civil liberties are not only important as means for reaching the goal of transforming social injustices, but also for the transforming effect they have on the protesters. Poor people publicly protesting their condition are rising up to deny their powerlessness, making a start to assert their rights to develop their potential to determine their lives and thus to regain their self-respect as people who refuse to be treated in humiliating ways. Michael Walzer calls mobilization for collective protest action against the violation of their humanity through protest movements action by virtuous citizens and refers to protest movements as the 'breeding grounds of self-respecting citizens' (1983: 311). When poor citizens demand to deliberate with their fellow citizens, start to take responsibility for their views on economic and social change and publicly protest the violation of their rights, they are exercising political power in defence of their rights. Such citizens respect themselves by not allowing fellow citizens or governmental authorities to violate any of their rights through either acts of commission or omission.

If poor people can assert their rights and demand social change to rectify their situation, part of the change must be to determine who had any responsibility for causing poverty and thus needs to compensate poor people in an effort to restore them to mutually interdependent, self-sustaining, equally respected, fellow citizens.

Conclusion

In this chapter I have explained the meaning of justice in the context of modern constitutional democracies by looking at the possibilities of a liberal-egalitarian conception of justice to function as a powerful deterrent to prevent poverty from occurring or to enable citizens to eradicate existing poverty from their midst. I have shown how such a conception of justice can counter and prevent some of the obvious harmful effects of poverty. A strong conception of justice duly adhered to can effectively rid a society of poverty, judged to be a major disabling privation.

The idea that an effectively implemented theory of justice can prevent poverty suggests that shared collective values must guide social organization and direct core governance functions. Although lots of opportunities exist for individuals and smaller groups to deal with poverty, ultimately the various tenacious manifestations of poverty require team work by a whole society for their long-term eradication. At least, that is what the complex configuration of symptoms, effects, consequences and causes of poverty thus far discussed suggest and what I want to argue for in the next chapter.

10 · Do We Do This Alone or Together?

I have thus far made a very important assumption that has nowhere been explicitly addressed and justified yet. Let me try to do so now. The assumption is that certain human problems cannot be effectively dealt with by individuals only. We cannot by ourselves build a road for all the routes we want to travel. We cannot set up a state-of-the art medical facility for our own heart operation through our own individual ingenuity and innovation. We cannot build a computer for our own use by first manufacturing all the materials and the equipment needed to extract and synthesize the materials, or by first designing and producing the machines we need for the manufacture of the parts. Certain human tasks can only be conceived and effectively done as cooperative ones that must be done collectively by teams of individuals working in close cooperation. How can I argue for a position that dealing with poverty is a similar kind of human challenge?

Threats to the idea we must do this together

There are several views that threaten the idea that poverty is a human condition that can best be dealt with through collective human action. Not everyone sees poverty as a human condition that we can fully prevent or heal, depending on the way we construct a social order or, more accurately, the values we institutionalize to guide our economic exchanges, guard financial transactions and direct our social policies. These threats are (1) the idea that poverty can best be addressed through individual people who must fulfil their duties of charity, (2) the notion that poverty is something that is inevitable and will always be part of human society no matter what and (3) the unfortunate fact that in many cases people with the responsibility to eradicate poverty are corrupt, incompetent or unwilling. Let us briefly look at each of these in turn to determine their worth.

Many people believe that poverty should be addressed through charitable work by individuals or non-governmental organizations. I always find it sad that those well-intentioned individuals, who try their best to fight poverty through helping poor individuals so often, though not always, become disillusioned through lack of success or meaningful signs of progress. However, the complexity of poverty and the complex configuration of factors involved in a specific case can paralyse and demoralize well-meaning individuals who do not have specialist knowledge. The limited role for such individuals still allows them useful things to do, such as offering poor people temporary relief from the distress poverty so often causes. But they often cannot accurately identify the causes of a specific case of poverty nor do they know exactly what interventions are needed to eradicate a specific case of poverty, or they do not have sufficient resources to address specific cases of poverty on an adequate scale.

The power of humans to collectively determine the nature of their shared social structure is often denied by people that claim the social order is determined by laws, fate, nature or the heavy weight of history, tradition and custom. This denial has been employed with such power to excuse appropriate, urgent action to do something about poverty that it must be looked at more closely. Note how poverty researchers have battled this seemingly plausible excuse in the past, an excuse that was referred to in an earlier chapter as the fallacy of false fixity.

Tawney sees in the British society of his time a general and 'almost unquestioning acceptance of habits and institutions, which vest in particular classes a special degree of public influence and an exceptional measure of economic opportunity' (1952: 71). Note how the unquestioning acceptance is the mechanism that allows the privileged elite the power and space to operate and exploit others in society.

Partha Dasgupta (1993: 128) says that the claim 'that "historical forces" have led poor societies to their present plight is one which, however true, [is] not only a conversation-stopper, but also a plank that has often been used by social scientists for condoning the most predatory of political regimes and oppressive of social practices'. He believes that to take this claim too literally, that is, historical forces determine our shared lives, is to 'overlook the existence of choice and thus responsibility. And that is to deny persons the respect that is owed to them.' Dasgupta's point is telling: acceptance of human subservience to 'historical forces' is demeaning and disrespectful to ourselves, as such an excuse requires us to deny some of the characteristics that make us uniquely human.

More often than not the collective power of ourselves in reshaping society is denied by inaction, through refusing to take responsibility for preventive or corrective action. Gunnar Myrdal (1970: 208–9) uses the concept of a 'soft state' to further explain why poverty is often ignored.

He defines a soft state as one that is lax in implementing and enforcing public controls. The lack of discipline that results in such states from arbitrary rule enforcement is 'exploited for personal gain by people who have economic, social and political power'. Obviously this laxity can be overcome, as we see in countries where poverty is reasonably effectively addressed.

At other times we deny our shared powers to determine social life by avoiding recognition of social problems affecting others that could be ameliorated through collective efforts. For example, how do we square our inaction with our moral values that implore us to act timeously and fittingly to reduce the suffering of our fellows? Thomas Nagel claims that other people's lives matter 'so hugely' from an impersonal standpoint that 'the recognition of it is hard to bear and most of us engage in some degree of suppression of the impersonal standpoint in order to avoid facing our pathetic failure to meet its claims' (1991: 19, 20). He calls this action a 'self-protective blocking out of the importance of others', which means 'denial of our full humanity'. Elsewhere Nagel (ibid.: 64) says that we are 'so accustomed to great social and economic inequalities that it is easy to become dulled to them'. Again, this dullness can be eliminated so that we can act on our most cherished values.

Our human power of reshaping society can also be disabled through corruption or lack of capacity. The UNDP claims that some well-intentioned socio-economic reforms fail because of a lack of proper governance. They have found that 'inept or unresponsive governance institutions can nullify the effect' of policies in favour of the poor, as also happens when 'a local elite diverts the resources for its own interests' (UNDP, 2000: 54). While this might sound like mild criticism of corruption, the report later on (55) states clearly that corruption 'directs income away from them and robs society of resources that it could deploy to combat poverty'. Effective strategies to minimize and eliminate governance failures are available and often successful.

Privileged elites furthermore often choose to do nothing to eradicate poverty, as they see the burdens suffered by poor people and the long-term disadvantages that poverty entails for society counterbalanced by their short-term personal and group interests privileged by current social arrangements. In such cases the rich are rich exactly because the poor are poor. Once again, democratic protest can call elites to account and restrict their space and opportunity to exploit others.

If these excuses for inaction all fail, what does the view of collective human responsibility for the social order imply for our dealings with poverty? We can now look at the eradication of poverty as follows. Poverty is the result of the choices humans make about the structures of their society, about the social forces they allow space to operate. Poverty exists by the grace of the collective choice of citizens that allows it to be. The levels of poverty and riches in society are thus the shared responsibility of its citizens. Poverty reflects a condition in which human beings live lives below those their fellow citizens think constitute an appropriate minimum for humans. Poverty, as a condition that either causes a decline in physical health or an inability to share in human social activities typical of our species, is entirely remediable. The continued, unabated existence of poverty reflects that non-poor citizens do not care enough about victims of poverty to change the social order to prevent, ameliorate or eradicate poverty. It is really as simple as that.

Let's suppose it is correct that poverty is a human condition that can be addressed through collective human action. Why, then, are so many human societies so ineffective in the ways they deal with poverty? Why is it so difficult to eradicate poverty in any sustainable way? The effects and consequences of poverty on individual lives show many overlaps and similarities with other conditions we know and deal with more effectively. If the consequences and effects of poverty show similarities with those of illness and disease, gross injustices, political domination and oppression, why do we not have institutions, resources and expertise to deal with poverty as effectively as we deal with these other conditions?

Perhaps someone will say that the medical facilities and personnel, political and judicial institutions and social policies in contemporary constitutional democracies are designed to deal with various distinct aspects or dimensions of poverty that are analogous to the other conditions mentioned. Poverty might thus be the collective name for a syndrome of interrelated human conditions, but each is worthy of being called the kind of hardship it independently is (see Halleröd, 2000: 183).

Let's suppose that is true. Let us suppose further that liberal-democratic institutions, facilities providing medical care and disciplinary institutions like schools and prisons are all designed to deal with one or more of the problematic conditions generated by poverty. The basic question then still remains: why do so many societies nevertheless have large numbers of poor people in their midst? If the right mechanisms, institutions and policies are in place to combat poverty and all the negative effects it entails, yet poverty persists on a significant, bothersome scale, how do we cross-check the sensitivity and workability of the precautions we have put in place? Why don't these institutions and policies eradicate poverty?

Perhaps the answer lies in the fact that we cannot adequately understand what poverty means unless we understand how poverty fits into a
broader understanding of society. A strong tradition of social thought
links the existence of poverty directly to the social order created within
a particular society or, more broadly, created within a broader region
or even the world as a whole. If this link between poverty and the social
order is correct, it implies that the eradication of poverty on a sustainable basis can only be accomplished through fundamental changes to
the social order. Let's look at some examples of major thinkers of the
past who argued for such links.

Note how the great poverty researcher J. Seebohm Rowntree interprets
the poverty he saw as part of the kind of society he lives in. Look at
how deeply disturbed he was about the results of this investigation. At
the end of his book, *Poverty: A Study in Town Life*, Rowntree refers to
'the gravity of the facts which have unfolded themselves' (1901: 304). He
consequently stresses the need for deep reflection 'by the nation about
the wellbeing of its own people' (ibid.).

What is the matter concerning the well-being of people that he thinks
requires such serious thought? That 'in this land of abounding wealth,
during a time of perhaps unexampled prosperity, probably more than
one-fourth of the population are living in poverty, is a fact which may
well cause great searchings of the heart' (ibid.). The issue disturbing him
so much is the simple fact of the huge contrast between 25 per cent of
citizens living in poverty with all the harmful effects he has just depicted
in fine detail, whilst he can simultaneously describe his country as
going through a period of 'unexampled prosperity' making it a 'land
of abounding wealth'. His observation that some have it so good in
terms of material possessions and wealth, while others suffer so much
as a result of their deprivation – this matter is so important to con-
template as the dominant humans in society allow this to be and do
nothing to relieve the suffering that could so easily be taken away through
the excessive resources employed for luxurious lifestyles.

Jean-Jacques Rousseau provides a good example of a philosopher
who explored this theme long ago. In his project to 'trace the origin and
progress of inequality', he concludes that 'all the inequality that now
prevails owes its strength and growth to the development of our faculties
and the advance of the human mind and becomes at last permanent
and legitimate by the establishment of property and laws' (1913: 221).
Rousseau blames 'society and law' for bounding 'new fetters on the poor'
and giving 'new powers to the rich'. In the process society 'subjected all

mankind to perpetual labour, slavery and wretchedness' for the 'advantage of a few ambitious individuals' (ibid.: 205). Note how harshly Rousseau condemns the ways in which human intelligence and ingenuity enabled a minority to privilege themselves at terrible cost for others, whilst they abuse social institutions and mechanisms to justify their unfair acquisitions.

He launches an attack against the social order that allowed poverty to persist in his time, directly addressing supposedly rich readers,

> Do you not know that numbers of your fellow-creatures are starving, for want of what you have too much of? You ought to have had the express and universal consent of mankind, before appropriating more of the common subsistence than you needed for your own maintenance. (1913: 204)

Note his accusation: people next door to you starve because they need things you have too much of. You have no right to your wealth that is so much more than you need for a decent life. You also do not have the consent of others to possess so much. Thus, by implication you have stolen your wealth from others who are now paying the price through suffering from hunger and all other kinds of deprivation.

Karl Marx made us aware how dominant groups exploit the labour of others to appropriate the surplus value thereof for their own sake. His focus on the harsh material conditions of the lives of the underdogs of society and his use of the results of the human sciences for understanding the causes and effects of those conditions are still accepted methods for dealing with problematic human conditions today. Marx pointed out how lack of economic resources, coupled with difficult work conditions, dehumanized people and alienated them from the product of their labour and their fellow human beings. One of the lasting legacies of Marx is his view that massive social forces manipulated by a powerful elite cause privilege and deprivation and only well-organized, collective human action can significantly redirect and change the effects and consequences of such forces.

Although Marx thought certain social laws would drive transformation of social structures towards a life where alienation and dehumanization would be uprooted, he also emphasized the indispensable role of the mobilization of exploited classes for collective political action. A change in consciousness to enable different ways of understanding society and perceiving their own power through collective agency were prerequisites for successful political action to alter power relations and redefine social organization to benefit those exploited by powerful elites.

Tawney (1952: 44–5) argues in similar vein to Rousseau and Marx that the distribution of resources, that eventually determines the rate of poverty in any society, depends largely on societal institutions. These institutions are determined 'not by immutable laws, but by the values, preferences, interests and ideals which rule at any moment in a given society'. These determining factors 'have changed repeatedly in the past and are changing to-day; and the distribution of wealth has changed and is changing, with them'. Tawney is clear: a ruling elite imposes their values, preferences, interests and ideas on other members of society to acquire much more economic resources than any human being needs at the expense of the rest of society who are left to suffer the effects of poverty.

Note the strong language he uses to condemn such exploitation that stunts people's development, deprives them of their cultural heritage and cuts them off from genuine human interaction so that elites can benefit from an excess of economic resources. Tawney (1952: 90) states it thus: 'A civilized community . . . will insist . . . that institutions which stunt the faculties of some among them for the advantage of others shall be generally recognised to be barbarous and odious.' Elsewhere he launches a more principled attack, stating that he is not that much bothered by some having more than others, but what he finds repulsive is 'that some classes should be excluded from the heritage of civilization which others enjoy' (118). This is not his only complaint against a society that allows poverty. More fundamental is his lament that 'the fact of human fellowship, which is ultimate and profound, should be obscured by economic contrasts, which are trivial and superficial' (ibid.). What does this comment suggest? We as human beings must have fundamental relationships with one another that are on a level where we build and share a common life that enables everyone to make a minimally decent life worthy of being human. This obligation ought to trump all other considerations that might be relevant to constructing a proper human society.

Very few researchers today would ascribe poverty to the functioning of natural or social laws of any kind. Pete Alcock is one of a group of contemporary social science thinkers who calls the collective organization of human societies to account for the existence of poverty. For Alcock, a contemporary British researcher, poverty is 'part of the wider question of the structure and distribution of resources in society and the power to control and use these' (1987: 9). He explains poverty as a consequence of 'structural social forces', defined as 'classes and groups and agencies and institutions which operate to reproduce a particular social order in which some are poor' (1993: 28). He acknowledges that national and international economic forces can influence people's levels of poverty, but even these economic forces he judges to be 'largely the products of decisions taken by people and the consequences of those decisions are to a very large extent predictable' (ibid.: 32). Alcock is crystal clear on why some are rich and others poor: some have power through being part of some or other collective human agency, to determine the unequal distribution of economic resources in their favour. This abuse of power for own benefit can be contested and redirected, surely.

John Rawls is not the most influential political philosopher of the past four decades for no reason. He combined a strong justification of the intellectual foundations of liberal democracies with an equally strong focus on the ways humans have power to shape the fundamental institutions of society ('the basic structure') to ensure adequate all purpose means for every citizen to build a decent life. Not only should the political, economic, social and family institutions ensure that everyone in society enjoys a social minimum to have a minimally decent life, but those institutions must only allow inequalities that are to the advantage of the least well-off members of society.

From this brief overview of how some influential thinkers view poverty in a broader context it is clear that (1) humans have full decision-making power over the fundamental societal institutions through their collective human agency and (2) that the distribution of economic resources and opportunities can be fully determined through our collective agency. Thus, poverty is the full collective responsibility of the decision makers in society.

Why we must do this together

I claim that we can fully prevent or heal poverty if we take our nature as human beings seriously. Poverty is a uniquely human phenomenon through which people's human dignity is negatively affected and their health threatened. Let us review what I have thus far tried to establish about poverty in this book.

1. Poverty is a complex phenomenon with a multitude of dimensions that gets uniquely configured in each individual case.
2. Poverty is a complex phenomenon with a wide range of symptoms, effects, consequences and causes that can only be untangled in each specific case through a particular judgement that accurately determines

the weight of the factors involved and the dynamics of their interplay.
3. Some of the causes of poverty can be the behaviour of other indi-
    viduals, the actions or inaction of governments at different levels,
    things that happened in the distant past or patterns of discrimination
    that run through a society.
4. Individuals working in isolation cannot implement the ethical values
    of empowerment and agency development or restoration required
    for full eradication of poverty.
5. Individuals working in isolation cannot ensure that appropriate
    principles of justice are properly accepted and enforced for poverty
    prevention.
6. Humans have both the power and responsibility to eradicate poverty
    and to prevent its recurrence.

While anyone can acknowledge that some resilient individuals can work
their way around many of the factors responsible for their specific case
of poverty, anyone can also see that many dimensions of poverty require
teams of dedicated specialists if their effects and consequences are to
be neutralized.

Poverty is indeed a condition that humans can deal with effectively
through their collective powers unique to our species. What is clear is
that we cannot imagine a group of cats meeting in a tree, discussing
rules for regulating cat behaviour in their area. We cannot visualize dogs
gathering in an open field discussing the best ways to improve productivity of food gathering, nor negotiating the fairest ways of distributing
bones found at human rubbish dumps.

We humans have unique capacities to engage in communicative action
through dialogue to set and enforce guidelines to shape the plasticity of
our natures into desired reciprocal actions for the well-being of everyone. This much has been proven in some of the northern European
countries that have drastically minimized the incidence of poverty.

How we must do this together

The condemnations by prominent social thinkers, discussed earlier, of
how humans allow poverty in society as a result of how they collectively
construct their society or just simply allow things to develop are not
my direct concern now, other than to note that they betray a strong

belief that we have power enough to change societal structures to eradicate poverty. The question now is: if we have the power to collectively fashion unequal societies containing high levels of extreme poverty, how can we again change a society through collective action to eradicate poverty completely?

My general explanation is as follows. Citizens create a social order through different processes. Sometimes, though rarely, citizens have the unique opportunity of recreating their social order through a revolutionary reconstruction of their society by means of negotiation or violent over-throw. More often an inherited social order gets gradually rebuilt over time through smaller policy changes, legislative renewal, innovative social practices and the enforcement of shared moral values.

One can usefully explain the role of individuals by highlighting the concept of responsibility, as citizens have a moral responsibility to do something to eradicate poverty in their society. Responsibility within this context has three meanings.

1. Responsibility means that persons or groups are held accountable for the actions over which they have control. To be held responsible for their actions is an integral part of a democratic society. Citizens must demand that politicians, bureaucrats and ordinary citizens explain or justify any kind of conduct that they regard as dubious. In the context of eradicating poverty it means that people exacerbating poverty, or using economic resources for their own benefit whilst harm-ing others must justify their actions or face public censure.

2. Responsibility refers to people's actions that are based on careful consideration of all interests involved. Only when people's actions are based on careful judgement of the relevant facts, circumstances, norms and possible consequences can they describe their actions as responsible. A democrat must have a concern for the rights and wel-fare of others, as well as for the public interest. To be responsible in this way means carefully to take into account other people's rights in whatever a person does.

3. Responsibility means that a person has to respond to whatever a situ-ation demands. Citizens can expect a lot of the state; that is why they vote in elections, criticize politicians and pay taxes. Citizens in a dem-ocracy must also be prepared to respond to any situations that they are able to handle themselves and where they can make a difference.

We should not assume that every citizen ought to play exactly the same role as everyone else. In some of the most successful human enterprises, like modern science or universal health care provision, some play the role of experts, some are publicists, some make policy, some fulfil specialized functions, others donate time or money and most pay taxes or insurance. Just imagine the input of millions of individuals into the collective goal of proper health care through all the processes of political decision making, paying taxes, building and maintaining hospitals, educating and training medical personnel, providing support services, developing and marketing medicine, ensuring proper diets and preventative health care, providing emotional and other support to patients and their families and getting rid of medical waste.

Through these kinds of collective organization, specialized functions and role division humans have achieved astounding successes in the modern era with the provision of sophisticated health care to all citizens and by exponentially expanding the frontiers of medical knowledge and technology. Is there any reason why it is impossible to tackle the problems and challenges of poverty in similar ways, especially if some northern European countries have already led the way?

Do individuals then have a role in the eradication of poverty? As citizens individuals comprise the collectives that determine the rights and duties of every citizen and decide the policies on employment and provision of means to fulfil basic needs. Some individuals have direct roles with respect to poverty eradication as scientists, policy makers, politicians or specialized social science practitioners. As ordinary citizens many individuals can lobby, campaign, organize, protest, write and co-operate to change the fundamental social order and support policies that determine how poor people are to be treated humanely. Or they can donate money, clothes or their time and care to ameliorate the lot of poor people.

Can individuals fulfil roles other than political ones to change society's dealings with poor people? Again the answer is obviously yes. Some citizens have expertise, means and caring to effectively address smaller problems of poverty through individual or small group effort. Citizens can get involved with the lot and lives of poor people in various ways as individuals or through voluntary organizations. In these ways they can effect smaller or larger changes that might add up to make a significant difference to the lives and attitudes of poor and non-poor people alike.

Citizens in groups can play crucial roles to eradicate poverty. Note how I quoted Michael Walzer in an earlier chapter referring to political protest as the breeding ground of self-respecting citizens. Few things can be as important for poor people as to engage in meaningful political protest that will reinforce their sense of self-respect and human dignity when they experience themselves insisting on decent treatment that respects their humanity and their legitimate rights. Protest marches, signing petitions and resistance against unfair policies can all contribute to a sense of legitimate moral outrage against any kind of treatment that reinforces poverty or stifles dissent about neglect of the poor. The resilience of poor people that shows in the ability of some to make the most of minimal opportunities to enhance their lives becomes the subject of legend in many cases. Despite meagre resources to nourish their poor lives, these people can form alliances across social differences and local or national boundaries, mobilize support, establish new organizations and committees, show passionate resistance to unfair treatment, get influential public figures to be on their side and sometimes speak on their behalf, use the courts to stop or slow down bureaucrats and attract media attention through persistent protest (see Ballard et al., 2006; Desai, 2002).

Sometimes citizens organized into non-governmental associations can serve needs far better than state institutions. Such organs of civil society as interest groups, sport clubs and service organizations provide valuable training ground for potential leaders. Membership is voluntary and organizations are largely self-supporting and independent from the state. They are nevertheless public, constrained by all the societal rules, rights and regulations that apply elsewhere. In the organs of civil society, people get opportunities to articulate their interests, formulate mutual goals and strategies for implementing them and opportunities for commenting on and sometimes demanding, governmental action. Participation in civil society stimulates the development of democratic values in citizens, such as tolerance for differing viewpoints, equal respect and consideration of the interests of other citizens and willingness to engage in dialogue as peaceful means of dealing with conflict. It also develops democratic skills such as persuasive rhetoric, abilities to criticize and respond to criticism, capabilities and experience of organization and skills for leadership, such as responsiveness and accountability. Thus, civil society becomes a training ground for true democracy. Some community or issue-based organizations in post-apartheid South Africa exemplify exactly what can be done by resilient poor people insisting on a better life of human dignity for themselves (see Ballard et al., 2006; Desai, 2002).

Note how a culture of human rights can strengthen public mobilization and protest in support of the eradication of poverty. A right to freedom of association enables citizens to form associations with whomever they want. The right to freedom of expression allows citizens and their associations to speak their minds, provided they do not propagate war, incite imminent violence or advocate hatred of other groups. A right to assembly, demonstration, picket and petition gives citizens and their associations opportunity to gather publicly and communicate their viewpoints to people who care to listen. Rights to equality and non-discrimination are particularly relevant here, as they impress on everyone the status of every citizen as a human being with dignity. These rights assist in creating and sustaining expectations that a better deal for poor people *must* be forthcoming.

Citizens associated through civil society must help solve problems as far as their abilities and resources allow, as no state can do everything for its citizens. In this way, citizens can create a society closer to their needs and wishes sooner and much more effectively than waiting on the state and its bureaucracies. Associations of civil society are able to organize, 'get resources, achieve goals, mobilise pressure, negotiate and express policy positions' (Camerer, 1996). Using these capacities for development make civil associations 'vehicles of reconstruction and development' (ibid.). Organizations of civil society also have a role to ensure that government and its bureaucracies are 'accountable and responsive to the claims and concerns of citizens' (ibid.).

Thus, responsibility means that citizens in a democratic state should always be prepared to respond to requests, accusations, suggestions and criticisms about their role to eradicate poverty on a sustainable, long-term basis. They must also be responsive to the demands of justice in whatever they do and be prepared to take the initiative to solve problems within their capabilities.

Conclusion

The point of this chapter is that poverty can only be understood – and best dealt with – within the context of the social order of a society and its underlying fundamental values. Thus, to efficiently address poverty, the core governance functions within society must be appropriately organized to sustainably prevent poverty in all possible futures that await us. In some European countries this has apparently been done. Schulte (2002: 123) says that in Europe, nearly 100 million people 'are lifted out of poverty', through 'income distribution and other benefits, reducing relative poverty by more than half'. He adds later that the right to a minimum income 'which is unconditional' has become 'a cornerstone of the modern European welfare state'. Let's look at an example to help us determine whether this might be the way to go. What values did Denmark use to modify their social order to virtually eradicate poverty?

Hans Christiansen (1996) gives an explanation for the even better success of the Danish welfare state in dealing with poverty. He says Denmark incorporates two values that are basic to the European welfare state, that is, the government has responsibility 'to alleviate genuine poverty by guaranteeing all residents a minimum living' and that 'risk of temporary or permanent loss of income should be shared collectively' through the tax system or a general insurance scheme. The Danish welfare state combines two further values with the ones above: 'that no individual should against his or her will be excluded from participation in the labour force and that no household should be excluded from full participation in social life on economic grounds'. Implemented together, these four values go a long way towards fully eradicating poverty. Note that these successes in the eradication of poverty depend on specific governmental functions aimed at issues directly related to the causes, effects and consequences of poverty. Thus, in the Danish society collective efforts to eradicate poverty have resulted in changes to governance to focus expertise and resources at the core issues of poverty.

To redefine the core governance functions fittingly to sustainably prevent poverty over the longer term implies that the legitimate interests of every citizen must be considered and duly taken care of. If the interests of poor and vulnerable people are prioritized above those of everyone else, resentment might follow that could scupper the project of eradicating poverty completely. Is it possible to design governance functions for the different levels of states and regional, continental or global organizations in such a way that the best interests of those who are poor and everyone else could be fairly accommodated? This topic will be explored next.

11 · Re-Imagining Governance to Eradicate Poverty Permanently

One of the most powerful mechanisms humans have for collective action is the governance functions that find their strongest embodiment in the state. Not only is the state the institution through which humans wield enormous power over one another's lives, but it also creates the space, sets the boundaries and oversees the impact of all other forms of power we exercise through the economy, civil society and international institutions and organizations. For this reason I focus on state institutions as symbol of governance functions in a society. Despite this focus, I intend that the re-imagination of the state and the re-definition of its goals and functions ought to apply to all governance functions that we employ for self-governance from local to global levels.[1]

Many examples from history show that humans have used the state in various ways to increase or decrease poverty. Sometimes small powerful groups have exploited the state as a vehicle for their own enrichment by confiscating the fruits of people's labour for themselves. Fewer examples can be found to show the opposite, that is, where humans have employed state power to strengthen weak and vulnerable citizens through establishing equally accessible opportunities for growth and more equitable distributions of income.

How must we re-imagine the state to turn it into a responsive complex of institutions that can prevent poverty from occurring without detracting from the life chances of any citizens? In this chapter I want to rethink the fundamental ends of the state so that it can protect every citizen's interests and thus also prevent something like poverty happening to anyone.

Perhaps some people might object to the prominent position afforded to the interests of poor people. Why should concern about their fate be central when one re-imagines the ends of the state? This objection assumes to know exactly who poor people are or thinks poor people are fixed in number, a well-established group with defined boundaries. Both these ideas are wrong.

Every human being is at risk of becoming poor and therefore can benefit from looking at the ends of government from this perspective. Non-poor people cannot shrug off concerns about poverty as if they will never be affected. In this respect, poverty is like disability: every person faces the risk of becoming poor. John D. Jones (1990: 16) says that non-poor people 'face a variety of forces that can break into their world, disrupt it, tear it apart and plunge them into poverty'. A sudden natural disaster, such as a flood or a human disaster, like war, can impoverish the most afflu-ent members of society. Unexpected loss of employment, sudden death or serious illness of an economically active household member can impoverish even rich people. More likely at risk of suffering poverty are those with few resources who cannot absorb the impact of sudden changes, like a down-turn in the economy, retrenchment, death, disability or illness of a house-hold member. Poverty thus matters to every non-poor person, as a possibility they might encounter in future. They must imagine themselves to be poor, if not now, then perhaps sometime in future.

To give priority to the interests of poor people through safeguarding them against the harms of poverty is simultaneously to protect everyone in society. If a society puts in place safeguards against the kinds of harms and suffering caused by poverty, the whole society will benefit from the development of the full potential of all people oppressed by poverty. Further-more, measures for the eradication of poverty and safeguards for preventing any recurrence will simultaneously protect the life, health, liberty and full set of capabilities requisite for the pursuit of happiness of every citizen, poor or not.

I

Philosophers are typically concerned about the legitimacy of state insti-tutions in general and governments in particular, asking questions like the following. Did a government gain power via a duly authorized set of procedures? Do the composition and organization of the government reflect all interests, allow proper political activity and limit abuse of power? Does a government fulfil the rightful purposes that its citizens judge fitting for its serious pursuit? Do government bureaucracies fulfil their functions without fraud and corruption, or without the abuse of power? Simply put, philosophers question the ends a government ought to pursue to allow and enable us to live the good life.

I want to focus on the fundamental ends legitimate governments ought to fulfil in twenty-first century societies so as to ensure opportunities for every citizen to live a good life. As I explained above, I use the concept government in the broader sense of governance, which means the way we humans collectively organize ourselves to take care of our human interests and coordinate our shared lives in ways that benefit us all, whether it be through governments, regional and international organizations, the economy or the organs of civil society.

I assume that we, as citizens who share a country, have a kind of highest level social contract – in the sense used by John Locke – with one another about the nature and functions of our collective organization and governance of each other. We revisit and renegotiate this 'contract' in the light of shifting values and changing circumstances over time. We thus periodically collectively decide what functions and roles we want government to take, revise what we want organizations of civil society to be and do and rethink what restrictions and regulations to impose on the freedom we allow markets.

We never have final blueprints to determine exactly what the nature, functions and jurisdictions of governments, markets, organizations of civil society or individuals are to be. We modify, adjust and redefine their roles and functions as we go along in the light of long-standing traditions, best practice, innovative ideas and altered conditions in our world. In this vein I endorse the approach by John Stuart Mill on how to determine which governance functions properly belong to state institutions and which not (see Mill, 2003). We must judge on a case-by-case basis in the light of relevant considerations, inter alia about the strength of competing institutions, what would be the most efficient solutions that will empower the body of citizens most.

I assume that every inhabitant of a specific geographical area governed by a particular state ought to have some kind of input in legitimizing the ends, functions, structure and election of their government. The authorization of government can be done through the revision of a genuine social contract or through any sufficiently participatory process that encourages free political activity and requires the consent of the governed to modify the fundamental ends of government (see also Hegel, 1991: § 258).

I first present my interpretation of the fundamental ends of government philosophers have argued for in the past as background check for my discussion on what appropriate ends would be for us now. I then briefly indicate how we humans have changed our world since the Industrial Revolution and the Enlightenment in ways that significantly complicate governing a society. Finally, I will set up a thought experiment to determine whether the fundamental ends of government identified by earlier philosophers are still adequate as broad guidelines for contemporary societies. I argue that these ends need revision to deal with the complexities of twenty-first century societies.

In my discussion I take note of two remarks by Hegel about studying the state. One is about the intricacies of understanding the state and the other warns us how easily we miss the crucial influence of government on societal well-being. Hegel is in no doubt about the complexity of understanding the state: 'We should . . . realize that, if it is difficult to comprehend nature, it is an infinitely more arduous task to understand the state' (1991: § 272). This observation rings even more true in contemporary societies, where governments play bigger roles in more complex human environments than ever before. Hegel also alerts us how easily we become unaware of the impact of governments on our daily lives. Note his example:

> It does not occur to someone who walks the streets in safety at night that this might be otherwise, for this habit of [living in] safety has become second nature and we scarcely stop to think that it is solely the effect of particular institutions. (§ 268)

To respond appropriately to this remark, I will set up a thought experiment that will help me imagine a contemporary society with all traces of government erased. In this way I hope to gain awareness of the deep, sometimes hidden, impact of government on society. If one imagines a contemporary society without any form of government in place, the complexities of the multifarious functions of contemporary states will become apparent as well.

II

Are the fundamental ends of government argued for by philosophers in the past still adequate for twenty-first century post-industrial and post-Enlightenment societies? I will explain four main ends that philosophers from different historical periods have assigned to the state and then proceed to test their contemporary validity through the rest of the chapter.

Allowing and enabling us to preserve our lives through provision for basic necessities is the fundamental end of the state often discussed by philosophers in the past. Some examples are as follows. Plato articulates the interdependence we have and the mutuality we require for providing in our basic needs so as to prolong and preserve our lives (1993: 369b, c). Aristotle also refers to the household's role 'for the satisfaction of basic needs' (1981: 1252b9), the state's role as a 'means of securing life itself'

(1252b27), as facilitator of 'the exchange of goods' (1280a34) and as an association to 'enable its members, in their households and kinships, to live well' (1280b29).

Hobbes similarly values the role of government to secure citizens so that 'by their own industrie and by the fruits of the Earth, they may nourish themselves and live contentedly' (1968 [1651]: 227). For Locke preservation of human life is also crucial, as 'natural reason . . . tells us that men being once born have a right to their preservation and consequently to meat and drink and such other things as nature affords for their subsistence' (1966 [1690]: 14). Rousseau (1968: 50) thinks 'man's first law is to watch over his own preservation' and therefore he formulates 'the prosperity of its members' as part of the 'object of any political association' (130).

For most of these philosophers governments must allow citizens to procure necessities for a good life. Hegel, however, marks the change to a world with a burgeoning human population placing ever-growing demands on agricultural land. For this reason he saw that the family no longer had a 'comprehensive effectiveness' (1991: § 238). Citizens now had claims on civil society like those they formerly had on families, because of the 'immense power' of civil society 'which draws people to itself and requires them to work for it, to owe everything to it and to do everything by its means' (ibid. See also § 230).

Closely linked to preservation as end of government is the well-known end of protection. This is the second common theme explored by many philosophers. Plato assigned his guardians and auxiliaries twin roles to 'ensure that neither the desire nor the capacity for harming the community arises, whether from external enemies or from internal friends' (1993: 414b). Note that Plato formulates this end primarily in terms of pro-active action to prevent the desire or capacity for such harm from arising, rather than in terms of dealing reactively with manifest harm. For Aristotle, protection, formulated as 'arms . . . both for internal government . . . and to repel attempts at wrongdoing coming from the outside', is one of six things without which he thinks there can be no state (1981: 1328b2).

Hobbes is famous for his emphasis on the core function of protection. He refers to the role of 'a common Power to keep them all in awe' to prevent 'that condition which is called Warre' in which 'every man is enemy to every man' (1968 [1651]: 185, 186). Hobbes does not only have civil war in mind, but explicitly mentions defence against 'the invasion of foreigners and the injuries of one another' (227). Locke formulates a law of nature, to be implemented by government, that clearly illustrates the link between protection and preservation, that is, no citizen may 'take away or impair the life, or what tends to the preservation of the life, liberty, health, limb, or goods of another' (1966 [1690]: 5). Rousseau (1968: 130) simply argues that governments exist for the 'protection . . . of its members'. Hegel similarly articulates as an end for a government's administration of justice that 'the *undisturbed security* of *persons* and *property* should be guaranteed' (1991: § 230). These philosophers concur that a government must protect the lives of its citizens.

Many philosophers have discussed liberty as one of the ends a state ought to pursue. Plato does not show much appreciation for the role of liberty in society, despite his astute observations of the nature and role of liberty in democratic societies. He is aware how liberty functions in a community that is 'informed by independence and freedom of speech and everyone has the right to do as he chooses' (1993: 557b). He realized the exercise of liberty in a democracy will produce a diverse population, making it a society with 'the most gorgeous political system . . . adorned with every species of human trait' (557c), although he ultimately rejects this model of governance in favour of his ideal state to be ruled by philosopher-kings.

Although Aristotle seemingly endorses Plato's views when he defines a state as consisting of 'similar persons whose aim is the best life possible', he shows more appreciation of the value of diversity resulting from freedom of choice. Conceded, his awareness might be addressed more to groups of persons than to individuals. He defines the best life as happiness through the 'active exercise of virtue', adding the discerning observation that 'different sets of people seek their happiness in different ways and by different means and so make for themselves different lives and different constitutions' (1981: 1328a33). To do so, they need a certain minimum of liberty.

Hobbes offers much stronger emphasis on liberty, defining the *Jus Naturale* (the Right of Nature) as 'the liberty each man hath, to use his own power, as he will himselfe, for the preservation of his . . . own Life; and consequently, of doing anything, which in his own Judgement and Reason, hee shall conceive to be the aptest means thereunto' (1968 [1651]: 189). Liberty thus becomes fundamental to ensure preservation, though guided by judgement informed through reason.

Locke is well known for his strong emphasis on the motivation of people in the state of war to unite into a political society for 'the mutual preservation of their lives, liberties and estates' (1966 [1690]: 63), thus portraying safeguarding of liberty as one of the core functions of government.

For Rousseau liberty gains such importance that he equates renouncing one's freedom with renouncing 'one's humanity'. Loss of freedom of the will, Rousseau claims, means 'you strip a man's actions of all moral significance' (1968: 55). Hegel (1991: § 260) calls the state 'the actuality of true freedom' and argues that the 'essence of the modern state' is that 'the universal should be linked with the complete freedom of particularity (*Besonderheit*) and the well-being of individuals'. Thus, for these major philosophers ensuring an adequate degree of liberty is crucial as a main function of government.

In many cases philosophers provide overarching aims for the state, pointing to the specific qualities of the state that expresses the unique nature of communal life that human beings share that strongly contrast with the less complex associations of other living beings. This is a fourth common theme often debated by philosophers where they depict the state as a manifestation of the uniqueness of human beings in contrast to life in the animal kingdom.

Plato argues for justice as the overarching aim through which a community becomes good and happy, both qualities he regarded as typically human (1993: 433b, 427e, 427d). Aristotle locates the difference between humans and animals in the human perception of 'good and evil, just and unjust', adding that a common view on such matters is a prerequisite for a state (1981: 1253a7). Humans establish a state not only as 'a means for securing life itself', but to 'secure the good life' (1252b27). The most successful state would thus be one in which 'the possibilities for happiness are greatest' (1331b39).

Hobbes refers to the role of the state in assuring citizens 'a contented life', or a life lived well (1968 [1651]: 161, 212), something that can typically only be done through human reflection on the nature of worthwhile goals and the extent to which they are realized. Similarly, for Locke the overarching goal of the state is 'the good of mankind' (1966: 114). Rousseau (1968: 64) emphasizes how the transition from the state of nature into political society changes human beings from being driven by instinct to being guided by justice. The result is a transformation from a 'narrow, stupid animal' to a 'creature of intelligence', whose 'faculties are exercised' 'mind is enlarged' 'sentiments so ennobled' and whose 'whole spirit so elevated' (ibid.: 64, 65).

Thus for these philosophers the state shows why humans are different from animals through our collective choice to express our humanity in the shared ends we establish for implementation by means of our state institutions. Note that this overarching goal of the state goes to the heart of the fundamental harm poverty inflicts on humans, that is, a denial and violation of the human dignity of its sufferers.

III

Are both (1) this overarching goal of government to establish the humanity of the inhabitants of a particular human community and (2) the three broadly defined subsidiary ends of government, that is, the preservation of human life, the protection of citizens against harm and the guarding of individual liberty still adequate for the governments of twenty-first-century nation states?

Before answering this question, I want to briefly touch on the sweeping changes brought about by the moral and political transformation of the Enlightenment and the scientific and technological revolutions that originated in the European Renaissance. Have these changes brought about such new human worlds that the ends of governments formulated by these philosophers need drastic revision?

Enlightenment social philosophies brought increasing emphasis on the equality of citizens and the freedom of individuals, who want to acquire opportunities for growth and development and have the chance to express their autonomy. A growing awareness of how many ways humans find to abuse power and to what extremes they can do so might also require a reformulation of the ends of the state. But do these new social visions and political analyses necessarily require qualitatively different ends for the state? In this case I will argue throughout the rest of the chapter that a careful reformulation and fitting modification of the ends of government as already articulated by philosophers over many centuries will be enough to satisfy the need citizens in the twenty-first-century societies have for the state.

The scientific discoveries of the European Renaissance initiated the development of scientific technology that set in motion unprecedented continuous societal change that gradually spread throughout the world. New sources of energy, new materials for manufacture, new production processes, new ways of cultivating food, new forms of transport, new sophisticated means of communication, specialized and organized labour practices, complicated financial instruments and services, astounding record-keeping and calculation devices and new scientific fields and amazing technological innovations have jointly created new human worlds beyond the wildest fantasies of humans in earlier ages.

These fantastic new worlds have enlarged human choice of worthwhile lifestyles beyond belief and created countless new ways in which humans and their most comprehensive sets of interests can either be improved or harmed. Environmental degradation that threatens human survival, economic decline leading to mass unemployment, high-tech warfare that can destroy whole populations and even life on earth and vulnerable dependence on energy sources and technology for normal everyday functioning of societies are some of the challenges that complicate the role of governments. However, to complicate the role of governments does not necessarily mean governments have any new purpose to fulfil in addition to those identified and argued for by philosophers in the past.

There are two new factors that require careful consideration. One is the huge increase in the volume and kinds of knowledge available about the nature of human beings and the functioning of human societies. The other factor to consider is the increasing complexity of highly differentiated industrialized societies with ever increasing impact on our global biosphere. These changes are driven by the similarly huge increase in the volume and kinds of knowledge available about natural resources and their productive use in the service of human survival and flourishing. Note that both kinds of knowledge can be crucial for attempts to eradicate poverty: some kinds of knowledge illuminate poverty as part of the dynamics of human societies and the other kind depict more productive and efficient use of natural resources for human survival and flourishing.

Both these factors require serious thought. Do they require the ends of the contemporary state to be redefined? Their indispensable contribution to the lifestyles of contemporary societies and their huge impact on both humans and their environments suggest we must look closely at the ends we assign to the state in the twenty-first century.

How can we work out what ends are most appropriate for state institutions in our world that will ensure the well-being of every citizen? In what follows, I will use a thought experiment that aims to unearth the ends governments ought to serve in times like ours.

IV

Imagine international terrorists develop sophisticated military capabilities, acquiring command of intercontinental ballistic missiles. Suppose they breach the defences of a First World country to target a joint

session of local, regional and national governmental leaders at government buildings. Imagine the chaos with all political leaders eliminated!
Imagine further that the terrorists have missiles focused on all governmental bureaucracies and insist that the missiles will be fired unless all
governmental functions are abandoned. Their aim is to subject this
country to total loss of all governmental services so that they can plunge
the country into anarchy and anomie as revenge for colonial domination,
cultural imperialism and economic exploitation their people suffered
in the past.

Imagine further the effects and consequences of the gradual implosion
of services and functions usually provided by all levels of government.
With all leaders and officials of local, regional and national government
immobilized or eliminated, what would result? No police officers will
enforce law and order, creating space for anarchy. No refuse removal will
be done, increasing risks of disease and plagues. Water supply will dry
up and public health care will shut down. All sources of energy will be dis-
rupted and consequently all technological applications using electricity
or fossil fuels will be made obsolete. All forms of communication other
than person-to-person communication will become disabled and all kinds
of transport except walking have become impossible. The terrorists insist
they will not allow any maintenance, repairs or reconstruction of any
kind. They back up this command with satellite surveillance and thousands
of missiles aimed at towns and cities. The terrorists want citizens to suffer
the humiliating loss of their luxurious lifestyle to pay for centuries of
imperialism, domination and exploitation.

Are we capable of imagining the result of the losses described above?
If we lose all levels of government and all the technological advances
brought about by modern science whilst maintaining current high levels
of population, what crises would we have to face? Lack of food and water,
security, transport, communication and medical care would immediately
place such a society in the deepest crisis imaginable. Without the option
of restoring any form of government, a desperate and vicious struggle for
survival will ensue, a state of war far worse than Hobbes or Locke could
ever imagine. Our dependence on governmental functions as foundation
for our normal, everyday activities has become so overwhelming that our
survival will immediately be threatened if our government, its bureaucracies
and agencies collapse.

Is this an impossible scenario? Perhaps not. After 9/11 this thought
experiment has sufficient plausibility to guide an exploration as to what
twenty-first-century citizens want governments for. Suppose the terrorists

have a five-year plan for making the descendants of their colonial masters suffer, what would be the main reasons why the suffering citizens would want some form of government to return? What would these citizens set as the ends they would want their government to focus on? In what follows, I want to evoke, clarify and systematically present the fundamental intuitions citizens in modern societies have about the ends governments ought to serve today.

V

We can easily imagine that humans in such dire circumstances will organize themselves to make the best they can out of the desperately few opportunities that remain. They might succeed in producing food for survival, organizing protection against crime and establishing minimal social cooperation akin to what was available centuries ago in far less developed areas with much less inhabitants. However, without basic governance functions a wide array of normal human services and typical human lifestyles would merely become impossible.

Suppose a small group of citizens starts an initiative to prepare their society to turn the situation around and restore government after the five years have elapsed. To do so, they arrange a meeting for a select group of citizens to determine what would make a new government legitimate and what fundamental ends it must pursue to gain acceptance from the traumatized population. Their fundamental guiding question would be: 'What must a future government do to enable and allow us to live the good life as we see fit?' These citizens know that any discussion could be thwarted by many issues which divide their fellow citizens. They are fully aware that an extraordinarily high amount of groups have organized themselves as interest groups on various sides of social conflicts that emerged or were exacerbated by their traumatic experience of being without a government.

To defuse conflict, they decide to gather a group of 1,000 citizens with the sole purpose of identifying the fundamental ends a government ought to pursue. This group of 1,000 citizens must be representative of all the citizens in the country. To accomplish that, they employ the services of their best statisticians to select a sample of 1,000 citizens that would be representative of all possible parties to every kind of conflict that disrupt their country. For this reason, the sample of 1,000 citizens includes men and women, rich and poor, rural and urban citizens, people with different languages, people from different religions, people with varying sporting and leisure interests, managers and workers, people from different generations, environmentalists and industrialists and so on. Obviously most of the selected citizens would be parties to more than one of these conflicts and thus be aware how many of their society's conflicts penetrate and influence one another.

When this group gather at a suitable venue, their task is to discuss the areas of conflict in their society with the aim of finding a consensus on the most important issues to be addressed by the group of people that must take up the role of government in future. The citizen sample must help define the problems and priorities a new government must address so that this new government will gain credibility and attain legitimacy in the eyes of the citizens of this severely troubled country.

The citizens selected bring with them their full knowledge, history and insight of all sorts that they have gathered by means of experience and imagination throughout their lives in their country and elsewhere. They are citizens like us and are fully aware of the diversity of people found in their own society. This diversity includes people with different languages, cultures, religions, moral values, political beliefs and so on. They know they live in a contemporary mass society that is partly industrialized, urbanized and dependent on all kinds of technology for its survival and continued well-being. They have intimate knowledge that their country is in a state of moderate scarcity, with a fragile environment strongly affected in various ways by human activity.

The citizens are also fully aware that their country is part of the global village and has all manner of complex ties with a wide variety of other countries, based on various interests and histories. Links through trade, tourism, language, religion, sport and communication media abound. The continuing processes of globalization, such as more sophisticated communication media, economic and trade links and multilateral agreements open up markets everywhere. Increased international cooperation through a multiplicity of organizations, treaties and agreements affect their country in varying degrees.

The contributions the sample citizens bring to discussions will be biased and prejudiced, but that is what the organizers prefer. The organizers want the limited perspectives of particular citizens that were formed through the interaction of their backgrounds, histories, knowledge, prejudices and values with those of their fellow citizens in the conflicts taking place within the particular circumstances of that society. They also want citizens' honest assessment of life in a contemporary state without a government. The rich textures of their selective memories and the bias of their interested standpoints are the basic material needed for discussions, as the interrogatory deliberations between diverse partial and limited perspectives will best contribute towards open-ended, fallible social truths. Note how Sen (2009: 45) similarly argues that 'reasoned scrutiny from different perspectives' is an 'essential part of the demands of objectivity for ethical and political convictions'.

The organizers need to ensure that discussions take place. They must therefore prevent participants carrying disabling conflicts with them into the discussion room. For this reason they will allow talking as the only means of interaction between citizens. They will insist that anyone can raise any issue and that every issue raised must be addressed to the satisfaction of the one who raised it, regardless of the time it takes. The one who raised the issue must get opportunities to respond to the reactions of other citizens. Anyone saying anything must be willing to be questioned by the others to improve understanding and to have the quality and strength of supporting arguments and reasons examined.

Citizens must be willing to provide information about themselves if asked. They must allow others to ask questions about their lives, circumstances, values, ideas and proposals. They must enable other citizens to gain insight into their lives and to glimpse aspects of the everyday experiences in their world. In this way the citizens can open up their worlds to let the moral imaginations of their fellow citizens roam into the often concealed, hidden or neglected worlds of especially marginalized people whose lives are often invisible and whose voices are frequently inaudible.

In their discussions the citizens would have access to a panel of diverse experts and well-meaning outsiders whom they themselves nominate. This panel will advise the citizens on any issue they find necessary or useful. The experts must be willing to present their expertise in easily understandable terms and they must be prepared to face detailed questions and challenges concerning their considered opinions.

These ground rules are minimal enough so as not to embody too many values that citizens might not want to feel pressurized to accept. Still, these rules ought to let discussions flow and will allow every citizen the opportunity to be heard and to be taken seriously. Any other rules to enable improved communication must be made through consensus by the sample of citizens themselves.

VI

What would this sample of citizens present as their list of priorities that any government has to attend to first? How would they articulate the fundamental ends appropriate for a government of the twenty-first century? How could I know what they would think if such an experiment in popular thinking about political matters is never carried out? The fact that the discussants are people like us who have knowledge and experiences like us in countries similar to ours makes it easy to infer what the upshot of their discussions could be. I could draw inferences about the possible outcomes of their discussions by making use of the following sources of information, accessible to anyone who would want to check whether my interpretation makes sense. One source is the overlaps in actual functions that governments perform with legitimacy throughout many countries in the world. Another source is to look at the demands citizens all over the world exact from governments and the way they blame governments when things go wrong. This information will direct us towards the intuitions contemporary citizens have about the fundamental ends governments ought to fulfil. A final source is to scan political theory to determine the functions legitimately ascribed to governments, whilst ignoring the specific conceptual categories of frameworks those functions are placed in. If one puts together all this information in a way that seems reasonable, what picture would emerge of the fundamental ends citizens expect from state institutions?

I imagine that the priorities of my group of representative citizens could be organized into five main categories. They are as follows. They would first ask for zones of ordered security. What does this mean? The concept security has meanings such as to guarantee something, to protect something or someone to make them safe from harm. John Stuart Mill argued that security is 'to every one's feelings the most vital of interests' (2003: 226). Why? For Mill 'no human being could possibly do without security', because humans depend on security 'for all our immunity from evil and for the whole value of all and every good, beyond the passing moment' (ibid.).

Order means that things are done according to settled and fixed rules that people have internalized to facilitate ways of doing things that have been found to work best. Order thus implies that citizens can have legitimate and stable expectations of how other citizens ought to treat them or not. Zones of ordered security thus mean areas in human society where specific fundamental human interests would be properly arranged, guaranteed safety and protected from harm. What are these interests that they want secured?

The sample citizens would judge the protection of their lives and bodies as high priority. They would not want to be killed, assaulted or physically injured in any way. The reason is simple. To be killed means all opportunities of living any kind of life falls away, whilst physical injuries curb or lessen one's ability to engage in some activities one would want to have the option to choose for oneself. Whether such threats come from within their own household, neighbourhood or anywhere else in their country does not matter, as such threats can be just as destructive and threatening as threats from foreigners, whether individuals, groups or governments. To ward off such threats, governments must operate security services and exercise border control to filter out dangerous people and goods from entering a country.

Citizens would also not want to be injured or killed in avoidable accidents in human or natural environments. The reason is the same: they do not want to die prematurely or be deprived of bodily capacities to engage in any activities they might prefer. They would not want a government to expose them to human or natural disasters, as far as possible. The zone where they want this done would obviously be the whole of their country that is reasonably accessible to all citizens. Some parts of a country may be zoned for security reasons, making impossible climbing dangerous mountains, entering nuclear power plants, running across shooting ranges or highways, or walking through national parks where dangerous predators roam. Governments must warn citizens of the dangers of unrestricted access to high risk areas so that citizens can take responsibility to protect their lives and physical security.

This major priority for citizens means a government must protect them against the possibilities of harm and damage to themselves and their property resulting also from the use of violence or from accidents and disasters. A government would have to do various things to protect citizens against such eventualities, such as setting up effective mechanisms for dispute resolution, erecting fences and barriers to keep citizens from dangerous areas, maintaining an effective protection and security service to enforce laws prohibiting harm to persons and damage to property, running early warning systems that guard against natural and human disasters befalling citizens and so on.

Zones of ordered security include more than this kind of protection of lives and property or the guarantee of places where citizens can live and move around in safety. Human lives need protection and guarantees in at least two other ways, as threats to their continued existence, or the quality thereof, can also come from other sources. All citizens are vulnerable to the vicissitudes of life such as unemployment, poverty, disability, ill health and so on. Such personal disasters can drain resources and impoverish citizens to the extent that their lack of resources have all kinds of secondary negative consequences, such as loss of life through preventable disease, hunger, loss of shelter, etc. Although many citizens have some form of guaranteed support for such personal disasters, many do not. Even those with the best insurance or those with strong family ties are vulnerable to disastrous personal circumstances and would want a government to step in when they are in dire straits. This protection aims to secure their physical survival and avoid bodily harm, as well as the associated psychological trauma and negative emotional impact.

Not only do citizens want governments to coordinate certain activities in order to enable them to participate freely and safely in them, but they also want a government to enable them to participate as competent adults in their society's activities. Thus, in addition to safeguarding zones of ordered security, citizens want state institutions to provide them opportunities for development that will empower them to participate fully as interdependent equals in society.

If it takes a village to raise a child, as a proverb claims, it takes the resources, planning and foresight of a whole community to enable children to become full participants as adults with shared responsibility for their communal life. Thus, our sample citizens would list enablement through education and training as an important issue that a government must add as priority, to complement parental upbringing. A government must either provide us with educational services, or oversee them, train us for jobs, educate us to share and develop our culture and teach us the values and virtues of citizenship. Only through such opportunities collectively developed and funded can citizens hope to acquire the competencies and capacities to become useful participants in social life.

For this role the select group of citizens want a government to establish regions of empowering enablement, that is, places where citizens can engage in activities of learning, growth and development that can crucially affect the quality of their everyday lives. This empowering function equips citizens with knowledge, skills and insight to manage various aspects of their lives successfully to secure the prerequisites for survival and flourishing.

Besides chances to engage in comprehensive education and lifelong learning, governments must play their role in regulating and coordinating our use of all manner of vehicles, for example. Governments must enable citizens to use their vehicles through providing the necessary infrastructure such as roads, traffic laws and officials who can enforce those laws. The government must license us and our vehicles to certify that we are capable of safely utilizing transport opportunities and enforce safety standards for road use, vehicle specifications and maintenance. Similarly, a government must provide, regulate or monitor the infrastructure and the specifications for safety and reliability, for whatever technological devices we have available to enhance the quality or productivity of our lives.

How to deal with property is another example of a government enabling citizens and this example is relevant to most societies throughout history. To make a living to stave off poverty and the disasters that could follow in its train, citizens need security of home ownership and land tenure. A government must set up rules and laws that regulate ownership or use of property: enabling citizens to use, rent, buy, own, sell or transfer property, or to make legitimate use of property in other ways with the aim of making a living. Citizens need to have their activities concerning land use and property coordinated so as to avoid conflicts about ownership, rights to use and income from property. Not only should a government regulate ownership and use of land, but also protect public properties that have special significance in terms of biodiversity or guard against any property being threatened by human pollution or destruction. Through protection of national treasures of natural or cultural origin a government enables citizens to appreciate the natural wonders and the cultural achievements of their part of the world that came into being through millennia.

Another form of enablement comes through the administrative functions of a government that record births and deaths and certify individuals through identification documents to be who they rightfully are. In an anonymous mass society where most people are strangers to one another these administrative functions verify our personal detail and enable us to get access to all kinds of governmental, educational or economic services. Through these same functions service providers are partly protected from fraudsters. A government's role in licensing, regulating or legislating can ensure that professions provide valuable service competently, safely and ethically to benefit the best interests of citizens.

Citizens want their government to enable them to travel abroad, whether by providing them with legitimate passports, through having good relations with other countries, by regulating the acquisition of foreign currency through a national bank and by ensuring safe cross-border travel. Enabling such international travel is important for the value of contact between citizens in our global village, for observing lifestyles of other cultures, for mutual learning between citizens from different countries and for appreciation of the scenic landscapes and diversity of life in our global biosphere. Through this contact citizens of the world interact when we entertain, learn, compete, trade and share with others. Furthermore, citizens want their government to play a significant role in international organizations, enabling their voice to be heard on many issues pertinent to their interests as global citizens deeply affected by people's actions in other parts of the world. To be part of international forums provides opportunities to bring the interests of a country to the attention of fellow global citizens and to negotiate mutually beneficial agreements that regulate and legislate human interaction across national boundaries such as trade, sport, cultural exchange or crime.

Citizens would define a third set of issues as priority for a government. These issues can be categorized as areas of constrained liberty. Liberty has to do with our ability to make our own choices, to have alternatives to choose from, to respond to life's challenges in appropriate ways and to be free to pursue a lifestyle according to our best judgement. Individuals judge that they have unique lives they are responsible for and would thus prefer to decide themselves how they choose to live those lives. Liberty, though, is always constrained, limited by the mere presence of others. Others, whether human or otherwise, also claim liberty and security for themselves, hoping thereby to enable their continued existence and make it meaningful.

Our sample citizens will define the issue of how much liberty individuals can have in the diverse areas of life as a major issue that a government must resolve. They would argue that human beings simply find it important to have certain personal freedoms, such as the liberty to choose their own friends from the numbers of people whom they have contact with, or to choose their own values in areas such as household budget priorities, consumer spending, the number of children and the nature of family life, the decoration of themselves and their property, the choice of personal moral values, the interpretation of the world with or without religion and so on. Within the confined space of the boundaries of a national state, citizens would want the freedom to decide for themselves with whom they want to associate, with which groups they want to identify and how strong that identification is to be. Within the almost unlimited possibilities of our planet, citizens would want to judge for themselves where to travel, with whom to do business and where they want to relocate. They find these liberties important, as the choices they make when exercising such liberties determine who they are, what kind of human beings they become and what they can do with their lives, or not.

The sample citizens would furthermore claim that citizens want at least a degree of liberty to participate in all kinds of communal affairs, whatever the size or nature of the community. Citizens would want to have opinions about matters of interest concerning however small or big a community they are part of and they would like to express those opinions to other people. They would want to comment on matters of shared, mutual interest and would like to discuss such issues with a broader audience. As they understand that humans are deeply influenced by their contact with other humans, they would want all options available to engage in any kind of communal life they can imagine.

Within this context, our sample citizens would want their government to step in where liberties are denied, violated or abused. A government ought to have as task to define liberties where they have become disputed, protect liberties where they have been violated, guarantee liberties where they are denied, restrain liberties where they are being abused and balance liberties where they are in conflict. Through establishing, maintaining, interpreting and enforcing liberties a government defines and enforces the aim, nature, scope and boundaries of the liberties citizens are allowed.

The discussions between the sample citizens might be impossible to imagine without them having at least a modicum of liberty. They have to be free to speak their minds about issues, to ask questions and expect answers, to inquire about other people's lives, to have opinions on priorities for governments and to challenge what others think and say. Similarly, their discussions would be virtually impossible if they did not feel safe and secure in their discussion room. If they feared reprisals for the content or manner of their speech, their speech could not have been honest and free. A certain minimum of security and liberty is already assumed in the imaginary device of discussions between a representative sample of citizens after the government of their state has collapsed for a considerable time. So too we must assume a degree of enablement for citizens to have language competency and a basic understanding of how their society works.

The same goes for the fourth category of issues that the sample citizens would list as priority for a government to restore decent living in their society. No discussions would have taken place without at least an inkling of equality among citizens in the sample. Without assuming to be equal at some level or another, discussants would find it difficult to make contributions to debates, question others, raise issues and propose novel ideas. I want to call the fourth category of issues spheres of focused equality, a category not adequately addressed by most pre-Enlightenment philosophers.

What does the expression spheres of focused equality mean? Equality is typically applied in a specific way in a certain sphere of life, often expressed or practised primarily in certain focused physical areas or intricate sets or combinations thereof, such as a sports field, a class room, a parliament building or the myriad shops, banks, traders, etc. that are collectively called the economy. Citizens in the sample would insist on being treated as equals. They would claim that they all belong to the species *Homo sapiens*, which means they have shared characteristics that distinguish them from all other living beings. Mere membership of this species qualifies them to be treated as equals, although what equality requires in all the multiple possibilities of human treatment in our highly differentiated social world is known to be highly contested.

One way of looking at equality is to say that to treat people as equals means to treat them the same. The citizens would insist that the concept of equality as treating similar things similarly acquire different meanings according to the focus of the sphere of life where this interpretation of equality is applied. To be citizens in a constitutional democracy means to be regarded as equals before the law. This focus in one aspect of being a citizen is that citizens are all subordinate to the laws of a state in the same way. To be equal thus means that laws should be applied similarly to individual cases that are the same in crucial, determining aspects. To be equal citizens also implies having the exact same set of political rights that provides citizens equal chances to participate in all facets of politics.

Another example of equality at work in a focused sphere is found in competitive sport. At international level, the focus is simply on who is the best in the sport. When selecting a team to represent a country, the focus of equality in this case is the standards that measure best performance in the sport. Equality is not the only value operative in either the practice of sport or the appreciation thereof. Although the selection of members of a national team requires equal treatment of every contender, the sample citizens would not want to be restricted to praise winners and losers equally, nor to admire excellent sports people equally to those who are average or mediocre. Similarly, sports people would not want to share a first prize equally, unless their performance was of equal standard and no other means of determining a winner is allowed. Sports people would also not appreciate being prescribed equal training programmes that do not take into account their individual talents, strengths, weaknesses, physical characteristics, mental abilities and so on.

The sample citizens would thus insist that a government help determine what treating citizens as equals means in the different spheres of societal life. A government must play a role when sharp differences of opinion about equality prevail and must step in where citizens are not treated as equals, but as people of lesser worth.

Citizens in the twenty-first century who have experienced (1) the collapse of societal infrastructure, for example the collective provision of water, electricity or roads, (2) the loss of the productive cultivation of food, (3) the impossibility to extract raw materials for all manner of technological application and (4) the implosion of organized social cooperation to accomplish complex multidimensional tasks will insist that the state has the end to establish life-sustaining cooperation.

The complexity of the organization of various aspects of contemporary societies where individuals work together as nodes in intricate networks is astounding. For example, to manufacture one motor vehicle requires many inputs of raw materials, electricity, equipment, space, transport, administration, food, shelter, training and so on. All these inputs require networks of people and specialized organization in turn.

Although most large organizations are reasonably good at maintaining their networks, the state can provide a holistic view of caring oversight that can safeguard the optimal functioning of all networks and their elements. If one element or network suffers or underperforms, let's say water provision is intermittent, electricity supply is interrupted, traffic is heavily congested or the climate changes in detrimental ways, then whole operations by many large organizations can come to a virtual standstill.

VII

The imaginary discussions of the sample citizens identified five categories of issues that they want a government to deal with as ends for their political society in order to sort out the anarchical mess their country is in. How do their issues relate to the ends articulated by the philosophers discussed earlier? Those philosophers identified the ends of the state as the overarching goal to acknowledge and respect the humanity of the inhabitants of a particular human community, the preservation of human life, the protection of citizens against harm and the guarding of individual liberty.

The imaginary discussions of the citizens trapped in enforced anarchy had led to an overlapping consensus with all four ends of the philosophers mentioned above. Two new emphases have emerged, the focus on enablement and the need to keep life-sustaining networks intact. Both these ends relate directly to the increasing complexity of contemporary societies that require much better and more specialized education than ever before.

These five sets of issues are not limited to contemporary societies only, but they form a kind of matrix that define universally problematic issues that people in any society throughout history had to respond to. These responses have differed throughout history and still differ for various reasons. Although there probably are no right answers and solutions to these problems and issues, some ways of answering these perennial challenges are better than others. To determine the better ways might require, amongst other things, to judge whether an appropriate answer is given to the specific historical manifestation of a set of issues, taking into account how the set of issues is configured into a complex set of problems through combining with specific factors pertinent to that time and place.

Another criterion to determine how appropriate responses are to the perennial challenges for governments would be to get the judgement of a representative sample of the people at the receiving end of political governance in that society. As Aristotle incisively responded when discussing whether ordinary citizens can judge a government: 'the user of a rudder, the helmsman, is a better judge of it than the carpenters who made it; and it is the diner not the cook that pronounces upon the merits of a dinner' (1981: 1282a7). My thought experiment is an attempt to implement Aristotle's advice on the capacity of citizens to have strong opinions on what they expect from governments in the twenty-first century.

From the issues that our sample citizens raise as fundamental matters for state institutions to focus on, several have direct bearing on the eradication of poverty. Note how the fundamental aims identified for the state include matters that would rid a society of poverty. For example, to acknowledge and respect the dignity of human beings, to preserve life, to protect individuals against harm, to enable citizens to become agents who are competent performers and the injunction to keep life-sustaining networks intact. Successful implementation of all these ends contributes directly to prevent or eradicate poverty. Note this: all five ends selected for governance must be implemented simultaneously with equal priority for poverty to be effectively eradicated and successfully prevented. The complexity of causes and consequences of poverty can only be effectively countered through a similarly complex series of governmental actions that accurately targets all possible factors involved in causing or perpetuating poverty.

Although I am not pursuing the issue which particular responses to this matrix are appropriate, an important issue does arise from the previous paragraph. Within the context of our contemporary world, we have specific political instruments available to implement responses to these sets of issues, that is, human rights and modern constitutional democracies. The sample citizens, if asked for an opinion, would insist on the best available political mechanisms to safeguard their fundamental interests. After consulting and interrogating political experts, the citizens would demand that their fundamental interests, that would enable them to build a good life of their choice, be secured by means of a set of basic rights. This set of rights must be embodied in a Bill of Rights in a constitution that has the status of fundamental law in their country. Their rights would thus become justiciable rather than being merely aspirational.

What would be included in this set of basic rights? Basic rights are those rights that protect citizens from any kind of harm, secure their means of living in the context of a human community, guarantee their liberties to make their own choices and ensure that they be treated as equals. Thus, the five categories of issues identified by the sample citizens are issues of the utmost importance for any person who wants to live their own life in a minimally meaningful way. This does not mean that a government itself must always provide all these goods, services, opportunities, liberties and decent treatment to citizens – it simply means that when these fundamental interests of citizens are threatened, a government must step in and ensure through proper oversight that citizens have what they need to live their lives meaningfully. A government could provide products or services themselves or through other agents, depending what would serve the long-term interests of citizens best as judged in terms of the fundamental ends of state institutions articulated above.

Note that not one category of rights consists only of so-called non-interference rights or so-called rights that require provision of goods and services. In all cases there are explicit demands that citizens should not interfere with one another's rights and in all cases governments must step in to provide something appropriate when needed in emergencies, whether it be protection, food, infrastructure, traffic regulations, mechanisms for conflict resolution and so on.

The common practice to give political rights priority – and its theoretical defence – makes sense in a way. Political power is an especially dangerous kind of power that easily leads to major kinds of abuses that negatively affect citizens. For this reason it might make sense to give citizens political rights to ensure they can check abuses of political power and participate in political decision making about the priorities they want a government to address. However, they could not participate in meaningful ways if they die from unnatural causes or are disabled through injury or disease. Neither could they participate in politics if they are so desperately poor that making a living exhausts their available energy. Similarly, their participation in politics and their ability to influence decision making is directly influenced by whether they are regarded and treated as equals. Various kinds of inequalities can debilitate citizens in their quest to demand fair treatment of their high-priority issues in any society.

Amartya Sen (1999) is thus right in arguing for the reciprocal influence that different kind of rights have on one another and for the mutual support that the acknowledgement and enforcement of one kind of rights give to the successful implementation of others. The point can be made even stronger. The five categories of rights are all required in contemporary societies for safeguarding citizen's interests, because they work together as combinations or configurations that are dependent on one another. They are co-original, in the sense that together they are the origins of the opportunities of choosing, making and living a life that a person judges to be the best possible option within available resources and current circumstances. In arguing for the value of socio-economic rights, Nickel says if all rights are perfectly realized, 'they would make it possible for every living person today to have and lead a life that is minimally good' (2005: 391–2).

Although the exact details of a set of rights and a package of policies and laws keep citizens and governments endlessly busy in every country all over the world, citizens would argue for a set of basic rights that would keep them alive and well, give them leeway to follow their own judgements, avail them of sufficient space to choose and practise what they judge as the good life and make them feel like human beings of equal worth.

VIII

The thought experiment elicits what twenty-first-century citizens value enough to demand that governments provide. The results of the thought experiment are mere speculations of what ordinary citizens judge governments are for.

Where does this discussion leave us? I claim that if we would consult a representative sample of citizens in a contemporary society, they would insist on such a range of services from a government, guided by the five ends discussed above. They would choose such roles for governments as these roles would best create spaces, conditions and circumstances within which citizens can select how they want to live their lives according to their own judgement.

Will a commitment to these ends eradicate poverty? The answer must be yes. These ends will ensure that equal respectful treatment, proper education, productive use of available resources, effective coordination and maintenance of life-sustaining networks and adequate assistance for people in need will be available for the benefit of everyone. Fulfilment of these ends gives us our best shot at building a society without poverty ever emerging.

Once a society is governed effectively in accordance with these goals, poverty will be prevented. However, in some cases poverty might persist as the result of injustices that occurred years, if not decades, ago. How should these difficult cases of poverty be dealt with? In the next chapter I explore the controversial matter of compensating people for injustices of the past that have left them impoverished.

12 • Compensating for Impoverishing Injustices of the Distant Past[1]

Calls for compensation are heard in many countries all over the world. Spokespersons on behalf of formerly oppressed and dominated groups call for compensation for the deeply traumatic injustices that their members have suffered in the past. Sometimes these injustices were suffered decades ago by members already deceased. How valid are such claims to compensation and should they be honoured as a matter of justice?

The focus of this chapter is on these issues of compensatory justice. I want to look at the issue from the perspective of the eradication of systematic poverty affecting particular groups – where injustices of the distant past can reliably be identified as one of the major contributory factors to people's current poverty. This perspective brings realism to the discussion. To eradicate poverty requires more resources than most societies have easily available and therefore the discussion must take limited resources for the purpose of compensatory justice into account. The harmful characteristics and consequences of poverty add a sense of urgency to dealing with issues of compensatory justice as well.

Legal systems in democratic societies embody strong moral values that specify that no injustice ought to be done to a fellow citizen. If someone commits a clearly identifiable injustice to a fellow citizen, the injustice must be stopped and the offender reprimanded or punished. In such cases an injustice means an objective wrong, usually defined as a violation of a person's rights that results in injury, harm, loss or damage. Stopping or punishing an injustice is, however, not enough. If serious harm or injury has been done to the victim of injustice or damage done to someone's property, the wronged person must be compensated.[2] Compensation means that the victim's original situation must be restored (see Barnett, 1991: 313; Sunstein, 1991: 281–2; Wade, 1978: 457).

Compensation can take different forms, although they express the same underlying principle. The principle is that the person who commits an injustice to another incurs a special moral relationship to the victim of the wrongdoing, that is, a relationship of owing the victim, of being indebted to the victim for the injury, harm, loss or damage caused (Fullinwider, 1975: 310). The fundamental idea of compensation is to restore the balance of justice between victim and perpetrator of injustice, to somehow make good the victim's loss. Compensation is partially aimed at restoring the victim's former position or state and thus tries to undo the wrong in such a way that the victim would be in a position similar to what the person would have been had the injury not occurred (Paul, 1991: 102).

There is more to compensation, however. Compensation also aims to restore the balance of equality between victim and perpetrator of injustice. Compensation implies acknowledging and honouring the rights of the victims that have been violated by a perpetrator. The perpetrator has illegitimately assumed and exercised power over the victim through committing the injustice.[3] Compensation thus symbolically restores the equality between victim and perpetrator as citizens of equal dignity and worth (see Paul, 1991: 102 ; Wilson, 1983: 523).[4]

Compensation can full or partial. Full compensation requires (1) attempts at repairing damage or harm as well as (2) restoring the moral status of victims as citizens with rights and dignity.[5] Partial compensation occurs when only one of these elements is involved. Compensation can often be partial in another sense, that is, not fully rectifying the wrongs committed. Reasons are the difficulties involved in some cases of either determining what would be appropriate to offer as compensation, or the enormity of the injury, harm, loss or damage suffered that cannot in any way be fully compensated.

These ideas about compensation are firmly entrenched in legal practice in democratic societies and regulate relationships between individual citizens, relationships between representatives of the state and individual citizens and relationships between individual citizens and organizations or companies.

However, attempts to apply these moral values about compensation to relations between groups of citizens (or between citizens of different countries) with a shared, but problematic and contested history are very difficult.[6] Why? There are several reasons. Note the following troubling questions that need to be resolved in order to make a convincing case for this kind of compensation.

1. What kind of injustice is at stake? Many kinds of injustices happen and nothing is ever done about them. How serious must an injustice be and why must this particular one be compensated and others not? How far back in history must one go?[7] How should such injustices be reliably identified?

2. If it can be established that there are injustices that occurred in the past that deserve to be compensated, who should be compensated? If the original victims of these injustices have already died, should their children or their grandchildren be compensated?[8] Are there grounds on which a person can be said to inherit the right to compensation from their ancestors? Is compensation due only to individuals who personally suffered an injustice, or should members of a group who suffered the injustice be compensated, as the group persists through time?

3. Similar issues are encountered when one asks who should be held responsible for the injustice and who should thus compensate the victims of an injustice. Are the individuals who perpetrated the original injustice the only ones who should compensate the victims? Should their descendants in any way accept responsibility for these wrongs? Maybe the responsibility for some injustices is a collective one that must be borne by a group, an organization or by society rather than by individuals. When should we judge that an injustice was perpetrated by a society or a group, rather than just being a series of smaller injustices committed by a loose collection of unrelated individuals?

4. If compensation is due in some cases, what kind of compensation should be given and for what purpose? Affirmative action is often used as a method of compensation. This practice grants victims of discrimination and oppression preferential treatment when applying for jobs. The purpose is to give victims of injustice a chance to get a job they were earlier denied for unacceptable reasons, despite their qualifications not being the best now amongst the pool of applicants for that job. Another purpose is to increase the representation of a formerly discriminated against group in the workplace and to provide role models for young people to aspire to. But are these kinds of compensation and the reasons provided in support the best ways of dealing with this issue?

In the rest of the chapter I will examine the following issues: (1) what kind of injustices qualify to be remedied by means of compensatory justice? (2) Should there be a limit to how far back in history one should go to compensate for injustice? (3) How can an injustice from the distant past be reliably identified as a cause of current problems? (4) Who should be compensated? (5) Who is responsible for compensation? (6) What form should compensation take? (7) Is the concept of compensatory justice backward looking or forward looking? I will argue for a moral obligation to the effect that serious injustices, perpetrated long ago against a group of people that caused poverty amongst them, ought to be compensated by society in a variety of ways to the original victims (if still alive) and their descendants.

I

What kind of injustices qualify to be remedied by means of compensatory justice? I defend the claim that a compensable injustice is a gross violation of the most important human rights, such as rights to life, to bodily and psychological integrity, to be free from all forms of violence and to own property.[9] Why use violations of human rights as indicators of compensable injustices? The vocabulary of human rights offers an already shared way of defining matters impartially that liberal democrats regard as high priorities that deserve governmental protection. If denied, the violation of these priorities leads to the various forms of serious harm that human rights are generally designed to avoid.

A group usually experiences such gross violations of human rights as deeply traumatic. Why this claim? Deeply traumatic injustices cause serious wounds to the bodies and minds of members of a group, or to the fabric of their social bonds.[10] Such injustices cause severe harm to individuals, from physical injury and deep psychological trauma to loss of life. Injustices of this magnitude have traumatic effects and disabling consequences on primary victims that are often transferred to succeeding generations, making them secondary victims. It is intuitively plausible that people responsible for such events with disastrous consequences for the lives of victims should be held responsible for compensating victims. In Nozick's terms, if past injustices have shaped present holdings and determined current lives, whatever property has been unjustly acquired or fundamental human rights have been violated, must be rectified.[11]

Major injustices with strong negative consequences and devastating effects on victims may consist of large-scale events such as a war of conquest, or they may consist of a cluster of smaller events equivalent to a major injustice, such as domination and oppression of a group based on irrational prejudice.[12] Some major injustices consist of a combination of both large-scale and smaller events.

A major injustice that qualifies as a compensable injustice is one that a group remembers with feelings of moral outrage and resentment.[13] Such remembrances usually form part of living memory. The injustice in dispute raises issues and generates debates that excite emotions that refuse to die or sink into oblivion. When told to descendants of victims, the experiences associated with the injustice come alive again and excite protesting emotions. Why is remembrance important? These memories and their associated emotions provide the spark for mobilization by the victims, or others on their behalf, to demand that debilitating injustices be acknowledged and rectified, however long the road to the eventual resolution of these issues might be. These memories give a rough indication of how serious and deep the group judged the harms they suffered.

I argue that the current effects of past injustice, or lack thereof, make a difference to our judgement whether full compensatory justice is called for. The kind and scope of the compensation called for are partially determined by the debilitating effects still reverberating through the members of the affected group. Noticeable negative effects persisting as a result of the injustice strengthen the case for full compensation for compensable injustice.

The way the effects have been dealt with by victims can influence the kind of compensation owed to them, whether it be full or partial compensation. Partial compensation is appropriate in the following cases. If the effects have been countered and reversed and the trauma has by and large healed, compensation to deal with trauma is no longer called for, though compensation for the suffering endured might still be needed. If human agency has been restored, if skills and levels of competence have been developed to levels similar to those of other groups and if moral responsibility can be fully employed again, then compensation to restore these things is no longer needed, but compensation for expenses and efforts in restoration might be relevant.[14] If the victims have recovered in these ways by themselves, it is to their benefit and psychological health: they have strongly proven and affirmed their independence and self-reliance. They can take pride in their ability to rise above their circumstances through healing themselves and reconstructing their skills to make a meaningful and worthwhile life. However, compensation acknowledging the harm, damage or loss caused by injustice, recognizing the efforts of victims to heal themselves and awarding money for costs incurred should still be on the agenda. So too should be compensation that restores the moral worth and human dignity of victims.

One could argue that full compensation would be required in cases where negative effects persist through generations and where those effects are traceable to the original injustice. Their traceability usually results from the fact that the injustice has been reinforced or maintained in the intervening years. The reinforcement and maintenance of injustice in subsequent years often have the result that the original sufferers of that injustice and their descendants have no reasonable chance to get rid of the negative effects and consequences. Increased opportunities were not available for empowerment through generally available mechanisms of redress, or through improved access to societal resources. Sufferers of injustice could thus not create decent lives for themselves on a par with what is available to and enjoyed by other citizens.[15]

In cases of justified full compensation, the situation of victims (group members) and their descendants in the time between the original event and its current effects did not change substantially or sufficiently. Sufficient change would mean that they could have acted autonomously and independently to empower themselves to rid their lives of the negative effects and consequences of the injustice. This means that some kind of injustice, oppression or prejudice kept the injustice or its consequences firmly in place or made it impossible to acquire resources, education or opportunities to nullify the effects. It may also be that the persisting effects result from the harm done to their person, agency or community, or from their social structure that was so devastated as to make recovery very difficult. If they consciously and deliberately made choices not to use meaningful opportunities to improve their lives, that would diminish the strength of their claims to full compensation.

II

Should there be a limit to how far back in history one should go to compensate for injustice? The answer depends largely on what has already been said. I claim that one should go as far back in history as (1) there are major injustices that have effects persisting to the present and (2) there are clearly defined and describable victims of those injustices. It stands to reason that no claim will be forthcoming if there is no victim. Thus, if there are claims for compensation by people who can demonstrate a reasonable possibility of a link between current poverty and past injustice, we have a moral duty to investigate such claims.

If claims for compensation go back to injustices that occurred more than a decade or two ago, the question arises when dealing with a compensable injustice becomes the responsibility of no one else but the victims themselves. A stage may be reached when effects of compensable injustices on victims indeed become the responsibility of the victims themselves and their descendants – a time when they ought to become agents of their own healing and recovery. Why this point of view? The argument hinges on the intuitively plausible ideas that (1) human beings can be or become agents of their own healing and recovery, (2) being such an agent depends on resources available before and after the traumatic event and (3) even deep harm does not totally extinguish human resilience in the face of adversity.

To determine the stage when effects of compensable injustices become the responsibility of victims themselves requires a complex judgement. In this judgement we must take into account the scope and consequences of the trauma caused by the injustice, the physical, mental and social resources available to the victims before the event and the extent of the damage to these resources. One must determine which aspects of their resources survive after the traumatic injustice to enable the victims to deal with the trauma. The levels of prejudice, discrimination and oppression must be noted that remain in place after the injustice, or newly develop in the wake of the injustice, that contribute to diminish the victims' opportunities for recovery and their access to support to deal adequately with their situation.

III

An important issue of compensatory justice is how a compensable injustice from the distant past can reliably be identified as a major contributory factor to people's current misery or poverty. I believe such a reliable identification can be made. It is possible to establish how one event, or a series of events, can have effects on or consequences for individuals, communities, groups or societies. These effects and consequences, if left untended or if reinforced by human action, persist as events creating further effects and consequences. These new effects and consequences can be similar to their predecessors, or be new distortions and perversions that affect the lives of the primary victims. These effects can be so drastic that secondary victims are created from people in close association with primary victims. These primary victims often cannot avoid transferring effects and consequences to others, as their own lives harbour too many debilitating effects that have sprung forth from the original injustice.[16]

How can a compensable injustice from the distant past be identified reliably? First, one must determine the current level of poverty of victims through standard measurements and indices of levels of poverty developed in the social sciences. Next, we need to identify that a particular group of poor people has been poor for quite some time. Their poverty is often not as recent as five or ten years ago, but more often than not goes back a generation or two. The history of individuals, families and communities can be traced easily – this information is often public knowledge – to verify claims of conditions of poverty transferred from one generation to the next. The inability of individuals, families and communities to escape traps of poverty that result from major injustices and other factors reinforcing the consequences of injustices is an important indicator of the need for full compensation.

The next move should be to investigate the major injustice from the distant past that is allegedly responsible for causing poverty that has been plaguing a group of people for more than a generation. This injustice must have been a major event with serious consequences and strong effects on the group. It must have inflicted significant wounds on their agency and diminished their means to develop their capacities and grow their life skills. The injustice should furthermore have dealt them psychological wounds that strongly affected their self-confidence, self-reliance, self-image and self-respect to such an extent that the impact of these psychological wounds detrimentally affected succeeding generations as well.

We should thus establish the harm done to the agency and autonomy of victims, their self-reliance and their capabilities for effective functioning and the reduction in their level of well-being. A trustworthy case must be presented that shows convincingly that such harms resulted from the consequences and effects of a major injustice. Major injustices typically have effects and consequences such as loss of life, serious bodily injuries, deep emotional scars, damage to property or loss thereof, destruction of interpersonal or communal relationships and loss of opportunities for personal and communal development and growth. These are all deeply traumatic events and their effects on the primary victims and their offspring must be established through independent investigation. Not only must we determine that these things have happened, but also how deep the harm was, how comprehensive the damage and to what extent the trauma affected their personal and collective agency and their abilities to make a good life for themselves as individuals or as community. How these disabling effects were carried over to the next generations must also be reliably established.

Typical examples of injustices with major, deeply traumatic consequences and effects are the following. Conquest in an unjust war, as in colonialism, is an example of a major single event or a series of bigger events. Political domination and oppression are examples of a mixture of smaller and larger events, as could be seen in a comprehensive series of injustices over many decades directed at black people through apartheid in South Africa. Women's oppression is another example of a series of injustices of different ranges, with the cumulative effect of oppressing and dominating women into disempowered human beings, deprived of equal developmental and growth opportunities. Persistent poverty must surely also be a part of this list.

While sufficient evidence of the broad outlines of compensable in-justices is available, detailed evidence or abundant first person accounts might not exist. This need not be a problem. The nature of these compen-sable injustices as deeply traumatic events is so well known that any person can form an idea of what it means to lose a loved one in war, to have your house burned down or flattened by a bulldozer, to be tortured whilst in detention without trial, to be raped by strangers or to be continuously humiliated by your partner in a love relationship.

Slightly more detailed examples of how philosophers depict two major events as injustices with continuing effects might be illuminating. Onora O'Neill (1987: 80) describes the enslavement, invasions and dispossession of indigenous peoples during European colonialism as consisting of serious harms and injuries resulting from gross violations of human rights that would today be judged as crimes against humanity. The effects of these human rights abuses are still 'all around us' and those effects are 'immeasurable, complex and intricate' (ibid.).[17]

Thomas Nagel (1973: 381) depicts the effects of racial discrimination in the USA as creating a group whose social position is 'exceptionally depressed, with destructive consequences both for the self-esteem of members of the group and for the health and cohesion of the society'. Bernard Boxill (1978) elaborates on this injustice by characterizing racial discrimination as in part 'judgemental injustice'. This consists in letting black people know that they deserve less consideration and respect than white people do. An arbitrary characteristic, their skin colour, is the reason why they are denied opportunities, excluded from participation in societal activities, treated with disrespect and judged to be inferior. Judgemental injustice also condemns them to the uncertainty of not knowing when they will suffer abuse for being black. As a result of these attitudes and actions against them, they lose self-confidence and self-respect.

We now have access to the two outer limits of the investigation into compensable injustices: the original deeply traumatic injustice and the current poverty. Perhaps the more difficult part is to convincingly show that the original injustice is a causal factor in the genesis of current poverty. I want to present an argument in support of the possibility that such a case can be made.

For poor people to make a convincing case for full compensation of a major injustice of the distant past, we should first examine the already gathered evidence of the impact of the major, deeply traumatic injustice on the group immediately after its occurrence. On the one hand we should note what coping skills, mechanisms and resources the victims had available and how these were affected by the trauma. Next we should investigate forms of oppression, discrimination and prejudice that continued afterwards that made their recovery and healing difficult, if not impossible. We should examine how oppression, discrimination and prejudice manifested in laws, attitudes, overt and covert behaviour, policies, priorities in budgets, etc. To demonstrate such a link between a major injustice and current poverty, information about the following factors must be presented: (1) seriously affected coping skills, mechanisms and resources, (2) continuing injustices denying them space for mobilization of human and other resources for recovery, or (3) cramped political space forcing them into stunted political growth and resulting in severely curtailed influence on society.[18] Thus, they must demonstrate an inability for healing and recovery, as well as for reduced capacity for mobilization to achieve self-renewal.

To establish the case for compensation convincingly, a group must thus be able to point to obstructions that impeded their recovery in the years between the initial impact of a major, deeply traumatic injustice and their current state of poverty.[19] Obstructions would mainly result from the denial of political rights which is profoundly disabling, continued oppression and discrimination which close opportunities for growth and shut off chances to have a voice being heard and a lack of human and economic resources which stifles attempts to engineer one's own recovery. A group must also show that such obstructions constrained their attempts to provide children a better future in which such obstructions would have no adverse effects on the development and growth of the children to mature self-realization.[20]

If such obstructions can be shown present to a degree significant enough to make any form of recovery difficult, a strong presumption exists in favour of acknowledging (1) that both primary and secondary victims have a strong case for compensation and (2) that not only the first generation of perpetrators of injustice are guilty and thus responsible for the plight of the poor. Obstruction that impeded recovery from a major injustice suggests that the descendants of the original perpetrators of the major injustice have committed further obstructing injustices. Through these injustices they have become complicit in the plight of the victims, in the sense that they are also participants in a continuing process of committing injustices against the victims. They are thus co-responsible for the plight of the descendants of the original victims.

IV

Who should be compensated? Individuals or groups? Only the original sufferers of the injustice or their descendants as well? Only their direct descendants? Whom should be compensated when most of the original sufferers from injustice have already died? Is there a cut-off point for how far the rippling effects of a traumatic injustice can reach through the complex histories of families, communities and distinct social groups? What are the links between continuing rippling effects and the strength of human agency capable of arresting and eliminating those effects?

Compensation for major injustices of the distant past – those responsible for contemporary poverty – is almost exclusively a group thing and not an individual matter.[21] The major injustices that qualify as compensable injustices, regardless of the fact that they occurred long ago, carry a distinct social or group aspect.[22] Two examples will suffice to explain this social or group dimension. Major injustices, such as wars of conquest, were fought in the name of and for the benefit of a country, or a particular group or community of distinct people. The soldiers fighting the war did so in their capacity as representatives of a government or a group, acting on commands of such principals. They fought against a community owning valuable land or a society in control of valuable resources.

Even major injustices, such as racism or sexism, that consist of a series of smaller events perpetrated by individuals and groups against other individuals and groups manifest an inescapable group dimension. Racism and sexism are perpetrated against identifiable groups of individuals, marked by specific visible characteristics they cannot control. The perpetrators of racism and sexism practise their prejudice from within constructed identities based on specific, preferred social or group characteristics.

In both examples the targets or objects of the injustices were not individuals in their personal capacity, but individuals as representative of their group, marked by their characteristic identifications.[23] Compensable injustices were committed against *groups* and we have already established that the results and consequences of these injustices can be transferred from the directly affected generation to the next one who did not themselves experience the injustice. A major injustice – or cluster of ongoing injustices – can have serious and debilitating effects on the primary victims. Through injuries and harms to body and mind, damage to possessions and property, loss of life, liberties and functions and ruptures of the social fabric of communities, primary victims may lose any one of a series of capacities that contribute to making a worthwhile human life.[24] These effects of a major injustice can be perpetuated and transferred from one generation to the next if sufficient space and resources for recovery are not available. Thus, all those adversely affected by a compensable injustice – even those more than one generation removed from the original injustice – must be compensated in some or other way.

If members of a group must be partially or fully compensated, what should the aim be? The aim of compensation must surely be one or more of the following: to repair their capacities to make a good life; to give them something equivalent in return for their injuries and losses; to restore relationships and resources; to acknowledge symbolically the serious violations of their rights and restore their dignity as equal citizens, whether it be through apologies or memorials.[25] Compensation must empower people disadvantaged by injustices of the past to take up their place as citizens of equal worth and dignity with at least a minimum decent lifestyle. Victims of injustice must have their agency restored, so that they can take proper care of themselves within a community of interdependent free and equal agents. Compensation ought to be due to (1) the original sufferers and (2) their descendants who have suffered as a result of the injustices done to their ancestors and still have to deal with the after-effects of the original injustice.

Although the injustices concerned affect groups in particular, that does not imply that all members were affected equally. The effects and consequences of an injustice do not strike everyone similarly and some people escape most of them or overcome them more easily than others can. A lot depends on how a person can dodge or overcome the way that injustices from the distant past have been reinforced or maintained. Can the exact extent of the harm, injury, loss or damage of each individual thus be determined so that each individual's exact amount of compensation can be calculated? No, for two reasons. One reason is that it would be virtually impossible, highly controversial and also too costly to make such fine-grained, specific investigations and detailed judgements about degrees of individual loss, harm and damage.[26] Another reason for being unable to determine exact amounts of compensation is that although some individuals might have been less directly affected by injustice than others, this does not adequately reflect the harm and suffering they may have experienced indirectly.[27] They were often also strongly negatively influenced by sharing the traumas that friends, family and colleagues have experienced, or they may have been affected by living in an atmosphere where their kind were despised and emotionally or physically abused. They lived with the awareness that the possibility of becoming a victim of trauma or abuse was always alive. Furthermore, ideological abuse, where a system of ideas with its accompanying justification reinforce injustices by deprecating and degrading victims, often legitimates physical and emotional abuse and contributes to low self-esteem.

V

Who is responsible? Individuals, groups or the state? Can the descendants of the people who originally committed the wrongs be held responsible for the injustices of their ancestors? If so, under what conditions? Can compensation only be provided by the perpetrators of injustice, or can someone else provide compensation vicariously?[28]

I want to argue that the state must take primary responsibility for compensable injustices.[29] The reason is that the state has failed to treat all its members fairly and equitably, albeit in a previous era and in a different manifestation.[30] That the state treated some members unfairly and unjustly is clear (1) from injustices perpetrated by governments, (2) from group behaviour sanctioned by a government or (3) from acts knowingly allowed by a government willingly watching how a particular group of citizens were unjustly and unequally treated and dominated into a desperate social position of vulnerable subordination. For this reason a government representing the state was responsible for the inequitable and unfair treatment of a group of its citizens in the past.[31] Therefore the current government as representative of the state must take over the responsibility to rectify this wrong, albeit that the injustice was committed by a former representative of the state. Thus, the government – and indeed society as a whole – must accept responsibility for the plight of the victims and the need for compensation.[32]

Yet, even individuals can and should be held responsible, if they are or have become complicit in committing an injustice or through their everyday behaviour maintained and reinforced the negative consequences of a major injustice. How could they have become complicit? They became complicit through acts of commission, that is, by adopting or acquiring prejudice, or through acts of omission, that is, by ignoring the plight of the vulnerable sufferers from injustice. Through these acts of omission or acts of commission individuals may have become accessories in maintaining the original injustice or its negative effects and consequences. They did not instead become aware of the immorality of the injustice being done to the victims, nor did they protest it, try to stop it, or undo its effects. This view assumes the commonsense notion that as human beings and fellow citizens we expect a certain level of moral agency from one another: we ought to have the moral capacity to judge certain practices, states of affairs or acts as unjust or unfair and act on those judgements. To act on such judgements might require us to condemn and remove injustices and their consequences, or do so when made aware of them by fellow citizens, especially victims of injustice. If not, we stand guilty before our fellow citizens and have to give an account why we have failed to respond, why we refused to see their plight as expressed on their faces, why we chose not to hear their cries of suffering, or why we have violated or ignored the implications of the values of our shared humanity.

There is another way in which individuals can be held responsible for compensable injustice, although to a lesser degree. They are at least partially responsible even if they had no part in committing the original injustice or if they did not participate in any activities reinforcing or maintaining current injustices or the effects thereof, but they have nevertheless willingly and knowingly enjoyed the benefits resulting from an injustice and its consequences. How can this claim be supported? Compensable injustices are often committed to strip a group of financial, property, social and other resources or to limit their access to these resources so as to transfer the resources to the dominant group. So-called innocent members of the dominant group mostly willingly accept their better-off position whilst being aware – or being made aware by victims or others on their behalf – of the worse-off position of members of the disadvantaged group. Many such beneficiaries may presume their societal arrangements to be natural and fixed, or may protest that in their innocence they knew nothing about those unfortunate events that occurred long ago. However, in most unjust societies sufficient voices of protest and cries of suffering are available to appeal to the conscience of every citizen.[33] As beneficiaries of injustice, they should thus have been aware of their privilege. Most possibly the beneficiaries were morally confronted by the victims of injustice

to reject and remove the negative disempowering and disabling consequences of the injustice committed by the forebears of the beneficiaries.
Not responding to victims and exploiting their own privileged position
make the beneficiaries at least partially responsible for the continuing
presence and consequences of a major injustice, though they are not
responsible for the original injustice.[34]

I am arguing for degrees of responsibility. The original perpetrators
of injustice have full responsibility for committing the injustice. Their
descendants might have lesser responsibilities for their roles in either
perpetuating the effects and consequences of the injustices or by refusing
to listen to the cries of suffering and voices of protest directed at them.
The government as representative of state and society incurs a long-
term responsibility to take care of the well-being of its citizens and thus
to restore their position once the government has either allowed or committed injustice against a specific group of members.[35]

VI

What form should such compensation take? Many forms of compensation
are possible: their aim should be to restore victims of compensable injustice
to full citizenship as persons (1) with dignity and worth and (2) who can
function as interdependent agents who take full responsibility as equals
for themselves and others in society.

The different forms of compensation depend on the kind of loss, injury,
harm or damage done to victims of injustice. What is clear, though, is
that compensation imposes a twofold obligation on the former perpetrators
and reinforcers of injustice. The first is to restore, rectify or compensate
for the victims' loss, injury, harm or damage (see Kershnar, 1999: 84).
In this case in kind compensation should take preference – if land had
been stolen, return the same land or something similar and acceptable.[36]
In cases of loss of life or trauma the harm cannot be undone, but some
of the effects and consequences can be softened. For example, the loss of
a breadwinner can be compensated by means of an income grant, financial
assistance for health and education, provision of adequate shelter and
so on.

In many cases where an injustice cannot be undone and in cases of
loss of land, a large part of what is at issue is the loss of the means to
make a livelihood, to establish meaningful relationships within a community, the loss of caretakers and breadwinners who should have provided

livelihoods, caring upbringing and life chances and the lack of role models who could have facilitated job training, social skills and practical intelligence. For these reasons it would make sense to compensate people through special education and training programmes or through special access to education, empowerment opportunities in business to develop their human agency and access to life skills to make successful lives for themselves as full and equal citizens.[37] The lives of primary and secondary victims might eventually turn out to be different from the ones they would have had without the injustice occurring, for example, they might not be able to be farmers as their ancestors or live as hunters in exactly the same area as their forebears. Such differences resulting from their compensation suggest that complete restoration might never be possible, despite full compensation.[38]

The second obligation compensation imposes on the perpetrators and reinforcers of injustice is to equalize the relationship between victim and perpetrator. The inequality in relationship results from the perpetrator assuming a relationship of power and dominance over the victim. This enforced relationship had destructive consequences for the victim, although the victim never gave informed consent for it to exist. What must be done to equalize the relationship between victim and perpetrator? The dignity and worth of the victim must be restored through an acknowledgement of the rights of the person that have been violated. This can best be done by means of an apology or through enforcement of those rights by a court of law. To acknowledge guilt, to ask forgiveness and to pursue reconciliation based on shared moral rejection of the injustice facilitate the equalization of the relationship. Part of this restoration of the equal dignity of victims as citizens is to negotiate the nature of all aspects of compensation with them and to make decisions concerning the manner of compensation only through eliciting their consent.

Some forms of compensation might not succeed in replacing losses or repairing damage, as some losses are irreplaceable and some harms are irreparable. In such cases, like the loss of loved ones, compensation must acknowledge the intensity of suffering, the loss of a valuable human resource and symbolically restore victims to equal citizenship. Other forms of compensation might not be successful in restoring harms or injuries, because the injustices might have been devastatingly destructive in their harm to human lives. In such cases, like permanent disabilities, compensation must aim to ease unbearable pain, to make someone's nearly destroyed life at least somewhat easier and to symbolically acknowledge the gravity of the injustice done.[39]

VII

Is the concept of compensatory justice backward looking or forward looking (see Boxill, 1978: 249)?[40] Are backward-looking justifications that aim to remedy harms done to people in the past better than forward-looking justifications that aim to improve future life for everyone? What exactly are the differences between these two justifications?

I want to argue that a backward-looking perspective is crucial. There must be some backward-looking justification, spelling out in detail the injustice done and how it was maintained and reinforced through the intervening years. There must be a justification of how some people are still suffering today because of what was done to their ancestors and reasonable evidence must be presented to support these links between present poverty, misery and suffering on the one hand and past injustice on the other. In this sense a backward-looking justification is an explanation of how the present came to be (see Amdur, 1979: 238; Paul, 1991: 100).

Although looking backwards is crucial, this does not mean that the past is the main issue in demands for compensation of injustices of the distant past. These demands are not to change the past so much as a desperate cry to change the present. People judging themselves victims of injustices long ago experience themselves and their group as inferior or disadvantaged or unequal *now*, when they compare the average position and standing of their group members with the current average position and standing of other members of society.[41] They judge themselves and their group in need of compensation to make up their accumulated losses, to improve their relative standing in society as measured by several indices and to gain respect as equal functioning and contributing members of their diverse society.

A forward-looking justification is important as well – anything done in the name of justice must raise the future well-being of society and improve the quality of cooperation within a community of citizens for the better. To establish and maintain justice in a society ought to secure the interests of every citizen. So compensation must not only improve the lives of a group of marginalized people, but enhance the quality of life available to all citizens in their country.

The backward- and forward-looking perspectives can be joined in a metaphor: compensation must clear up a festering wound in the body of society for the benefit of improved functioning of all component parts. Such a societal wound will have at least three parts: (1) a certain group suffers a decline in life chances and opportunities for personal betterment and this decline manifests in poverty, (2) discrimination based on group characteristics shows in humiliating and denigrating behaviour towards members of the group, in the silencing of their voices and concerns and in the consequent prevention and inhibition of healing and recovery and (3) the contents of propositions (1) and (2) are directly linked to a compensable injustice from the distant past.

A societal wound is not something that strikes a number of individuals randomly or naturally, but members of a dominant group inflict it on a vulnerable group for reasons such that the dominant group dislikes the subordinated group for some of their shared group characteristics, wants their resources or exploits their labour and services. I thus want to argue that injustices of the distant past are actually issues of the present,[42] showing that current inequalities, domination and oppression have histories of being brought into existence and being nurtured by dominant groups. Through healing such wounds, society itself will grow into a better state of moral health in future and become more sensitive to the voices, issues and plight of any new category of marginalized and vulnerable people that might arise.

At times it seems plausible that the contents and implications of this view of compensatory justice for aggrieved groups can be transposed into something like John Rawls's theory of justice without loss of content, but with gains in simplicity.[43] The two foci of compensatory justice can be captured by the two Rawlsian principles that secure equal dignity, fair equality of opportunity and improvements of the position of the least advantaged members of society as prerequisite for justified inequalities of income and wealth. This transposition seems to have the advantage of discarding the backward-looking justification.[44] Why not rather work on these Rawlsian principles that can secure similar results as the principles of compensation? Why not just forget about the ugly past, as so many of the perpetrators of injustice and their descendants fervently wish? Or is this advantage of ignoring the past a dubious one?

The main reason to stick to the principles and ideas of compensation is that such a transposition to Rawlsian principles would deprive victims of injustice of their personal and collective narratives that make sense of their experiences and the condition of their lives.[45] These narratives also construct their history that gives them identity and they offer them stories that give them hope for liberation with dignity from oppressive circumstances. Also, why should descendants of former elites be satisfied to be classified as poor or least advantaged with little state aid forthcoming to improve their position if through compensatory justice their descent from, and position as, elites in the past might be recognized and restored in the present?[46]

VIII

There is a strong emotional reaction against compensatory justice by former perpetrators, reinforcers and beneficiaries of compensable injustices. They either deny responsibility for past events or claim new injustices are being committed when a group is compensated for past injustice. Perhaps they will view the issue differently if they interpret compensatory justice as a special case of transformatory justice.

Transformatory justice deals with issues Rawls[47] assigns to non-ideal theory or partial compliance theory. Such issues deal with injustice in societies and how best to transform a society to reduce or eliminate injustice. The term transformatory justice implies that existing political institutions, policies, practices, ideas and citizens of unjust societies must be changed, modified, reformed and reshaped to embody and express the newly defined or negotiated values of justice fundamental to a new or revised constitution.

In the case of the comprehensive transformation of a radically unjust society into a just one, the acceptance of a theory of justice as foundation for the new society is a milestone. From this point onwards, the accepted theory of justice functions as a Rawlsian ideal theory guiding further processes of transformation. Compensation for injustices of the distant past is merely one of those further processes of transformation and not so different from the others.

The way in which other aspects of transformation share many goals and characteristics with compensatory justice can be explained as follows. For example, when assigning formerly disenfranchised and oppressed people rights to equal liberties as part of transforming an unjust society, a government is rectifying injustices that might have existed for decades or even centuries. Assigning these rights has enormous implications. In new institutions of governance, new interest groups demand and formulate new policies to change the present that was shaped and formed by many injustices from the past. Such policies could include setting up a truth commission to identify victims and perpetrators of serious human rights violations, implementing affirmative action to rectify patterns of racial prejudice in job appointments, changing priorities of governmental budgets to benefit those disadvantaged for many years by the neglect of unjust governments and so on. Compensating for impoverishing injustices of the distant past is merely one part of a comprehensive set of policies to undo the injustice of the past.

Compensatory justice starts with the acknowledgement that all members of society are now regarded as citizens of equal dignity, but many were not treated as that in the past. A lot of current misery and suffering can be traced directly to acts of fellow citizens based on assumptions about the supposed inferiority of the victims. If governmental representatives of the new foundational theory of justice have the power to show they disagree with past injustices and they have the capacities and means to ameliorate the consequences and effects thereof, then to refrain from doing so is equal to condoning and perpetuating past injustice.

Compensatory justice is thus tied to an ideal theory of justice and the ways this theory gets embodied and expressed in a transforming society on a quest to establish justice for everyone.

Conclusion: A Theory of Poverty and its Eradication

In this book I have developed the following ideas about poverty that collectively form a theory of poverty that presents its core issues, interprets it, explains it and provides guidance for how to interact with or react to it.

The core argument

In Part 1 of this book, I have presented arguments, ideas and evidence to establish the following: poverty has a wide range of dimensions complexly assembled in every case. To understand poverty properly, we need a comprehensive grip of the multidimensional nature of poverty that highlights the diverse range of harmful impacts poverty might have on individual humans. Only such an understanding provides an appropriate illumination of the salient issues for moral evaluation as a prelude for aid and action. Such a moral evaluation shows how the many dimensions of poverty violate a wide range of generally accepted moral values.

In Part 2 I have argued that the eradication of such a complex phenomenon like poverty in its myriad configurations, with the potential to inflict such a wide range of harmful effects on people, their relationships and institutions, needs a counter of aid and collective action consisting of a similarly comprehensive set of strategies and interventions based on appropriate moral values. I thus argued in defence of an ethically justified style of aid, I showed how a decent theory of justice can, at least in principle, counteract or prevent all manifestations of poverty, I indicated why poverty needs to be tackled through collective efforts, indicating eventually that only collective action through core governance functions can completely eradicate poverty and prevent its recurrence. Once these governance functions have been established effectively, it becomes possible in principle to uproot all forms of poverty remaining from events that occurred in the past.

The arguments of Part 1 establish the following positions. I first argue that the core harms that poverty inflicts on human beings are the loss of human dignity and a threat to one's health. I embody these perspectives in my definition of poverty. I revise the traditional distinction between absolute and relative poverty into a new distinction between extreme and intermediate poverty. The advantage of this distinction is that the focus is on the degree of harm involved in the two kinds of poverty, whilst in both cases there are universal elements embodied that make the definitions useful in any society. Both definitions nevertheless retain contextual elements as well that can only be specified meaningfully in terms of a particular society.

1. The main dimensions of the meaning of the concept of poverty in everyday language are as follows. The concepts poverty and poor refer to people who (i) have insufficient economic means to procure the necessaries of life or inadequate resources to participate in human social activities; (ii) lack essential properties, have deficiencies in desired resources, or have access only to inadequate or scant resources; (iii) have a low position in society without substantial influence; (iv) sometimes perform unworthy of their position or ability and (v) make a small, or no, contribution to society. The negative terms associated with poverty suggest at the very least that poverty in this sense is not something ever chosen easily by anyone. Social scientists typically use terms like the following in their descriptions of poverty, 'deprivation', 'exclusion', 'insufficient', 'lack', 'dependent', 'unable to', 'loss of assets', 'too little', 'shortage', 'disabilities', 'incapacities' and 'fall below'.

2. Poverty's core meaning is that human beings are without economic resources needed for survival or have too little thereof. They stand in need of basic requirements for a minimally acceptable human life. To be poor means to suffer as a result of all the consequences of not having enough economic capacities. Poverty as lack of economic capacities makes it impossible for its victims to develop and deploy their abilities to engage in social life as rich people do, disables people from giving their full input in employment, diminishes their range of activities as full members of society and restrains them from utilizing opportunities they would otherwise qualify for as rich people can easily do. For poor people a lack of economic capacities implies some things cannot be acquired, some activities cannot be engaged in because the prerequisites are not there, the enabling circumstances to make something of their lives are absent. They just don't have what rich people do. The things, support, circumstances and resources to acquire

what is necessary to engage in a fully human life are not accessible to support their life's project.

3. Poverty is a concept *uniquely applied to humans* to indicate when a specific person has fallen below the standard of life thought appropriate for someone in that culture.

4. *Extreme poverty* means that a person does not have enough economic capacities to provide adequate food, clothing, shelter, security and medical care to maintain their physical health. In everyday language this means people do not have enough means to procure even the necessaries of life. Such people mostly cannot secure their proper survival and are dependent on others for help.

5. *Intermediate poverty* means that although people have adequate economic capacities to provide adequate food, clothing, shelter, security and medical care to maintain their physical health, they cannot participate in any other activities regarded as indicative of being human in that society. People are unable to afford participation in characteristic aspects of human life, that is, they are people without sufficient money, wealth or material possessions to afford anything more than the barest necessities to keep themselves physically alive and well. Poverty, as a lack of economic capacities, can thus have the consequence that poor people cannot participate in the activities of their broader social context. Their poverty thus leads to *social exclusion*.

Descriptions and interpretations of poverty

In my description and interpretation of poverty I followed a holistic approach that offers a comprehensive grip of the multidimensional nature of poverty that highlights the diverse range of harmful impacts poverty might have. I show the diverse dimensions of poverty that play out uniquely in each individual case in a complexly assembled way. I present a profile of poverty as a complex phenomenon that can best be understood through a series of overlapping metaphors drawn mainly from the contexts of health, medicine and politics that best expresses the nature of this troubling condition.

1. Metaphors drawn from the medical and health world.

   (i) Poverty can be described as a *disabling condition* that places
        many restrictions on people's ability to determine their own
        lives and develop themselves. Poor people are *disabled* in their
        quest to live a life worthy of humans as defined by society. They
        cannot empower themselves sufficiently to exploit the oppor-
        tunities available to them as human beings seeking to live lives
        comparable to those of their rich fellow citizens. Poverty takes
        away opportunities for making a decent living and deprives people
        of life chances approximately the same as others have for making
        and implementing meaningful choices.

        Poverty is an example of a condition consisting of many pos-
        sible elements that can constrain people's lives significantly and
        disable them into lives far below their capacity. Lack of economic
        capacities to engage in empowering education or meaningful self-
        improvement immediately springs to mind. Greater susceptibility
        to disease and less economic capacities to care for one's personal
        health are other disabling factors. The lack of opportunities for
        participation in generally accepted social activities and sharing in
        the richness of social interaction with fellow citizens is another
        factor that disables poor people.

        Lack of self-respect, reinforced by public stereotyping, under-
        mines poor people's confidence to change their situation. Lack
        of basic skills as a result of inadequate access to educational
        and self-improvement opportunities make it difficult to design
        creative solutions to the problems of poverty. Lack of time and
        money places further constraints on people's ability to change
        their lives, as does the inability to tap into social and political
        resources that can help to address problems of poverty collectively.

  (ii) Poverty can often be described *as privation*. Privation is a con-
        dition where humans lack access to attributes or qualities they
        ought to possess for living lives that qualify as worthy for members
        of their species. It can also refer to a state where humans lack
        essentials needed for decent living according to an acceptable
        standard.

 (iii) Poverty is at times *akin to disease or infection*. Some cases of
        poverty become like *disease*, where certain human functions do
        not work properly and as a result the normal state of health is
        negatively affected. Like disease, poverty leads to discomfort or

a disturbance of health. Poverty can cause crucial human functions to derange and thus negatively affect various parts of people's lives. Like *infection*, poverty has primary manifestations, like malnutrition, that produce knock-on effects that can be transmitted throughout other areas of a person's life where further injuries or harms result. Lack of economic capacities thus exacerbates stress in human beings. This aspect of poverty resembles an *infectious spread* of something bad throughout different dimensions of a person's life.

(iv) Poverty can thus be characterized as *an ill or hardship*. As *an ill* it reduces a person's quality of life and becomes injurious to someone's health. The result often is that people experience their lives as miserable, troublesome or wretched. As *hardship* poverty is a series of painful challenges people find difficult to bear. Poverty inflicts harsh conditions on people that they find tough to endure or give meaning to.

 (v) In some cases poverty resembles *a syndrome*, that is, poverty is like a disease or condition where one finds a characteristic combination or concurrence of symptoms.

(vi) Some effects of poverty are similar to *the impact of the AIDS virus* on people's immune systems. Like the AIDS virus reduces the resistance and immunity of a human body to effectively fight disease, so poverty diminishes the capacities and options available for poor people to respond effectively to life's shocks and changes. As a result poor people are often reduced to *dependency*, which means they must rely on other people for support to cope with life's basic challenges. They become unable to do without assistance that gives them access to basic necessities required to cope with the demands of everyday living.

(vii) Poverty resembles the *common cold*. Most humans can easily and accurately observe when a fellow human suffers from the common cold, as the symptoms are clearly visible and easily identifiable. A further resemblance between poverty and the common cold is that both phenomena can be caused by a variety of factors. As the common cold is caused by a virus that constantly mutates so poverty results from one or more causes drawn from a wide-ranging set of factors.

(viii) Poverty resembles *a lack or deficiency*. For example, poor people often lack food, that is, they are without proper food for a healthy diet, or they have too little of it. They furthermore often have

deficiencies in their diet, that is, they have a shortage of adequate
nutrition necessary for a healthy human body.

2. Other metaphors used in the description and interpretation of poverty
    come from the socio-political world.

    (i)   In some cases researchers define poverty in terms of *lack of
          independence*, or self-reliance. The independence of people can
          suffer in different ways as a result of poverty. Poor people's in-
          dependence is restricted by the way that poverty curtails their
          ability to make decisions about their own lives for lack of resources
          they command and opportunities they are able to utilize. Poverty
          then refers to an inability to be self-reliant, which focuses our
          attention to the incapability of families to provide minimum
          means for living a decent life for themselves. Poor people with
          strong feelings of powerlessness tend to become dependent on
          other people, the state or relief organizations for aid or to take
          care of them.

    (ii) *Lack of power* is close to the heart of what poverty means to
          many poor people. Power means the ability to do something, to
          influence people, to have an impact on a community, to accomplish
          one's goals, to grab people's attention, to have freedom to explore
          different options or the ability to use ideas or resources to change
          people's lives. Poor people experience themselves as powerless,
          as they find themselves with no strength or ability to do many
          of the things they could legitimately want to, influence people
          to have a significant impact on the circles of human association
          they are involved in, or change anyone's life positively through
          using capacities whose training require adequate economic
          resources. Poor people are often aware of their powerlessness
          and the negative consequences thereof. They often experience
          themselves as powerless in the face of life's challenges and
          adversities.

    (iii) Poor people often define poverty as *violation of social norms*.
          Part of the explanation for this definition amongst poor people
          is that it expresses their inability to be equal participants in social
          events, as they cannot always 'reciprocate with gifts or partici-
          pate in community events'. Their inability to participate and
          reciprocate as equals has harmful consequences that range from
          'humiliation, loss of honor and psychological distress, to social

marginalization and exclusion from important social networks'
(Narayan et al., 2000a: 44, 45).

(iv) In some cases poverty is similar to *oppression*. If oppression
amounts to people not being given opportunities to develop their
talents and exercise their capacities where appropriate in their
social environment, then some effects of poverty are virtually
identical to oppressive social treatment.

(v) Poverty is sometimes *a trap*. Note the metaphors used to describe
some poor people's experience of poverty as entrapment, itself
a metaphor: being encircled, feeling trapped by the interlocking
strands of a web, being imprisoned and living in bondage. This
interlocking makes it difficult for poor people to rid themselves
of poverty.

(vi) Poor people in addition experience the *humiliation* of not being
able to live fully human lives as specified by their society. Poverty
entails the desolation of realizing that others do not demonstrate
care that you experience poverty in all its fullness.

Explanations of poverty

In my explanation of poverty I present a view of poverty as caused by a
complex configuration of factors that could jointly play a causal role in
any specific case. I place poverty in the broad context of myriad things
that can go wrong with the complex range of processes that humans must
engage in to ensure survival and flourishing through social cooperation.

1. Normal human activities can be derailed by myriad human actions
to produce poverty. Human resource dealing processes, that is, the
complex series of human activities consisting of the location, conversion, exchange and distribution of resources, can be short-circuited
and thwarted in a diversity of ways, some of natural and others of
human origin. Humans can directly or indirectly influence these activities through the use and abuse of any kind of power.

Poverty can be the result of any of *thousands of possible kinds
of failure or obstruction* somewhere in the highly complex series of
processes involved in the location, conversion, exchange and distribution of resources. Whole human societies become poor when the
highly complex processes of location, conversion, exchange and distribution of resources are short-circuited or fouled up on such a large

scale that significant parts of the population are classified as poor. Individuals are, or become, poor when they do not have, or cannot, find any rewarded role within these processes, or are excluded from them, for whatever reason.

Their poverty is due to the fact that they do not have roles or functions rewarded in their society's quest for the location, conversion, exchange or distribution of resources, nor are they compensated for this lack. They cannot realize the appropriate social activities characteristic of humans in their society. They also do not participate in the fundamental collective human quest for ensuring the survival and enabling the flourishing of human communities. In a double sense they are thus *excluded* from fully realizing their unique human characteristics.

2. Poverty is *a multidimensional complex human phenomenon* that in each case consists of a complex interweaving of contingent circumstances and factors. What does it mean to call poverty a complex human phenomenon? What poverty consists of, the effects it has on persons and the causes thereof, have many different parts related in many ways. Importantly, these parts combine to form a unique configuration in each individual case. Nevertheless, the configuration exhibits characteristics easily recognized as belonging to the complex, multidimensional phenomenon of poverty. The complexity of poverty can be seen in social science research by noting both its multiple indicators and causes.

3. In so far as poverty is a lack of knowledge and technology to find and use resources humans share this fate with other living beings, that is, being *unable to adapt successfully* to their environment. Inappropriate disturbance of the interlinkage between habitat, diet and species capabilities, coupled with inability to adapt timeously to changing circumstances, often result in a population crash or even extinction in the case of other living organisms. In humans the first result is poverty.

4. Poverty thus sometimes results from *a shortage of knowledge and skills* for proper cultivation of the earth's resources and smart innovation to productively transform whatever we have available into useful products for survival. This shortage of knowledge and skills is often the cause that large parts of the world's population are consistently in situations

where they cannot obtain sufficient economic resources as required for decent human living.

5. Many cases of poverty result from *an inability to transfer* to a younger generation what experienced, skilled people have learnt in their efforts to cope with our world in our quest for survival and flourishing.

Guidance for action

The complex configuration of symptoms, effects, consequences and causes of poverty thus far discussed suggest that although lots of opportunities exist for individuals and smaller groups to deal with poverty, ultimately the various tenacious manifestations of poverty require team work by a whole society for their long-term eradication. Only if shared collective values guide social organization and direct core governance functions can poverty be sustainably eradicated. How do the ideas of this part of the book fit together?

I point out the need for individual profiling to identify accurately the specific factors at work in a particular case of poverty and to examine how they interweave to determine a person's poverty. I focus on our collective responsibility for the nature of our society that either causes and legitimates existing poverty or enables us to eradicate poverty.

1. In order to understand each individual case of poverty, we must draw *a profile* that would do justice to the *complex configuration of indicators and causes* operative in a particular individual's case. Factors involved can be personal, communal, national, continental or natural. To profile individual or group cases, profilers must be conversant with current poverty research that provides checklists of possible intervening factors. Profilers must also be deeply attentive to all circumstances and conditions actually impacting on a specific case. Sachs states that only 'a close diagnosis of particular circumstances will allow an accurate understanding' (2005: 73).

In profiling cases of poverty, broader contexts must be accounted for. Often individuals, communities or countries find themselves in spaces where several complex societal systems, such as local, regional or national governments or economies intersect with regional, continental and global trends. The manner of such intersections could amplify the effects of some factors and strengthen their causal role.

Furthermore, it has to be determined why a specific individual, community or country was susceptible or vulnerable to the set of circumstances and factors that led to poverty. The combined results of such a detailed investigation, constructed to present a personal, communal, regional, national or continental profile are the necessary prologue to any appropriate and effective aid. Such profiles are also prerequisites for any detailed moral evaluation of the manifestation of poverty in a given context.

2. Poverty can be ascribed to *our collective human responsibility* for the social order. Poverty, as a condition that either causes a decline in physical health or an inability to share in human social activities typical of our species, is entirely remediable. Poverty exists by the grace of the collective choice of citizens that allows it to be. The continued, unabated existence of poverty thus reflects that non-poor citizens do not care enough about victims of poverty to change the social order to prevent, ameliorate or eradicate poverty.

3. *Every human being is at risk of becoming poor.* Non-poor people cannot shrug off concerns about poverty as if they will never be affected. In this respect, poverty is like disability: every person faces the risk of becoming poor. Poverty thus matters to every non-poor person, as a possibility they might encounter in future. They must imagine themselves to be poor, if not now, then perhaps sometime in future.

How to deal with poverty ethically

I have evaluated poverty in comprehensive ways in terms of generally shared universal moral values and in terms of the ideas of justice operative in modern constitutional democracies to provide a thoroughly clear and comprehensive picture of the harms poverty can do to people. I have shown how a consistent application of our core moral values can eradicate existing poverty and prevent all future cases. Furthermore, to deal ethically with all the complexities of poverty, I have proposed that the full implementation of core moral values would require an overhaul of institutions and a rethink of every individual's role in the struggle against poverty. In the process of providing poverty relief, I argue that emergency poverty relief is always required but never enough. In addition the agency functions of poor people need reconstruction and liberation.

1. Through *using all our moral values* – from general universally shared moral values to the specific values of justice underlying liberal egalitarian constitutional democracies – *to comprehensively evaluate* all dimensions concerning the causes, impact, effects and consequences of poverty, we can get a clear profile of what exactly poverty does to human beings.

2. All our moral values urge us to *assume a strong moral obligation* to eradicate poverty and to prevent it from recurring. By adhering strictly to treating every human being according to these moral values poverty cannot get a foothold in a human society. Only full ethical integrity will ensure that we do the right things and avoid what is wrong to prevent or eradicate every case of poverty that is not chosen voluntarily.

3. We can empower ourselves as human beings to deal with poverty fittingly if we properly understand *the value and power of collective human action* for addressing seemingly intractable problems that often persist through generations.

4. If we *redefine the core governance functions* in our human societies, we can enable ourselves as a species to optimally address a pernicious, destructive condition like poverty. Social reconstruction to properly address all the underlying causes of poverty is requisite.

5. *Aid for poverty relief* must take two forms, that is, (i) emergency poverty relief where no questions are asked of people in dire need and (ii) agency restoration where poor persons are enabled and empowered to deal appropriately and accountably with the effects, causes and consequences of their individual case of poverty as expressed in their unique profile.

6. Wherever poverty is a clear-cut result of injustice, *compensation* must be forthcoming.

Poverty is a complex, multidimensional phenomenon with many possible symptoms, effects, consequences and causes that can harm human beings in many different ways. Nevertheless, poverty is easily recognizable as a shortage of economic capacities that might threaten people's health and restrict their participation in commonly accepted social activities.

Poverty is the result of the choices humans make about the structures of their society, about the social forces they allow space to operate. The levels of poverty and riches in society are the collective responsibility of its citizens.

Poverty is entirely remediable, if the appropriate suite of actions are taken from a wide range of possible interventions based on a careful consideration of the configuration of factors that are involved, their weight and interplay that determine the dynamics of a particular case of poverty. To paraphrase Aristotle: to do the right thing at the right time for the right reason in the right degree with the right intention based on the right judgement can fully eradicate poverty on a sustainable basis. Only this kind of action will show proper respect for the human dignity of everyone involved: rich and poor.

The most important thing is that everybody should do something about poverty. The quality of the kind of human beings we are is at stake.

Notes

Are We One Another's Keepers Across the Globe?

[1] See Iris Young's conception of responsibility that she calls a 'social contention model' that is closely related to the view I try to articulate here in Young, 'Responsibility and global justice', *Social Philosophy and Policy*, 23, 1 (2006), 102–30.

Defining Poverty as Distinctively Human

[1] This chapter was published in an earlier form in September 2007 in *HTS* (*Hervormde Teologiese Studies*), 63, 3. An extract was used as a chapter in my book called *When I Needed a Neighbour Were You There? Christians and the Challenge of Poverty* (Wellington, South Africa: Lux Verbi).

[2] The number of poor people in the world is staggering. In 1995 it was said that more than one billion people 'live in extreme poverty, most of whom go hungry every day' (Copenhagen Declaration, 1995: 6). The United Nations Development Programme estimated in 1997 that 1.3 billion people were poor (UNDP, 1997: 3). William W. Lewis thinks the 'disparity between rich and poor is the most serious and the most intractable problem facing the world today'. He adds that the 'gap between rich and poor nations threatens global stability' (Lewis, 2004: 1, 3). Although poverty is a major issue now, it has been defined as one of the most serious issues facing humanity long ago. Already in 1970, Francis O. Wilcox said in a foreword that, 'As we move into the 1970s, two great problems stand out above all others . . .' The one was how to avoid nuclear war and the other 'how we can utilize world resources so that mankind may be able to meet the urgent challenge of poverty' (Myrdal, 1970: viii).

[3] David Gordon calls poverty 'the world's most ruthless killer and the greatest cause of suffering on earth' (2002: 74). He quotes the following statement from a 1995 report of the World Health Organization in support of his claim: 'Poverty is the main reason why babies are not vaccinated, clean water and sanitation are not provided and curative drugs and other treatments are unavailable and why mothers die in childbirth. Poverty is the main cause of reduced life expectancy, of handicap and disability and of starvation. Poverty is a major contributor to mental illness, stress, suicide, family disintegration and substance abuse.'

[4] As quoted above (Gordon, 2002: 74), the World Health Organization judges that 'Poverty is the main cause of reduced life expectancy, of handicap and disability and of starvation.'

⁵   In 1997 the Human Development Report of the United Nations Development Programme stated that we have 'the material and natural resources, the know-how and the people to make a poverty-free world a reality in less than a generation' (1997: iii). The authors added that this is 'not wholly idealism but a practical and achievable goal'. Political will is the missing factor, Gordon (2002: 73) thinks, as it is not 'a problem of lack of money or scientific knowledge on how to eradicate poverty'. He adds that the 'costs of meeting the basic needs of every person in the world are relatively small compared with the vast wealth available'. Furthermore, no new knowledge is required, as the 'practical policies and institutional mechanisms, needed to end world poverty are well known and widely understood' (74).

⁶   Gordon says there exists 'a strong desire amongst most of the world's governments to end poverty during the 21st century and a growing international momentum to take concrete action to eradicate poverty on a global scale' (2002: 53). He can make this claim partly because of events such as the following two. In 1995, 117 heads of state or government attended the World Summit for Social Development. The 'largest gathering yet of world leaders pledged to make the conquest of poverty, the goal of full employment and the fostering of stable, safe and just societies their overriding objectives' (Copenhagen Declaration, 1995: vii). In the declaration the heads of state commit themselves to 'give these goals the highest priority both now and into the 21st century' (3).The next event was even bigger. The Millennium Declaration, adopted in 2000 by the 'largest-ever gathering of heads of state', committed world leaders to do all they can 'to eradicate poverty'. These leaders promised through 'a global compact' 'to work together to meet concrete targets for advancing development and reducing poverty by 2015 or earlier' (UNDP, 2003: 1).

⁷   The World Development Report, *Attacking Poverty* (World Bank, 2001), laments the existence of 'deep poverty amid plenty' despite the fact that 'human conditions have improved more in the past century than in the rest of history'. Although 'global wealth, global connections and technological capabilities have never been greater', the report points out that the 'distribution of these global gains is extraordinarily unequal' (3).

⁸   Alcock thinks the 'issue of definition . . . lies at the heart of the task of understanding poverty' (1993: 57).

⁹   See Brian Fay's discussion of the issues in his book, *Contemporary Philosophy of Social Science: A Multicultural Approach* (1996).

¹⁰ An illustration of this approach can be found in the Second Carnegie Inquiry into Poverty and Development in South Africa (Wilson and Ramphele, 1989: 14). The leaders of the project sent their researchers into the field without any explicit theoretical or operational definition of poverty. Their reason was not to restrict the meaning of poverty to characteristics which researchers 'living within the sheltered walls of an urban university' think important.

Rather, field researchers were to go out in the country and listen to how people who experienced poverty and those who lived or worked with such people, understood the concept. From such an understanding of poverty they were to develop their indicators, make their measurements, give descriptions and interpret people's experience. Their assumption was that the use of the concept of poverty in everyday language – amongst those knowledgeable about the experience of poverty – is the one to be operationalized into reliable indicators of poverty. What must be noted, though, is that highly trained researchers selected the participants, collated the experiences and interpreted them. The process of theoretical construction is supplemented by duly taking into account empirical information from the right sources. However, this process does not imply that poor people define the concept themselves or advise the researchers. The researchers merely listen to one important group of voices.

11   See, for example, how moving poor people's self-descriptions of their own condition can be in Julian May (eds), *Experience and Perceptions of Poverty in South Africa* (1998b) and Narayan and Petesch, *Voices of the Poor* (2002). Note, however, that such self-descriptions depict harrowing experiences of severe poverty, but mostly do not contain neat theoretical definitions of poverty.

12   See Charles Taylor's discussion of these issues in his articles 'Interpretation and the sciences of man' (1985b) and 'Social theory as practice' (1985c) in his book *Philosophical Papers 2: Philosophy and the Human Sciences*.

13   There is a fascinating similarity between this definition of poverty and a recent definition of the underclass. Let us compare the two definitions. Ricketts and Sawhill (1988: 318) argue that it is behaviour rather than income that distinguishes the underclass from poor people. They define the underclass as those who engage 'in behaviors at variance with those of mainstream populations'. They set out (American) behavioural norms and show how people described as belonging to the underclass deviate from those norms and create 'significant social costs' (320). Townsend (1979: 567) gives a similar list of (British) behavioural norms and points out how people deviating from those norms might be abused by others. Poverty thus occurs when people fail to meet minimum societal standards for human living because they lack economic resources. The underclass consists of both poor and non-poor people who fail to meet behavioural norms for whatever reason. There is symmetry between the definitions as both groups fail to meet a societal standard. The reasons for the failure differ, some of the standards violated differ and sometimes the reasons for violating the same standard differ as well. This relationship deserves to be explored in more depth.

14   Peter Townsend (1979) made an attempt to define in detail what contemporary British society judge as minimal standards for adequate accommodation for human beings.

[15]   Note that although the concept of poverty has a moral evaluation built in, the minimum lifestyle standards referred to here are not moral. These standards refer to those aspects of human lifestyles that are only available through the legitimate use of economic resources.

[16]   Paul Streeter (1994: 234) explains why it can be difficult to specify nutritional requirements that apply generally to human beings. He says that food 'meets the needs of nutrition differently according to the rate of metabolism, the sex, the age, the workload of the individual, the climate, whether an individual is pregnant or lactating and whether she is ill, has parasites in her stomach, or needs the food for other uses than her own consumption, such as entertainment or ceremonies'.

[17]   Sometimes social scientists use the concept 'resource profile' to describe the basket of human, material and social resources available to an individual or group living in poverty. Alternatively, the concept of 'livelihood' can be used to depict the various ways and means through which individuals and households gather resources and employ capacities in their quest to make a living. Livelihood includes any kind of income, social institutions, assets, activities, support, skills, public goods, gender relations and property rights 'required to support and to sustain a given standard of living' (see Ellis, 1998: 4; Dovie, 2002). These concepts are useful when operationalizing concepts for measuring levels and severity of poverty, but not necessary for my purposes.

[18]   Tarp et al. (2002) discuss measuring absolute poverty by means of methods called Food Energy Intake and Cost of Basic Needs.

[19]   Halleröd also refers to 'differences in the ability to convert resources' which lead to the well-known phenomenon that 'the same amount of income can result in quite different outcomes' (2000: 168).

[20]   Hagenaars and de Vos note that these kinds of poverty lines 'will always be more or less arbitrary, because there will never be general agreement as to what basic needs are and how high these minimal amounts should be' (1988: 213).

[21]   See Dasgupta's (1992) detailed descriptions of destitution and its measurement in his book, *An Inquiry into Well-Being and Destitution*.

[22]   The significance of human dignity for poor people should not be underestimated. World Bank researchers found that when 'everything around them starts to deteriorate, the poor continue to invest in burial societies to ensure that they are at least taken care of in death' (Narayan et al., 2000a: 6), thus ensuring that they are at least buried worthy of human beings, if they did not have the economic capacities to live their lives that way.

[23]   John Veitch Wilson (2000: 158) judges that poverty means a 'lack of income resources adequate for socially defined participation'.

[24]   Note how my approach overlaps with Nussbaum's approach, but also differs from hers (see, for example, Nussbaum, 2000: 70–86). Nussbaum remarks

that similar to my definition of intermediate poverty, we sometimes judge a human life to be 'so impoverished that it is not worthy of the dignity of a human being' (72). In addition she makes a distinction similar to my version of extreme poverty when she remarks that at 'one extreme, we may judge that the absence of capability for a central function is so acute that the person is not really a human being at all, or any longer – as in the case of certain very severe forms of mental disability or dementia' (74). Furthermore, Nussbaum similarly emphasizes the importance of interdependent cooperation between humans when she says that her core idea is, 'of the human being as a dignified free being who shapes his or her own life in cooperation and reciprocity with others' (72). Her list of central capabilities are different from my list of social activities, as she includes individual capabilities with those that we share with others (78–86).

Why the Inequality of Poverty is Morally Wrong

[1]   See John Locke's *Second Treatise of Government* (1996 [1690]), for a political theory where this convertibility plays a very important role in its outcomes.
[2]   Robert M. Blackburn (1999) argues that there are good reasons for seeing poverty as 'the most important problem facing the world'. At the same time that many human beings 'are facing the real possibility of starving to death', 'a few individuals have control of enormous wealth'.
[3]   Alcock says bluntly that 'some would have to get less for the poor to get more' (1987: 7).
[4]   Jacques Baudot claims that it is 'an illusion, or worse a lie, to pretend that the question of poverty in a nation or in the world, can be solved without any sacrifice on the part of those who are in a privileged position' (2000: 33).
[5]   Jones wonders whether, from a perspective of social justice, we should allow 'some people to have means, opportunities and resources which allow them to not only meet needs but also numerous frivolous desires and wants while others, who might be regarded as poor and deprived, are unable to satisfy basic needs' (1990: 160). Tawney's expression of 'sensational extremes of wealth and power' (1952: 181) applies today even better to our massive inequalities than when he wrote it.
[6]   The 1997 Human Development Report is explicit about this issue, 'Poverty often serves the vested interests of the economically powerful, who may benefit from exploiting the pool of low-paid labour' (UNDP, 1997: 94).
[7]   Timothy Bates (1995/6) claims that the 'low wages paid to ghetto residents are embedded in the prices of products and services that the entire community relies upon'. In his comprehensive study of poverty, Townsend (1979: 588) has found that 'a large proportion of the poor are in work'.

[8]   Rowntree depicts this strong link as he observed it in late nineteenth-century England. His meticulously collected evidence suggested to him that the diet of the 'servant-keeping class is, upon the whole, in excess of that required for the maintenance of health'. The poor people, or 'labouring classes', in contrast, 'upon whom the bulk of the muscular work falls . . . are seriously underfed' (1901: 259). Rowntree's remarks suggest that the poverty of the labouring classes is closely linked to the riches of the servant-keeping classes. Alcock states that affluence and poverty 'are different aspects of the same question of the distribution of resources' (1987: 7).

[9]   Townsend thinks that to 'comprehend and explain poverty is also to comprehend and explain riches' (1979: 337). He argues that poverty must be understood not only 'as an inevitable feature of severe social inequality', but also as 'a particular consequence of actions by the rich to preserve and enhance their wealth and so deny it to others'.

[10]   See to what extent Townsend (1979) has employed the concept of deprivation to explain poverty. In *Overcoming Human Poverty*, the UNDP combines the concept deprivation with a focus on capabilities. Note how they do it, 'Human poverty . . . is deprivation in the most essential capabilities of life, including leading a long and healthy life, being knowledgeable, having adequate economic provisioning and participating fully in the life of the community' (2000: 22).

[11]   Bernd Schulte (2002: 119) says that the term social exclusion 'has replaced poverty in the European Community's law and policies' since 1995.

[12]   Note the range of negative words used in the Human Development Report (UNDP, 1997: 17) for describing poverty, including 'dependent', 'ill-being', 'lack', 'inability to participate', 'suffering', and so on.

[13]   John D. Jones claims that people 'commonly say that such people lack what is needed or are fundamentally unable to accomplish certain goals and ends or obtain a certain quality of life' (1990: 5). See also his use of the concept 'insufficiency' to illuminate poverty (ibid.: 104, 108).

[14]   The 1997 Human Development Report uses 'loss of assets' to describe one of the factors that 'transforms transient poverty into chronic poverty that can extend to the next generation' (UNDP, 1997: 64).

[15]   See also Schulte (2002: 120).

[16]   Spilerman and Elesh argue that poverty is 'associated with a range of disabilities, some spawned by low income, others producing this condition' (1971: 358).

[17]   Alcock uses Amartya Sen's views to describe poverty as exemplifying 'a lack of capability' and says that the 'commodities needed to avoid this incapacity would vary from society to society' (1993: 62).

[18]   Larry Temkin (1993) influenced my discussion on the relation between inequality and poverty. This discussion is indebted to his book and a limited response to some of the issues he raises.

Poverty Violates Fundamental Human Values

¹ This chapter was published in an earlier form in 2007 as 'The moral challenge of poverty's impact on individuals', in *Koers*, 72, 2.

Poverty's Impact on Human Environments

¹ This chapter was published in an earlier form in 2008 as a chapter in my book called *When I Needed a Neighbour Were You There? Christians and the Challenge of Poverty* (Wellington, South Africa: Lux Verbi).

Poverty as Threat to Democratic Values

¹ This chapter was published in an earlier form in *Public Affairs Quarterly*, 22, 2, April 2008, 175–93.

Why Poverty is Such a Complex Affair

¹ See Paul Spicker's (2007: 101–8) discussion of the ways many non-poor people blame those who are poor for their poverty and the way he dismisses such views.

Justice as Poverty Prevention

¹ David Schmidtz, for example, says that 'justice will always be about what people are due' (2006: 179).
² See, for example, the discussion John Rawls presents about this matter (1971: 10–11).
³ J. R. Lucas says justice is 'many-faceted' (1980: 31) and he shows this clearly in his book. He argues that although 'there are only partial and inadequate explications of the concept of justice, each takes up and develops a strand of reasoning that is integral to the concept as a whole. We need, therefore, to appreciate the force of the arguments for particular versions of justice, as well as their limitations' (170). See also David Schmidtz on this matter (2006: 3, 7–19). He says, for example, that no 'single principle of justice . . . is more than an element of justice' (102).

[4]   See the discussion of these issues by Nicholas Wolterstorff (2008: 4–6, 137–44).
[5]   See also the view of Iris Marion Young (2006).
[6]   See some of the following sources: Mary Albon, rapporteur (1992a; 1992b; 1993); Kader Asmal (1992); Sissela Bok (1989; 1990: 52–72; 1995); Allan Buchanan (1991); S. L. Darwall (1977: 36–49); Larry Diamond (1994: 3–17; 1995); André Du Toit (1994: 9–19; 1996); Ronald Dworkin (1978); Nancy Fraser (1995: 68–93); William A. Galston (1980); Alan Gewirth (1978; 1982); Jürgen Habermas (1994: 107–48); Will Kymlicka (1995); Kai Nielsen (1986–7: 222–53); Robert Nozick (1974); John Rawls (1975: 536–54); Ian Shapiro (1986); Judith N. Shklar (1990); Nicholas Tavuchis (1991); Charles Taylor (1994: 25–73); Hendrik W. Van der Merwe (1989); Michael Walzer (1980; 1983; 1994); Nicholas Wolterstorff (1983); Iris Marion Young (1990; 1996).

Re-Imagining Governance to Eradicate Poverty Permanently

[1]   I cannot discuss in detail how to deal with this issue on all levels from local to global. Note the valuable analysis of these issues by Nancy Fraser (2009: 21–9).

Compensating for Impoverishing Injustices of the Distant Past

[1]   This chapter was published in an earlier form in *Politikon: South African Journal of Political Science* in June 2005.
[2]   Taylor talks about the obligation for 'some form of compensation or reparation' that must be made to restore 'the balance of justice when an injustice has been committed to a group of persons' (1972–3: 179).
[3]   Wilson (1983: 523) refers to the fact that a perpetrator of injustice does not only gain a particular advantage, but such a person 'has adopted an unjust superior position' and 'infringed the rights or status of his (her) fellows as equal negotiators and deal-makers'.
[4]   Wilson (1983: 523) spells out the significance of repentance and apology in the metaphoric language of material compensation. He says repentance and apology restore equality, as the 'repentant person acknowledges the innocent's rights and the innocent thus gets his (her) own back'.
[5]   Amdur (1979: 241) articulates something of this aspect when he refers to the need that African-Americans should be compensated for the 'humiliation inflicted by segregation'. Waldron (1992: 7) suggests that 'a symbolic gesture may be as important to people as any material compensation'.
[6]   Wilson (1983: 522) articulates both the simplicity and the complexity of this issue. The simplicity of the issue is the idea that 'when another takes away

what is rightfully and desirably mine, he ought to give it back'. The complexity of compensation between groups is that it is 'not always easy to see what sort of, or how much, compensation A should give to B if A cannot restore the original situation'.

7   Waldron (1992: 15) refers to widespread beliefs that deny compensation for injustices committed long ago. He refers to the belief that 'after several generations have passed, certain wrongs are simply not worth correcting'. A further belief he refers to is that some rights 'are capable of "fading" in their moral importance by virtue of the passage of time and by the sheer persistence of what was originally a wrongful infringement'. However valid these beliefs might be, they do not affect my position which argues for compensation for major injustices with effects and consequences that persist through time, often as a result of being reinforced and maintained.

8   Paul thinks that 'some rights violations lapse with time and, therefore, are uncompensable' (1991: 103).

9   See Barnett's claim that we need objective criteria to 'distinguish . . . compensable from noncompensable injuries' (1991: 313).

10   O'Neill (1987: 80) refers to 'gross violations of human rights' and injustices that would count as 'crimes against humanity'. Nagel (1973: 361) identifies a group to whom compensation is owed as one 'whose social position is exceptionally depressed, with destructive consequences both for the self-esteem of members of the group and for the health and cohesion of the society'.

11   See Robert Nozick's theory of justice as entitlement, especially the part of rectificatory justice (1974: 150–3).

12   Jaggar (1977) shows the links between these smaller injustices when she says that overt job discrimination 'could hardly occur except in a social context where such discrimination was widely considered to be acceptable and where it could appear to be justified because of the existence of a universal covert discrimination'.

13   Waldron points out that great injustice has a well-known characteristic, 'that those who suffer it go to their deaths with the conviction that these things must not be forgotten' (1992: 5).

14   Note what Boxill says on this point: 'For if they have overcome their injuries, they have borne the costs of compensation that should be borne by those who inflicted the injuries' (1978: 249). He adds as reason for the remaining claims of victims to some form of compensation that a person 'who has worked hard and long to overcome an injury is not what he would have been had he never been injured'.

15   Waldron (1992: 19, 20) claims that often a 'long-stolen resource' no longer plays a significant part in people's lives, because they 'must have developed some structure of subsistence'. This implies that their claim to compensation loses credibility. Somehow Waldron ignores the point that people's lives often have deteriorated significantly through many generations as a result of the irreplaceability of 'long-stolen' resources. Besides being disabled by the original

injustice, their recovery is more often than not impeded by subsequent main-tenance and reinforcement of the original injustice. Waldron (27) acknowledges this possibility when he says it is a fact that 'many of the descendants of those who were defrauded and expropriated live demoralized in lives of relative poverty – relative, that is, to the descendants of those who defrauded them'.

[16] Waldron makes an argument against compensation for historic injustices based on his problems with the subjunctive approach that uses counter-factual reasoning to approximate 'what would have happened if some event (which did occur) had not taken place' (1992: 8). This hypothetical reconstruction of possible events is then the basis to 'change the present so that it looks more like the present that would have obtained in the absence of the injustice . . .' I will show that this approach is not the only one to establish a factual basis for compensation for historic injustices.

[17] See O'Neill's (1987) rejection of compensation, despite her vivid recognition of the harm done by past injustice.

[18] Sunstein's (1991: 297) reference to affirmative action as 'an effort to overcome the social subordination of the relevant groups' reinforces this point.

[19] The importance of this point can be illuminated by Barnett's remark (1991: 318) that the liberal conception of the rule of law requires 'that sufficient evidence of liability must exist and be presented before a remedy may be imposed'.

[20] Janna Thompson (2001: 114–35) uses this line of argument to justify com-pensation.

[21] See Sher (1976–7: 174–9) for a position that refuses to acknowledge any notion that groups are involved in issues of compensatory justice. For Wade (1978: 464) the matter in the case of African-Americans is clear: 'since the injustice the blacks have lived with was directed towards the group, reparation must follow the same pattern'.

[22] Taylor (1972–3: 181) also describes the victims as a group, because they 'were the *collective* target of an institutionalized practice of unjust treatment'. Perhaps he overstates his case when he says the group was '*created* by the original unjust practice'. The group with their specific characteristics might have been drawn into the spotlight, have been focused on in a special way, or they might have been forced to react in ways that strengthened their group identification and mobilization.

[23] My view coincides with one proposed by Taylor (1972–3: 148) when he says the following: 'For the injustices done to a person are based on the fact that he has characteristic C. His being C is, other things being equal, a sufficient condition for the permissibility of treating him in the given manner.'

[24] See Boxill's comment: 'In order to retain their sanity and equilibrium in impossibly unjust situations, people may have to resort to patterns of behavior and consequently may develop habits or cultural traits which are debilitating and unproductive in a more humane environment' (1978: 254–5). He calls

these cultural traits 'unjust injuries' and says they 'may be deeply ingrained and extremely difficult to eradicate'.

25 O'Neill (1987: 74) refers to symbolic modes of restitution that respond to a 'ruptured moral relationship' between victim and perpetrator. Modes such as apology, forgiveness and acceptance do 'not undo wrongs', she says, 'but (at best) they expunge them'.

26 See for example Nickel's point (1974: 148). Goldman, though, wishes to argue that fairness requires that damages be assigned 'as specifically as possible' and that individuals must be reimbursed 'always in proportion to the actual damages suffered under the unjust policy'. Goldman clearly denies the group aspect of such injustices that I am arguing for which does not demand these almost impossible details from victims. His position on the individualist nature of discrimination furthermore states that 'discrimination always affects particular individuals and reparation must be made to specific individuals'. This sentence, though true, needs to be qualified as follows: 'Discrimination always affects particular individuals *insofar as they are members of particular groups and* reparation must be made to specific individuals *insofar as they have been direct or indirect victims of the consequences of discrimination based on group characteristics*' (1977: 293, 296, my emphasis).

27 Goldman makes the point that 'broad social pressures and stereotypes affect different individuals in different ways' (1977: 235). He adds that although all women, for example, might encounter discriminatory attitudes, 'it is clear that when these differ in intensity and manifest form and when some females receive considerable support in their endeavors from others, the long-range psychological effects of such discriminatory effects can also differ'.

28 O'Neill argues that victims are compensated 'if *somebody* offers them *some* equivalent for the loss suffered' (1987: 75, emphasis in original). She adds that compensation 'can be done vicariously . . . it need not be provided by wrongdoers or by their heirs or representatives'.

29 Wilson argues for the view that it is 'the guilty who . . . are to "pay back" the innocent . . . who are to compensate or requite those injured by what they have done, or to make up for it' (1983: 521).

30 Kershnar (1999: 90) argues for the view that all citizens are responsible for compensation, as the government as their agent 'omitted to intervene to prevent private persons and state and local officials from committing unjust acts'. See also Fishkin's point (1991: 95) that some principle 'that holds contemporary institutions responsible for previous acts by those same institutions might be acceptable'.

31 Taylor (1972–3: 180, 181) argues for an obligation to compensate that belongs to every member of society except the victims of injustice. He says that it is 'the society in general that, through its established social practice, brought upon itself the obligation'.

[32] Goldman's worry is that 'specific individuals who have not caused or received benefit from discrimination will be forced to pay' (1975: 294). Paul (1991) has a similar worry about creating a 'new generation of victims' who must 'bear the burden of the remedy'. There might be individuals who did not cause the injustice, played no part in reinforcing the injustice and received no benefit in any direct or indirect way from the consequences or effects of the injustice. Would they have reason to complain that small proportions of their taxes are used to compensate victims? The assumption that they would have reason to complain misunderstands how governments differentially distribute tax income to the benefit of interest groups of citizens. If I had no part in any crimes, why should my tax money be used to compensate victims of violent crimes, for example? Alternatively, if I don't travel by road, why should I pay taxes for building and maintaining roads? If the argument is that taxes are used for the general interest of society, then compensation for victims of injustice that eliminates bitterness and rebuilds agency would surely also benefit society? Are we victims in any way if our taxes are used for such purposes? Amdur (1979: 233) adds to this view when he says the costs of compensation must be distributed 'just the way we distribute the costs of any public good'.

[33] Fullinwider (1975: 318) refers to the fact that the benefits of injustice may be received 'involuntary and unavoidable'. Although whether this is true in all cases might have to be settled empirically, I am strongly convinced that in most cases of injustice protest would be audible and suffering visible enough to argue that the beneficiaries had the moral responsibility of at least recognizing and enquiring about such issues.

[34] Sher (1976–7: 180) draws a slightly different conclusion about the beneficiaries, saying they 'may have *benefited* from past discrimination; but in a society in which such benefit can hardly be avoided, this is surely not a punishable offence' (emphasis in original). Sher too easily avoids appealing to the role of their moral agency in such circumstances.

[35] See also some of the distinctions made by O'Neill (1987: 81).

[36] Goldman defends a principle of compensation that says 'injured parties should be compensated and compensated in kind if possible' (1975: 291).

[37] Nagel proposes compensatory measures 'in the form of special training programs, or financial support, or day-care centers, or apprenticeships, or tutoring' (1973: 349–50).

[38] See Paul (1991: 101) and note her comment (103) about the limits of individual compensation when she says that 'especially with the passage of much time between the injury and the recompense, restoring the individual to his *ex ante* position will not fully erase the injurious event'.

[39] Goodin (1991: 155) thinks that 'little more than token compensation' can be offered in cases where 'harms are truly irreparable and the loss truly irreplaceable'. Without denying that some harms are irreparable and some

losses irreplaceable, I think compensation in such cases can have more value than being mere tokenism. The value of restoring the equal human value and dignity of victims should especially not be underrated. Creative ways of material compensation could ease a person's life to give compensation more value than mere tokenism.

[40]   See Ronald Dworkin's discussion of this issue in his book *Sovereign Virtue* (2000).

[41]   Wade (1978: 464) uses ideas similar to those of average position and relative standing to suggest a criterion when compensatory measures ought to be terminated. He says that point would be reached when victims of injustice (in this case African-Americans) 'would have risen to preferred jobs and positions in about the same proportion as other ethnic groups who did not suffer insulting discrimination'.

[42]   Waldron says part of the moral significance of the past is 'the difference it makes to the present' (1992: 7).

[43]   This is proposed by Joseph F. Carens when he says: 'I want to argue that . . . the best way to institutionalize the ideal of compensatory justice would be to adopt the familiar egalitarian strategy of progressive taxation of high incomes and supplemental transfers to low incomes up to the point where these taxes and transfers interfere too much with market incentives' (1985: 65). Onora O'Neill (1987: 87) takes a slightly different approach by arguing for addressing poverty through the restoration of agency rather than 'arguing about whether or not we can stretch notions of compensation for violation of rights to cover rectification of selected Third World problems'.

[44]   Waldron (1992: 27) seems to favour such an approach. He says the following: 'If the relief of poverty and the more equal distribution of resources is the aim of a prospective theory of justice, it is likely that the effect of rectifying past wrongs will carry us some distance in this direction. All the same, it is worth stressing that it is the impulse to justice now that should lead the way in this process, not the reparation of something whose wrongness is understood primarily in relation to conditions that no longer obtain.'

[45]   Waldron (1992: 7) emphasizes that material compensation can have important functions of recognition of injustice and confirming victims' historical identities. He gives an example of compensation in America which was 'a clear public recognition that this injustice did happen, that it was the American people and their government that inflicted it and that these people were among its victims'.

[46]   Goodin (1991: 143) makes the point that compensatory justice 'usually serves to restore some *status quo ante* . . . the notion of some preexisting state that is to be recreated virtually always seems to lie at the core of compensatory justice'.

[47]   See also Rawls (1971).

Bibliography

Albertyn, J. R. (1932) *Die Armblanke-Vraagstuk in Suid-Afrika: Verslag van die Carnegie-kommissie. Deel V: Sociologiese verslag. Die armblanke en die maatskappy*, Stellenbosch: Pro-Ecclesia Drukkery.

Albon, Mary, rapporteur (1992a) *Project on Justice in Times of Transition*, New York: Charter 77 Foundation.

Albon, Mary, rapporteur (1992b) *Truth and Justice: The Delicate Balance*, New York: Charter 77 Foundation.

Albon, Mary, rapporteur (1993) *Reconciliation in Times of Transition*, New York: Charter 77 Foundation.

Alcock, Pete (1987) *Poverty and State Support*, London and New York: Longman.

Alcock, Pete (1993) *Understanding Poverty*, Houndmills, Basingstoke, Hampshire: The MacMillan Press Ltd.

Allen, Jonathan (2001), 'The place of negative morality in political theory', *Political Theory*, 29, 3, 337–63.

Amdur, Robert (1979) 'Compensatory justice: the question of costs', *Political Theory*, 7, 2, 229–44.

Aristotle (1925) *The Nichomachean Ethics*, translated with an Introduction by David Ross, revised by J. L. Ackrill and J. O. Urmson, Oxford: Oxford University Press.

Aristotle (1981) *The Politics*, translated by T. A. Sinclair, revised and re-presented by Trevor J. Saunders, Harmondsworth, Middlesex: Penguin Books.

Asmal, Kader (1992) 'Victims, survivors and citizens – human rights, reparations and reconciliation' (Inaugural Lecture, University of the Western Cape, Bellville, South Africa).

Ballard, Richard, Adam Habib and Imraan Valodia (2006) *Voices of Protest: Social Movements in Post-Apartheid South Africa*, Scottsville: University of KwaZulu-Natal Press.

Barnes, Barry (2000) *Understanding Agency: Social Theory and Responsible Action*, London: Sage Publications.

Barnett, Randy, E. (1991) 'Compensation and rights in the liberal conception of justice', *Nomos*, 33, 311–54.

Baron, Robert A. and Scott A. Shane (2005) *Entrepeneurship: A Process Perspective*, Mason, Ohio: Thomson South Western.

Barringer, Bruce R. and R. Duane Ireland (2006) *Entrepeneurship: Successfully Launching New Ventures*, Upper Saddle River, New Jersey: Pearson Prentice Hall.

Barry, Brian (2005) *Why Social Justice Matters*, Cambridge: Polity Press.

Bates, Timothy (1995/6) 'Political economy of urban poverty in the 21st century: how progress and public policy generate rising poverty', *Review of Black Political Economy*, 24, 2/3, 111–21.

Baudot, Jaques (2000) 'The international build-up: poverty and the spirit of the time', in David Gordon and Peter Townsend, *Breadline Europe: The Measurement of Poverty*, Bristol: The Policy Press, pp. 25–34.

Benn, Stanley I. (1971) 'Egalitarianism and the equal consideration of interests', in Hugo A. Bedau (ed.), *Justice and Equality*, Englewood Cliffs, NJ: Prentice-Hall Inc. pp. 152–67.

Berlin, Isaiah (1969) *Four Essays on Liberty*, Oxford: Oxford University Press.

Blackburn, Robert M. (1999) 'Understanding social inequality', *The International Journal of Sociology and Social Policy*, 19, 9–11, 1–24.

Blackburn, Simon (2001) *Being Good: A Short Introduction to Ethics*, Oxford: Oxford University Press.

Bohman, James (1996) *Public Deliberation: Pluralism, Complexity and Democracy*, Cambridge, Massachusetts: The MIT Press.

Bok, Sissela (1989) *A Strategy for Peace: Human Values and the Threat of War*, New York: Pantheon Books.

Bok, Sissela (1990) 'Early advocates of lasting world peace: utopians or realists?', in Leroy S. Rouner (ed.), *Celebrating Peace*, Notre Dame, Ind.: University of Notre Dame Press, pp. 52–72.

Bok, Sissela (1995) *Common Values*, Columbia, Mo.: University of Missouri Press.

Booth, Charles (1892) *Pauperism: A Picture and Endowment of Old Age*, London: MacMillan and Co.

Boxill, Bernard (1978) 'The morality of preferential hiring', *Philosophy and Public Affairs*, 7, 3, 246–68.

Bratman, Michael E. (2001) 'Two problems about human agency', *Proceedings of the Aristotelian Society*, 101, 309–26.

Braybrooke, David. (2003) 'A progressive approach to personal responsibility for global beneficence', *The Monist*, 86, 2, 301–22.

Brundtland, Gro Harlem (1987) *Our Common Future. World Commission on Environment and Development*, Oxford: Oxford University Press.

Buchanan, Allan (1991) *Secession*, Boulder, Colo.: Westview Press.

Callinicos, Alex (2000) *Equality*, Cambridge: Polity.

Camerer, Marianne (1996) 'Party politics, grass roots politics and civil society', paper presented at a conference on 'Christianity and democracy in South Africa', Potchefstroom, South Africa: Potchefstroom University for Christian Higher Education, 12 July 1996.

Carens, Joseph H. (1985) 'Compensatory justice and social institutions', *Economics and Philosophy*, 1, 39–67

Christiansen, Hans (April/May 1996) 'The costs of the welfare state', *The OECD Observer*, 199, 35–6.

The Copenhagen Declaration and Programme of Action (1995), World Summit for Social Development, 6–12 March 1995, New York: United Nations Department of Public Information.

Cullity, Garrett (2004) *The Moral Demands of Affluence*, Oxford: Oxford University Press.

Darwall, S. L. (1977) 'Two kinds of respect', *Ethics*, 88, 36–49.

Dasgupta, Partha (1993) *An Inquiry into Well-Being and Destitution*, Oxford: Clarendon Press.

Davidson, Donald (1980) 'Agency', in Donald Davidson (ed.), *Essays on Actions and Events*, Oxford: Clarendon Press, pp. 43–62.

Davis, Lawrence H. (1979) *Theory of Action*, Englewood Cliffs, NJ: Prentice-Hall Inc.

Desai, Ashwin (2002) *We Are the Poors: Community Struggles in Post-Apartheid South Africa*, New York: Monthly Review Press.

Diamond, Larry (1994) 'Toward democratic consolidation', *Journal of Democracy*, 5:3, 3–17.

Diamond, Larry (1995) *Promoting Democracy in the 1990s: Actors and Instruments, Issues and Imperatives*, New York: Carnegie Corporation.

Diener, Ed and Robert Biswas-Diener (2002) 'Will money increase subjective well-being?', *Social Indicators Research*, 57, 2, 119–69.

Dieterlen, Paulette (2005) *Poverty: A Philosophical Approach*, Amsterdam and New York: Rodopi.

Dorling, Daniel and Jan Rigby, Ben Wheeler, Dimitris Ballas, Bethan Thomas, Eldin Fahmy, David Gordon and Ruth Lupton (2007) *Poverty, Wealth and Place in Britain, 1968–2005*, York: Joseph Rowntree Foundation.

Dovie, Delali D. K. (2002) 'Towards Rio+10 – Trend of environmentalism and implications for sustainable livelihoods in the 21st century', *Environment, Development and Sustainability*, 4, 1, 51–67.

Dowding, Keith (2004), 'Are democratic and just institutions the same?', in Keith Dowding, Robert E. Goodin and Carole Pateman (eds), *Justice and Democracy: Essays for Brian Barry*, Cambridge: Cambridge University Press, pp. 25–39.

Dryzek, John S. (2000) *Deliberative Democracy and Beyond: Liberals, Critics, Contestations*, Oxford: Oxford University Press.

Du Toit André (1994) 'Agtergrond tot die Waarheid en Versoeningskommissie', in Waarheid en Versoeningskommissie, Bylaag tot *Die Suid-Afrikaan*, 9–19.

Du Toit André (1996) 'Philosophical perspectives on the truth commission? Some preliminary notes and fragments', paper presented at the Annual Conference of the Southern African Philosophical Society, Stellenbosch, South Africa, 22–4 January.

Dworkin, Ronald (1978) *Taking Rights Seriously*, new impression corrected with appendix), London: Gerald Duckworth and Co. Ltd.

Dworkin, Ronald (1986) 'Liberalism', in Ronald Dworkin, *A Matter of Principle*, Oxford: Clarendon Press, pp. 181–204.

Dworkin, Ronald (2000) *Sovereign Virtue*, Cambridge, Massachusetts: Harvard University Press.

Ellis, Frank (1998) 'Household strategies and rural livelihood diversification', *The Journal of Development Studies*, 35, 1, 1–38.

Fabre, Cécile (2007) *Justice in a Changing World*, Cambridge: Polity Press.

Fay, Brian (1996) *Contemporary Philosophy of Social Science: A Multicultural Approach*, Oxford: Basil Blackwell.

Fishkin, James S. (1991) 'Justice between generations: compensation, identity and group membership', *Nomos*, 33, 85–96.

Foster, James E. (1998) 'Absolute versus relative poverty', *The American Economic Review*, 88, 2, 335–41.

Follesdal, Andreas and Thomas Pogge (eds) (2005) *Real World Justice: Grounds, Principles, Human Rights and Social Institutions*, Dordrecht, The Netherlands: Springer, 335–41.

Frankena, William K. (1962) 'The concept of social justice', in Richard B. Brandt (ed.), *Social Justice*, Englewood Cliffs, NJ: Prentice-Hall Inc., pp. 1–29.

Fraser, Nancy (1995) 'From redistribution to recognition? Dilemmas of justice in a "post-socialist" Age', *New Left Review*, 212, 68–93.

Fraser, Nancy (2009) *Scales of Justice: Re-Imagining Political Space in a Globalizing World*, New York: Columbia University Press.

Fullinwider, Robert K. (1975) 'Preferential hiring and compensation', *Social Theory and Practice*, 1, 307–20.

Galston, William A. (1980) *Justice and the Human Good*, Chicago: University of Chicago Press.

Gasper, Des (2004) *The Ethics of Development*, Edinburgh Studies in World Ethics, Edinburgh: Edinburgh University Press.

Gewirth, Alan (1978) *Reason and Morality*, Chicago: University of Chicago Press.

Gewirth, Alan (1982) *Human Rights: Essays on Justification and Applications*, Chicago: University of Chicago Press.

Gewirth, Alan (1984) 'Practical philosophy, civil liberties and poverty', *The Monist*, 67, 4, 549–68.

Goldman, Alan H. (1975) 'Limits to the justification of reverse discrimination', *Social Theory and Practice*, 1, 289–306.

Goldman, Alan H. (1977) 'Reply to Jaggar', *Social Theory and Practice*, 4, 2, 235–7.

Goodin, Robert (1991) 'Compensation and redistribution', *Nomos*, 33, 143–77.

Gordon, David (2000) 'Measuring absolute and overall poverty', in David Gordon and Peter Townsend (eds), *Breadline Europe: The Measurement of Poverty*, Bristol: The Policy Press, pp. 49–77.

Gordon, David (2002) 'The international measurement of poverty and anti-poverty policies', in Peter Townsend and David Gordon (eds), *World Poverty: New Policies to Defeat an Old Enemy*, Bristol: The Policy Press, pp. 53–80.

Gordon, David, Christina Pantazis and Peter Townsend (2000) 'Absolute and overall poverty: a European history and proposal for measurement', in David Gordon and Peter Townsend (eds), *Breadline Europe: The Measurement of Poverty*, Bristol: The Policy Press, pp. 79–105.

Grosskopf, J. F. W. (1932) *Die Armblanke-Vraagstuk in Suid-Afrika: Verslag van die Carnegie-kommissie. Deel I: Ekonomiese verslag. Plattelandsverarming en plaasverlating*, Stellenbosch: Pro-Ecclesia Drukkery.

Gutmann, Amy and Dennis Thompson (1996) *Democracy and Disagreement*, Cambridge, Mass.: Harvard University Press.

Habermas, J. (1994) 'Struggles for recognition in the democratic constitutional state', trans. Shierry Weber Nicholsen, in Charles Taylor, *Multiculturalism* (edited and introduced by Amy Gutmann), Princeton, NJ: Princeton University Press, pp. 107–48.

Hagenaars, Aldi and Klaas de Vos (1998) 'The definition and measurement of poverty', *The Journal of Human Resources*, 23, 2, 211–21.

Haksar, Vinit (1998) 'Moral agency', *Routledge Encyclopaedia of Philosophy*, Oxford: Routledge (CD Version).

Halleröd, Björn (2000) 'Poverty, inequality and health', in David Gordon and Peter Townsend (eds), *Breadline Europe: The Measurement of Poverty*, Bristol: The Policy Press, pp. 165–87.

Hampshire, Stuart (1989) *Innocence and Experience*, London: Penguin Books.

Hampshire, Stuart (2000) *Justice in Conflict*, Princeton, NJ and Oxford, England: Princeton University Press.

Harvey, Jean (2007) 'Moral solidarity and empathetic understanding: the moral value and scope of the relationship', *Journal of Social Philosophy*, 38, 1, 22–37.

Hegel, G. W. F. (1991) *Elements of the Philosophy of Right*, ed. Allen W. Wood, trans. by H. B. Nisbet, Cambridge: Cambridge University Press.

Hobbes, Thomas (1968 [1651]) *Leviathan*, ed. with an introduction by C. B. Macpherson, Harmondsworth, Middlesex: Penguin Books.

Hollander, Jack M. (2003) *The Real Environmental Crisis: Why Poverty, Not Affluence, is the Environment's Enemy Number One*, Berkeley, CA: University of California Press.

Jaggar, Alison (1977) 'Relaxing the limits on preferential treatment', *Social Theory and Practice*, 4, 2, 227–35.

Jones, John D. (1990) *Poverty and the Human Condition: A Philosophical Inquiry*, Leviston, Queenston and Lampeter: Edwin Mellen Press.

Jordan, Bill (1996) *A Theory of Poverty and Social Exclusion*, Cambridge: Polity Press.

Kabir, Md. Azmal, Ataur Rahman, Sarah Salway, Jane Pryer (2000) 'Sickness among the urban poor: a barrier to livelihood security', *Journal of International Development*, 12, 5, 707–22.

Kane, John (1996) 'Justice, impartiality and equality: why the concept of justice does not presume equality', *Political Theory*, 24, 3, 375–93.

Kershnar, Stephen (1999) 'Uncertain damages to racial minorities and strong affirmative action', *Public Affairs Quarterly*, 13, 1, 83–98.

Krause, Sharon (2001) 'Partial justice', *Political Theory*, 29, 3, 315–36.

Kymlicka, Will (1995) *Multicultural Citizenship: A Liberal Theory of Minority Rights*, Oxford: Oxford University Press.

Landmann, Michael (1966) *Filosofische Antropologie*, Utrecht, Antwerpen: Uitgeverij Het Spectrum N.V.

Lewis, William W. (2004) *The Power of Productivity: Wealth, Poverty and the Threat to Global Stability*, Chicago and London: University of Chicago Press.

Liebenberg, L. W. (1990) *The Art of Tracking: The Origins of Science*, Cape Town: New Africa Books.

Lister, Ruth (2004) *Poverty*, Cambridge: Polity Press.

Little, Daniel (2003) *The Paradox of Wealth and Poverty: Mapping the Ethical Dilemma of Global Development*, Boulder, Colorado: Westview Press.

Locke, John (1966 [1690]) *Second Treatise of Government: An Essay Concerning the True Original, Extent and End of Civil Government*, ed. with a revised introduction by J. W. Gough, Oxford: Basil Blackwell.

Lucas, J. R. (1980) *On Justice*, Oxford: Clarendon Press.

McDonald, David A. (1998) 'Three steps forward, two steps back: ideology and urban ecology in South Africa', *Review of African Political Economy*, 25, 75, 73–88.

Malherbe, E. G. (1932) *Die Armblanke-Vraagstuk in Suid-Afrika: Verslag van die Carnegie-kommissie. Deel I: Onderwys-verslag: Onderwys en die Armblanke*, Stellenbosch: Pro-Ecclesia Drukkery.

May, Julian (ed.) (1998a) *Poverty and Inequality in South Africa*, Report prepared for the Office of the Executive Deputy President and the Inter-Ministerial Committee for Poverty and Inequality, Durban: Glenwood Publishing.

May, Julian (ed.) (1998b) *Experience and Perceptions of Poverty in South Africa*, Durban: Glenwood Publishing.

Mill, John Stuart (1939) 'Utilitarianism', in Edwin A. Burtt, *The English Philosophers from Bacon to Mill*, New York: The Modern Library, Random House.

Mill, John Stuart (2003) *Utilitarianism and On Liberty*, ed. with an introduction by Mary Warnock, Oxford: Blackwell Publishing.

Millennium Ecosystem Assessment (2005) *Report: Ecosystems and Human Well-Being*, Washington, DC: Island Press.

Murray, W. A. (1932) *Die Armblanke-Vraagstuk in Suid-Afrika: Verslag van die Carnegie-kommissie. Deel IV: Mediese verslag: Die fysieke toestand van die Armblanke*, Stellenbosch: Pro-Ecclesia Drukkery.

Myrdal, Gunnar (1970) *The Challenge of World Poverty. A World Anti-Poverty Program in Outline*, Allen Lane: The Penguin Press.

Nagel, Thomas (1991) *Equality and Partiality*, New York: Oxford University Press.

Nagel, Thomas (1973) 'Equal treatment and compensatory discrimination', *Philosophy and Public Affairs*, 2, 348–63.

Narayan, Deepa and Patti Petesch (2002) *Voices of the Poor: From Many Lands*, New York and Washington: Oxford University Press and the World Bank.

Narayan, Deepa with Raj Patel, Kai Schafft, Anne Rademacher, Sarah Koch-Schulte (2000a) *Voices of the Poor: Can Anyone Hear Us?*, Oxford: Oxford University Press for the World Bank.

Narayan, Deepa with Robert Chambers, Meera K. Shah and Patti Petesch (2000b) *Voices of the Poor: Crying Out for Change*, Oxford: Oxford University Press and the World Bank.

Nickel, James W. (1974) 'Classification by race in compensatory programs', *Ethics*, 84, 146–50.

Nickel, James W. (2005) 'Poverty and rights', *The Philosophical Quarterly*, 55, 220, 385–402.

Nielsen, Kai (1986–7) 'South Africa: the choice between reform and revolution', *The Philosophical Forum*, 18 (Winter–Spring), 222–53.

Nozick, Robert (1974) *Anarchy, State and Utopia*, Oxford: Basil Blackwell.

Nozick, Robert (2001) *Invariances: The Structure of the Objective World*, Cambridge, Mass. and London: The Belknap Press of Harvard University.

Nussbaum, Martha C. (1995) 'Human capabilities, female human beings', in Martha C. Nussbaum and Jonathan Glover (eds). *Women, Culture and Development: A Study of Capabilities*, Oxford: Clarendon Press, pp. 61–104.

Nussbaum, Martha C. (2000) *Women and Human Development: The Capabilities Approach*, Cambridge: Cambridge University Press.

O'Neill, Onora (1986) *Faces of Hunger: An Essay on Poverty, Justice and Development*, London: Allen & Unwin.

O'Neill, Onora (1987) 'Rights to compensation', *Social Philosophy and Policy*, 5, 1, 72–87.

O'Neill, Onora (2001) 'Agents of justice', *Metaphilosophy*, 32, 112, 180–95.

Orton, Michael and Karen Rowlingson (2007) *Public Attitudes to Economic Inequality*, York: Joseph Rowntree Foundation.

Palmer, Guy, Tom McInnes and Peter Kenway (2007) *Monitoring Poverty and Social Exclusion*, York: Joseph Rowntree Foundation.

Paul, Ellen Franken (1991) 'Set-asides, reparations and compensatory justice', *Nomos*, 33, 97–139.

Peet, Richard (1975) 'Inequality and poverty: a Marxist-geographic theory', *Annals of the Association of American Geographers*, 65, 4 (December), 564–71.

Phillips, Ann (1999) *Which Equalities Matter?*, Cambridge: Polity Press.

Pitkin, Hanna Fenichel (1981) 'Justice: on relating private and public', *Political Theory*, 9, 3, 327–52.

Plato (1993) *The Republic*, trans. with an introduction and notes by Robin Waterfield, Oxford: Oxford University Press.

Pogge, Thomas (2002) *World Poverty and Human Rights*, Cambridge: Polity Press.

Ramphele, Mamphela (1993) *A Bed Called Home*, Cape Town: David Philip Publishers.

Rawls, John (1971) *A Theory of Justice*, Oxford: Oxford University Press.

Rawls, John (1975) 'Fairness to goodness', *The Philosophical Review*, 84, 536–54.

Rawls, John (1985) 'A Kantian conception of equality', in John Rajchman and Cornel West (eds), *Post-Analytic Philosophy*, New York: Columbia University Press, pp. 201–14.

Rawls, John (1993) *Political Liberalism*, New York: Columbia University Press.

Rawls, John (2001) *Justice as Fairness. A Restatement*, ed. Erin Kelly, Cambridge, Mass.: The Belknap Press of Harvard University Press.

Report of the Commission on Poverty, Participation and Power (2000) *Listen Hear. The Right to be Heard*, Bristol: The Policy Press.

Ricketts, Erol R. and Isabel V. Sawhill (1988) 'Defining and measuring the underclass', *Journal of Policy Analysis and Management*, 7, 2, 316–26.

Roll, Jo (1992) *Understanding Poverty: A Guide to the Concept and Measures*, London: Family Policy Studies Centre.

Rossouw, H. W. (1972) 'Die Mens in die Moderne Wêreld', in *Die Mens en die Moderne Wêreld*, Kaapstad: Tafelberg-Uitgewers.

Rossouw, H. W. (1995) 'Die Begrip Geregtigheid', unpublished paper.

Rousseau, Jean-Jacques (1913) *The Social Contract and Discourses*, trans. with introduction by G. D. H. Cole, London: J. M. Dent & Sons Ltd. (Everyman's Library), 1913).

Rousseau, Jean-Jacques (1968) *The Social Contract*, trans. and introduced by Maurice Cranston, Harmondsworth, Middlesex: Penguin Books.

Rowntree, B. Seebohm (1901) *Poverty: A Study in Town Life*, London: MacMillan and Co.

Sachs, Jeffrey (2005) *The End of Poverty. How We Can Make it Happen in Our Own Lifetime*, London: Penguin Books.

Sandel, Michael J. (1982) *Liberalism and the Limits of Justice*, Oxford: Oxford University Press.

Scanlon, Thomas (1998) *What We Owe To Each Other*, Cambridge, Mass.: The Belknap Press of Harvard University Press.

Schmidtz, David (2006) *Elements of Justice*, Cambridge: Cambridge University Press.

Schulte, Bernd (2002) 'A European definition of poverty: the fight against poverty and social exclusion in the member states of the European Union', in Peter Townsend and David Gordon (eds), *World Poverty: New Policies to Defeat an Old Enemy*, Bristol: The Policy Press, pp. 119–45.

Sen, Amartya (1984) 'Well-being, agency and freedom: The Dewey Lectures 1984', *The Journal of Philosophy*, LXXXII, 4, 169–220.

Sen, Amartya (1992) *Inequality Reexamined*, New York: Russel Sage Foundation and Cambridge, Mass.: Harvard University Press.

Sen, Amartya (1999) *Development as Freedom*, Oxford: Oxford University Press.

Sen, Amartya (2009) *The Idea of Justice*, Cambridge, Mass.: The Belknap Press of Harvard University Press.

Shapiro, Ian (1986) *The Evolution of Rights in Liberal Theory*, Cambridge, England: Cambridge University Press.

Shapiro, Ian (2003) 'Optimal deliberation?', in James S. Fishkin and Peter Laslett (eds), *Debating Deliberative Democracy*, Malden, MA, and Oxford: Blackwell Publishing), pp. 121–37.

Sher, George (1976–7) 'Groups and justice', *Ethics*, 87, 174–81.

Shklar, Judith N. (1990) *The Faces of Injustice*, New Haven, Conn.: Yale University Press.

Shue, Henry (1980) *Basic Rights: Subsistence, Affluence and U.S. Foreign Policy*, Princeton, NJ: Princeton University Press.

Singer, Peter (1981) *Practical Ethics*, Cambridge: Cambridge University Press.

Singer, Peter (1993) *How are We to Live? Ethics in an Age of Self-Interest*, London: Mandarin Paperbacks.

Smith, Noel and Sue Middleton (2007) *A Review of Poverty Dynamics Research in the UK*, York: Joseph Rowntree Foundation.

Spicker, Paul (2007) *The Idea of Poverty*, Bristol: The Policy Press.

Spilerman, Seymour and David Elesh (1971) 'Alternative conceptions of poverty and their implications for income maintenance', *Social Problems*, 18, 3, 358–73.

Squire, Lyn (1993) 'Fighting poverty', *The American Economic Review*, 83, 2 (1993), 377–82.

Srinivasan, T. N. (1994) 'Human development: a new paradigm or a reinvention of the wheel?', *The American Economic Review*, 84, 2 , 238–43.

Streeter, Paul (1994) 'Human development: means and ends', *The American Economic Review*, 4, 2, 232–7.

Sunstein, Cass R. (1991) 'The limits of compensatory justice', *Nomos*, 33 (1991), 281–310.

Tarp, Finn, Kenneth Simmler, Cristina Matusse, Rasmus Helberg, Gabriel Dava (2002) 'The robustness of poverty profiles reconsidered', *Economic Development and Cultural Change*, 51, 1, 77–108.

Tavuchis, Nicholas (1991) *Mea Culpa: A Sociology of Apology and Reconciliation*, Stanford, Cal.: Stanford University Press.

Tawney, R. H. (1952) *Equality*, London: George Allen and Unwin.

Taylor, Charles (1985a) 'What is agency?', in Charles Taylor, *Human Agency and Language: Philosophical Papers 1*, Cambridge: Cambridge University Press, pp. 13–44.

Taylor, Charles (1985b) 'Interpretation and the sciences of man', in Charles Taylor, *Philosophical Papers 2: Philosophy and the Human Sciences*, Cambridge: Cambridge University Press, pp. 15–57.

Taylor, Charles (1985c) 'Social theory as practice', in Charles Taylor, *Philosophical Papers 2: Philosophy and the Human Sciences*, Cambridge: Cambridge University Press, pp. 91–115.

Taylor, Charles (1994) 'Multiculturalism and "The Politics of Recognition"', in *Multiculturalism: Examining the Politics of Recognition*, Amy Gutmann (ed.), Princeton, NJ: Princeton University Press, pp. 25–73.

Taylor, Paul W. (1972–3) 'Reverse discrimination and compensatory justice', *Analysis*, 33, 177–82.

Temkin, Larry S. (1993) *Inequality*, New York: Oxford University Press.

Temkin, Larry S. (2004) 'Thinking about the needy, justice and international organizations', *The Journal of Ethics*, 8, 349–95.

Terreblanche, Sampie (1977) *Gemeenskapsarmoede: Perspektief op Chroniese Armoede in die Kleurlinggemeenskap na Aanleiding van die Erika Theron-Verslag*, Kaapstad: Tafelberg-Uitgewers.

Thompson, Janna (2001) 'Historical injustice and reparation: justifying claims of descendants', *Ethics*, 112, 114–35.

Townsend, Peter (1954) 'Measuring poverty', *The British Journal of Sociology*, 5, 2, 130–7.

Townsend, Peter (1979) *Poverty in the United Kingdom: A Survey of Household Resources and Standards of Living*, London: Allen Lane (Penguin Books).

Townsend, Peter and David Gordon (2002) *World Poverty: New Policies to Defeat and Old Enemy*, Bristol: The Policy Press.

UNDP (United Nations Development Programme) (1997) *Human Development Report*, New York: Oxford University Press.

UNDP (United Nations Development Programme) (2000) *Human Development Report. Overcoming Human Poverty*, New York: UNDP.

UNDP (United Nations Development Programme) (2003) *Human Development Report: Millennium Development Goals: A Compact among Nations to End Human Poverty*, New York: Oxford University Press.

Unger, Peter (1996) *Living High and Letting Die*, New York: Oxford University Press.

United Nations (Department of Social and Economic Affairs) (2009) *Rethinking Poverty: Report on the World Situation 2010*, New York: United Nations Publication.

Uys, J. M. (1990) *Relatiewe Deprivasie in 'n Swart Stedelike Gemeenskap*, Rand Afrikaans University, doctoral thesis.

Van der Merwe, Hendrik W. (1989) *Pursuing Justice and Peace in South Africa*, London: Routledge.

Van Kempen, Eva T. (1997) 'Poverty pockets and life chances: on the role of place in shaping social inequality', *The American Behavioral Scientist*, 41, 3 (1997), 430–49.

Van Peursen, C. A. (1972) *Strategie van de Cultuur: Een Beeld van de Veranderingen in de Hedendaagse Denk- en Leefwereld* (Tweede Druk), Amsterdam: Elsevier.

Wade, Francis C. (1978) 'Preferential treatment of blacks', *Social Theory and Practice*, 4, 4, 445–70.

Waldron, Jeremy (1992) 'Superseding historic injustice', *Ethics*, 103, 1, 4–28.

Walzer, Michael (1980) *Radical Principles: Reflections of an Unreconstructed Democrat*, New York: Basic Books.

Walzer, Michael (1983) *Spheres of Justice: A Defence of Pluralism and Equality*, Oxford: Basil Blackwell.

Walzer, Michael (1994) *Thick and Thin: Moral Argument at Home and Abroad*, Notre Dame and London: University of Notre Dame Press.

Willcocks, R. W. (1932) *Die Armblanke-Vraagstuk in Suid-Afrika: Verslag van die Carnegie-kommissie. Deel II: Psychologische verslag: Die Armblanke*, Stellenbosch: Pro-Ecclesia Drukkery.

Wilson, Francis and Mamphela Ramphele (1989) *Uprooting Poverty: The South African Challenge*, Report for the Second Carnegie Inquiry into Poverty and Development in Southern Africa, Cape Town and Johannesburg: David Philip.

Wilson, John (1983) 'The purposes of retribution', *Philosophy*, 58, 223, 521–7.

Wilson, John Veitch (2000) 'Horses for discourses: poverty, purpose and closure in minimum income standards policy', in David Gordon and Peter Townsend (eds), *Breadline Europe: The Measurement of Poverty*, Bristol: The Policy Press, pp. 141–64.

Wolterstorff, Nicholas (1983) *Until Justice and Peace Embrace*, Grand Rapids, Mich.: William B. Eerdmans.

Wolterstorff, Nicholas (2008) *Justice*, Princeton: Princeton University Press.

World Bank (1990) *World Development Report 1990*, New York: Oxford University Press.

World Bank (2001) *World Development Report 2001*, New York: Oxford University Press.

Young, Iris Marion (1990) *Justice and the Politics of Difference*, Princeton, NJ: Princeton University Press.

Young, Iris Marion (1996) 'Representation and communication in a democracy: are all voices heard?', Public Lecture at Rand Afrikaans University, Johannesburg, 25 June.

Young, Iris Marion (2003) 'Activist challenges to deliberative democracy', in James S. Fishkin and Peter Laslett (eds), *Debating Deliberative Democracy*, Malden, MA and Oxford: Blackwell Publishing, pp. 102–20.

Young, Iris Marion (2006) 'Responsibility and global justice', *Social Philosophy and Policy*, 23, 1, 102–30.

Zola, Irving Kenneth (1983) 'Toward independent living: goals and dilemmas', in Nancy M. Crewe, Kenneth Irving Zola and Associates, *Independent Living for Physically Disabled People*, San Francisco: Jossey-Bass Inc., pp. 344–56.

Index